ideas on film

ideas on

a handbook for the 16mm. film user

film

edited by Cecile Starr

Non-theatrical Film Editor, The Saturday Review of Literature

with a foreword by Irving Jacoby

Funk & Wagnalls Company, New York

I am ready to sit down and weep at the impossibility of my understanding or barely knowing a fraction of the sum of objects that present themselves for our contemplation in books and in life.

George Eliot

contents

preface

MOST of the articles and reviews in this book appeared first in the *Saturday Review of Literature*. Some have been expanded or shortened, with the intention of presenting as rounded a picture as possible of the American non-theatrical film field. If this book serves satisfactorily as a first attempt to present a variety of opinions and facts about the 16mm. "idea" film in this country, it will have accomplished the editor's aim.

The idea of organizing this material into book form came first from *SRL* readers who from time to time have asked for such a collection. To them the editor offers thanks for their sustained interest. In addition, she is indebted to the many contributors who have kindly made their articles and reviews available for use in this volume. Special thanks are due the editors of the *Saturday Review*, and to Jack Cominsky, William D. Patterson, Minna Elkind, and the others who have given special and much-appreciated support and assistance to the 16mm. film department.

The Institute of Adult Education of Columbia University Teachers College has given its permission to reprint freely from the pages of *Film Forum Review*, a quarterly publication issued from 1946 to 1949, with which the editor was associated for most of that time. Special thanks are due Morse A. Cartwright, former director of the Institute, and Dr. Paul Essert, its present director. In addition, it is important to mention each of the people connected with the film project at the Institute, since the reviews were the result of group work and were published without individual credit lines: Robertson Sillars, J. Roby Kidd, Harry Campbell, Monty Stearns, Carl Pettersch, Harry Miller, Miriam Zwerin, Gordon Smith, John Bass, John Friesen, Joyce Hazelhurst, Harold Goldstein, Herbert Maccoby, Melita Seipp, and Fred Windoes.

Special acknowledgment, further, should be made of the contributions of Raymond Spottiswoode, who initiated a systematic evaluation of non-theatrical films in this country, and whose reviews are well represented in this collection; and of the late Kenneth Edwards, whose energy and enthusiasm in support of the 16mm. field were always guided by the highest principles. Thanks also are due to Arthur Knight, who gave valuable assistance in choosing the illustrations; to the Museum of Modern Art Film Library, which gave permission to use its stills from *Hymn of the Nations*, *The River*, and *The City*.

Particular thanks are due to Frances Hickman and Amy Clampitt, who are often helpful in many ways; to my mother, Carrie Lightman Starr, who is a constant and interested reader; and to many other Starrs.

To all these, and surely some others, the debt is acknowledged, if not repaid.

CECILE STARR

New York
February, 1951

foreword

THE films this volume deals with are designed essentially to influence what people think. In these troubled days when our freedoms and our dignities are under attack from all sides, we may not at first like the idea of being "influenced" or even of "influencing," for the word carries overtones of violence, expediency, and even contempt for the object that is to be won, changed, and redirected: the human mind. Yet I believe readers will detect in these pages few signs of coercion, opportunism, or cynicism. For the films under consideration, contemporary American films for the most part, seem to try to influence people in the mildest, gentlest, most gradual of ways, the way that is based on respect for human values, the way that is the way of all good teaching and all art. And yet the purpose of influencing is their reason for existing and we must measure them by their achievement of this purpose. The ideas in these films must come across, must actually be transmitted to the audience, or the films are failures no matter how successful they are as entertainment. This book, therefore, is about education as well as about movies, and the two seem to have more in common than one might expect.

It was from Europe that we imported the concept of using film to change human attitudes and thus affect human behavior, but it is essentially an American success story that is revealed by the articles and reviews in this book. For a tool must be adapted to the job that it is to do, and to the people who are to use it. And so it is little wonder that in America the serious films quickly changed from propaganda to education, from an authoritarian approach to liberalism, from "avant gardism" to "popularism."

It is not accidental that many of our best films ask questions rather than give answers, that both in production and distribution our successes are time and again the result of cooperation and American organization, that the artistic standards of our films are not quite high enough, and even that the great bulk of our films are not keyed to a very advanced level of emotional and intellectual maturity.

The European documentary, beautifully made by one artist and used sharply by a single group, has changed into a cooperative but somewhat less beautiful effort, used broadly by many groups for many different purposes. One thinks of the difference in automobile making: Europe with its superb Rolls Royces and De La Hayes for a few drivers in contrast with America's production of serviceable Fords and Chevrolets that millions can afford. We may not like the comparison or its inference that we do not have the best. But we seem to have what we want and until we refashioned the "idea" film in our own image we did not really have it.

We have it now. How important it has become in the learning process of our people has been pointed out month by month in the *Saturday Review of Literature* whence most of this book is reprinted. It is now the foundation of our adult education programs and it is considered indispensable by our schools and colleges. Our government spends millions of dollars on it every year and groups interested in the advancement of ideas in areas as separated as art and political science, as religion and public health, use it constantly to reach the masses of our people. It has found its own place in America's intellectual life.

We Americans talked about the possibility of using motion pictures this way ever since their popularity became evident at the turn of the century. We talked and talked for the first quarter of the century and did nothing but make a few poor fact films that had neither cinematic quality nor ideas. Then in the early Twenties, Robert Flaherty made pictures that married facts to feelings and we were on the right path for the first time. His were idea pictures, even though the ideas were special and personal. In England, John Grierson appreciated the importance of the new development, coined the word Documentary to describe it, and went on to develop its second and most important step: the use of film to advance specific community ideas which were being advanced in other media and by other means. Film-making became a social process thereby, and the film maker a servant of the community.

As Cavalcanti, Rotha, Wright, Legg, Elton, Watt, and many others discovered, this does not mean the artist was less important as a creator or as an individual. If anything, his importance was increased by the responsibilities of leadership that he undertook, and his creative efforts benefited from the sharp increase in opportunities that he now had and from the focus automatically given to his work by his acceptance of a specific goal. Pare Lorentz probably found the same thing true in America when he tied his talents to the social changes brewing here in the Thirties. *The Plow That Broke The Plains* and *The River* were the first American films that united ideas (in emotion-provoking form) to possible community action. And it is interesting to note, in the following pages, that they live long after the New Deal has disappeared, in contrast to the British documentaries which were concerned with a social movement that prospered and thus naturally enhanced their popularity.

It was World War II, however, that was responsible for the great growth in the production and use of idea films in America. On one hand the audience, both in and out of the services, became accustomed to seeing thought-provoking films and, on the other, educators had a chance to learn how to use films effectively and to explore new possibilities of using them. To top it off, a generation of film makers was trained to work cooperatively with military and naval officers, government information advisers, economists, diplomats, and many other specialists, and was later available to work in the same way with educators, physicians, social and physical scientists, labor leaders, social workers, and the many other experts of the peacetime community. How they collaborate and what their collaboration has produced is the material of this work, interesting to a layman as the inside story of a new creative movement developing in his own time and in his own community, and even more interesting to those who will determine the future of the movement themselves by making films, causing them to be made, or using them.

Certainly a future for such films is now assured. But what that future will be is not something that can be predicted with ease.

As a matter of fact, those of us who have worked in the field have been constantly amazed at the twists and turns of the development. In the many years of guessing about its direction, we have been wrong more often than right. Where we looked for support, we found none forthcoming, and where we least expected it, we found the greatest interest and understanding. When many of us were tempted, either by Hollywood or less glamorous evasions, to retire from the field because of lack of opportunity, we suddenly found new vistas opened before us. When we thought that our hope was in the intellectuals and advanced groups in the country, we discovered that it was the ordinary audience Hollywood had always claimed for its own that really wanted to see our pictures. This kind of surprise is what makes the field exciting. The idea-film movement in America today is alive and hence not to be confined or pushed around or developed according to someone's pet schemes.

All one can venture to say is how one would like to see it develop. And I would put first on my list a hope that it will develop rapidly in terms of creative personnel. Since so many films are now being made in comparison with the production output of previous years, there is now considerable room for new talent.

This is particularly true in film-writing, which requires not only an understanding of the nature of film-making and an ability to write but also good intellectual training and a real interest in community life. As the use of sound, particularly dialog, has increased in modern idea films, more and more of the work has to be done in the script-writing stage, since dialog can almost never be prepared spontaneously on the set. The writer's importance has also grown in connection with the need to work with experts, who must make most of their contribution to the film in its planning and writing. By the time the director has his actors in front of him or the editor has his rushes on the moviola, there isn't much a consultant can do to give positively of what he knows. And so we find ourselves needing many more writers who like films and believe in them and who, like the young would-be cameramen and would-be directors, have found ways of training themselves so that they can be useful in the cooperative effort and earn both satisfaction and a living through the use of their skill. This increased importance of the writer (which incidentally has also grown in Hollywood during the last decade) does not seem to result in films that are any less cinematic in their values. As a matter of fact, the good directors, both in the entertainment and documentary fields, have turned out to be those who could work closely with their writers and could thus be helped to absorb ideas from outside their own personal knowledge and experience.

Certainly I do not mean to suggest, by stressing the growing importance of the writer, that the director today is any less the key creative talent in the production of a film. He is still supreme arbiter of the film and of the expression of the dramatic idea, and there can be no shackles on his creative authority if a vital, unified, and integrated work is to appear on the screen. As a matter of fact it is only that director who can cooperate with the expert and the writer without being overwhelmed or seduced by them who can make good pictures in this field. The moment he steps back from his creative responsibility, his films tend to become didactic, talky, intellectualized presentations of the subject-matter. He is still responsible for feeling through all the elements of dramatic presentation and only what he feels can he transmit to his cameramen, his actors, his editor, and thus, eventually, to his audience.

One big thing some of us have learned in twenty years is that you do not communicate ideas to film audiences by telling them something from the screen either in pictures or in words. Time and again we realize we must go back to men like Flaherty and to the poets, dramatists, novelists, and painters in whose tradition he worked. Films or any works of art can only help an audience tell itself something. The audience really does the work when the film sets the favorable emotional atmosphere and provides the insights and understanding in a simple, effective way. In any medium, ideas can be communicated and still not heard by audiences; or they can be heard and not understood; or they can be understood intellectually and not really learned. Idea films can do most by helping the audience to accept on the deepest level ideas which it has probably been made aware of intellectually in other ways. And that is probably why it constantly turns out that the best teaching films are also examples of the best film-making, that when the resources of the medium are used most honestly and creatively, they do the most useful and efficient job for the educator.

We also hope for greater knowledge of how and when films can teach on the part of those who cause films to be made—the producers, the sponsors, the administrative officials, and the subject-matter groups in our communities. They can learn to do a better job in coordinating film to other social expressions and can learn even more about the audience's reaction to the emotional, intellectual stimulation of an idea film. The audience is an integral part of the phenomenon of motion pictures; it has its own identity which must be known and understood if films are to be increasingly effective in transmitting ideas. When we have more knowledge about the intellectual and emotional development levels of the audience, our pictures can do a better job of meeting them half way. Otherwise, like Hollywood, there is a danger of seeking a lower and lower common denominator. Since the film maker himself cannot control the audience, he must accept it; and to accept it, he must first know it. He can only get his information about the audience from the producer and sponsor and too often they are unable to give it to him.

We can also hope that the future will see an increase in the number of people who use films effectively. I believe it cannot be said too often that using films well is at least as creative a role as the seemingly more glamorous job of producing them. A film and an audience are just as exciting components of the dramatic experience as are a camera and an actor. And when it comes to idea films the user is unquestionably as important as the maker. Already teachers, librarians, and community leaders in America can boast of a great number of individuals in their ranks who are really learning to use film, who can actually perform the most important function of all—recognizing a good film. They know how to get the most out of a film, they know at first-hand the pictures that are available, and they are gradually becoming able to express themselves on the films that are still needed. They are being helped by many lay and professional organizations, trade publications, general magazines such as the *Saturday Review of Literature* that publish news about films, and by distributors who are beginning to understand their responsibilities in the educational process. We can expect them to have a continually greater influence on the films that are made in the future.

What will these films be? The answer lies with the writers, directors, sponsors, and users that we have been talking about. For the films will reflect the life that they are living or want to live. As it has in the past, the idea film will continue to be a mirror to the problems, the aspirations, the growing-up process of the community that supports it. Documentary, when it is good and really doing its own job, is a moving picture of the hopes and fears of the people who are giving and receiving in a two-way communicative process. For idea films are not simply fact films.

That is probably the principal reason why they outlast the problems or the solutions that seem to be their subject-matter.

Today the people who are making and looking at idea pictures are concerned with democracy. We can expect to see on our screens many definitions of the concept, many descriptions of its workings, and many breakdowns of its background, its nature, its essential meaning in political, economic, cultural, and human terms. As we explore it with camera and sound recorder, we will probably unearth facets we are hardly aware of. As we dramatize it for ourselves, we will find ways of changing it, improving it, making it real for more and more of our people. As we present it in film for the rest of the world, we will rediscover what it really means to us, why we prefer it over other ways of life, why we must do what we can to keep it alive and growing. Such pictures will not be dull or didactic if we make them honestly and vigorously. They will be films about people, how they get along with one another, how they live and work together, what they like and what they hate, what they dream and how they try to realize their dreams. They will be pictures about us, as Documentary has been about us in the first quarter-century of its existence, and it seems we can be quite interesting on the screen. Certainly in these troubled days we Americans had better be reminded what we are, what we want, and what we are presenting as an answer to the confusion of modern man. In our idea films we can project, however tentatively and modestly, the light that we glimpse and the substance that is taking shape before our eyes.

IRVING JACOBY

I. FILMS—16mm. AND OTHERWISE

fifty years of film

Rudolf Arnheim

THOUSANDS of years ago man discovered the art of making signs on surfaces. Changes of pictorial style took place as different cultures explored the medium, but the technique remained essentially the same. Suddenly, in the nineteenth century, a machine offered new powers to the visual arts. Pictures could be made to move, and reality could be recorded with mechanical truthfulness. What have we done with the magic tool?

Movement added time to the picture. Now the picture could tell a story. But stories had always been told in words, and words were out of place in pictures. Thus the first film stories showed the absence of what had been lost rather than the wealth of what had been gained. Imagine a novel or a play deprived of the word, reduced to the mere skeleton of the plot. The husband opens the bedroom door and discovers his wife in the embrace of a lover. He throws up his arms in a mute rage, draws a gun, and shoots the guilty couple. Fifteen seconds of dehydrated drama—such were the early stories of the screen.

The first enlightenment came from the clowns. They were the

heirs of pantomime, used to expressing human tribulations visually
by gestures, fights, and staged accidents. As they stepped in front
of the camera they were not embarrassed by the absence of speech.
They merely spread their antics over the larger stage of real streets,
lakes, beaches. Instead of trying for the internal action of drama
and novel they engaged in outer conflict with the inhabitants and
objects of the everyday world. The waiter and his tray, the drunk-
ard and his lantern, the fireman and his ladder—these were the
tangible problems of their stories. Buster Keaton made a full-length
picture (*The General*) out of the maneuvers of a machinist whose
locomotive had got caught between the parties of the Civil War.
And when Charlie Chaplin, in *The Pilgrim*, had to preach a ser-
mon he chose as his theme the story of Goliath and David, which
could be told without words.

Much of the early pantomime was crude physical performance,
pie-throwing, blows over the head, and mad chase. This created a
tradition, which is still going strong with cowboys, gangsters, and
balcony-climbing Don Juans. But already in those years of infancy,
the great artists, Chaplin and Keaton, conveyed in their comedies
a deep sense of tragedy, which has rarely been matched in later
films. The manifestations of human striving and feeling had been
translated from speech into visible action. That was the beginning.

The clowns had discovered the object as a partner—the blind
stubbornness of furniture, the brainless violence of machines, the
malice of fixtures. Soon the object, enlarged by close-up shots to
the size of a mountain, revealed its expressive face and gestures.
The pendulum of a clock, a broken bottle, fluttering underwear
on the clothesline performed on equal terms with human actors.
In Stroheim's *Greed* the pathetic inventory of an apartment exposed the disintegration of a marriage. Von Sternberg cluttered
his sitting rooms with the expressive bric-à-brac of Victorian
baroque.

The charms of exotic landscape had already been exploited in
the earliest chases around the world in twenty minutes. Later the
documentary film poems of men like Robert Flaherty pictured the
Pacific islands, the Arctic snowscapes, and more recently the invasion of dreamy Louisiana jungles by gigantic oil derricks. The
Russians found the symbols of growth and labor in their corn-
fields and factories. They also had the people to match the simple
grandeur of nature. Peasants, laborers, watching, smiling, eating.
The spontaneity of these faces "projected" something the theatre
had never known.

The world was explored, but at the same time there was constant experimentation with the film technique. Camera and printing machine could transform reality into phantasy. Already in the days of the French magician Georges Méliès a man could suddenly disappear or change into a woman or fall upward to the ceiling or meet himself in the street. Later the audience could see a young woman shrink into an old one (*Lost Horizon*) and Dr. Jekyll turn into Mr. Hyde. Monsters and spirits walked the earth, walls became transparent, the invisible man played his extrasensory tricks, fairy tales and dreams came true.

And there was the element of light. At first light had been nothing but a chemical prerequisite. Without the sun or the flood lamps there could be no picture. But soon shadows were cast with purpose: beams of light fell through cathedral windows; the camera captured the glittering highlights of waves, jewels, tears. Melancholy romanticists in Germany and Scandinavia played with the mystery of what is hidden in darkness. It took the technicolor people to expel these bewitching nightmares, and have they given us anything worth the loss?

The great temptation came with sound. In the first decade of the century, films had been synchronized with disks, and famous tenors sang arias on the screen. But only in the late Twenties photoelectric recording made sound fit for mass consumption. The loudspeakers produced the noises of the streets, footsteps, bells, the voices of weather and animals, but also song and speech. Speech was the great temptation. It was the biggest step toward realistic reproduction since Daguerre and Lumière. There was no further need for paraphrasing the story by means of visible action. But precisely the creation of a world which was complete and intelligible without speech had been one of the great contributions of the film. Now the film became a branch of the theatre. The eyes of the spectator, which had become so proficient in the symbolic deaf-and-dumb language, relapsed into laziness. The burden of screen art shifted from the director to the actor. And the free exchange of pictures among peoples of different language was severely limited.

Looking backward and forward at the half-way mark of the century, we find that the medium has not let us down. It has given us powerful means of expression, information, and education. Rather have we let down the medium. We have used the movies mainly to reinforce bad taste rather than to improve it. Pictures have tended to distract people from thinking rather than to deepen thought by vision. Their convincing realism has made distortions and illusions more credible.

There have always been the few who, at great personal sacrifice, have made beautiful things. What are their tasks for the future? Artistically, there is the almost unexplored field of painting in motion. Disney, at his best, has created poetry of color and shape which went far beyond cartooning. From Oskar Fischinger to Norman McLaren, artists have tried to give movement to abstract art. The striking results suggest that on the screen abstractions are most likely to lose their character of noncommittal decoration and acquire the impact of music.

In the meantime, the camera will keep on recording reality, and it must be hoped that the incorruptible faithfulness of the machine will be matched more often by the honesty of those who use it. True pictures can add the weight of experience to the knowledge provided by the printed word. They are a remedy for the lack of imagination which prevents understanding and cooperation. People who see find it harder to hurt.

Rudolf Arnheim is the author of Film, *a systematic analysis of the artistic achievements and potentialities of the motion picture, published by Faber & Faber, London, in 1933. He teaches general psychology and the psychology of art at Sarah Lawrence College and the Graduate Faculty of the New School.*

documentary redefined

C. A. Siepmann

"THE difficulties of producing and distributing 16mm. films are enormous. A hodge-podge of agencies is now in the field. Most find it too uneconomic for large or sustained investment. . . . There is no steady flow of adult films. Moreover, distribution through scattered film libraries, occasional public libraries and dealers is unprofitable and ineffective." This is the summary conclusion of the most recent study of 16mm. films, *The Information Film,** by Gloria Waldron, a work marred by some unduly arbitrary comment —and a treatment of the documentary film which, on two counts at least, is so confusing and so damaging as to invite immediate challenge.

Confusion stems from a definition which, by fastening on purely adventitious attributes of documentary films, obscures what is distinctive and important about them. Documentaries are defined as including "all serious, adult, non-theatrical films." This gets us nowhere. Many non-documentary films are both serious and adult. Not all documentaries hit the theatre circuits, but some do. Industrial films come within this definition, but these are rarely documentary. The term evidently needs salvaging before its distinctive meaning is lost sight of altogether.

Makers of documentary films share with all film makers a delight in the experimental development of a unique medium. They are distinguished by their conception of the use to which their craftsmanship should be put. Like the poets and dramatists of ancient Athens, they conceive of art as constituting service to society by the enlargement of knowledge and refinement of attitudes. It is by this conception of the function of the artist that they are distinguished from most of their confrères in Hollywood. They are unwilling to subordinate their skill as craftsmen or their integrity as creative artists to the mere satisfaction of mass appetites or to the primary consideration of making money.

Beyond this the maker of documentary films has his eye on the exploitation of one among the many resources of the art of film. His concern is with the living scene and the living story. Such interest implies not merely the choice of one esthetic field of interest. It derives as much from a concern with social comment, and from perception of the fact that actuality is neutral in its significance until selectively interpreted by imaginative insight. These are the strands which, interwoven, constitute the essence of documentary film-making and lend validity to Grierson's original definition of the term as the "creative treatment of actuality."

The success of a documentary film depends on the extent to which the visual portrayal of life and its subjective interpretation by the film maker are integrated. It is this integral conception of what is

* THE INFORMATION FILM: A Report of the Public Library Inquiry. By Gloria Waldron. New York: Columbia University Press. 1949. 281 pp. $3.75.

seen and what it is intended to convey which makes of Robert Flaherty a supreme master of the art of documentary. In all his pictures what we see is an integral part of his message. Comment on his part would be superfluous and obtrusive.

Artists at all times have in one way or another been dependent upon patronage. Makers of documentary films are at a special disadvantage here because of the high cost of film-making. Today this factor of dependence unduly restricts the scope for self-expression, partly because of the now generally prevalent fear of ideas, partly, too, because of the concern of sponsors to get their own particular ideas across. The modern patron tends to attach strings to his patronage of a kind which are all too often a denial of the artist's integrity. This hits the maker of documentary films particularly hard in view of the fact that the richest field for documentary films is that of social comment. Such comment nowadays, other than in a most restricted sense, is virtually taboo. Hence the present tendency for the commissioning of documentary film makers to deal in life situations at an expository rather than at an interpretative level and the consequent increasing approximation of the documentary to the instructional film.

Consider the consequences in terms of the effectiveness of two films concerned with a common problem—psychiatry. *The Feeling of Hostility* (p. 183) is, properly speaking, an instructional film. It is non-documentary, being at one remove from life in that the situations are contrived and the visual images subordinated to clinical exposition on the sound track. *The Quiet One* (p. 175) is likewise at one remove from life. Exposition likewise accompanies the film. Yet, despite these resemblances, the impact of these two films is sharply differentiated—to the advantage of the latter. In the first the artist subserved the expert. In the second the subject was no less expertly treated, but the expert was (as he should always be) on tap but not on top. An artist's insight triumphed over the subject matter and lent it a new, compelling significance. It is thus that, without doing violence to their contractual obligations, artists at all times have transcended the limitations of their allotted tasks. It is thus that integrity is reconciled with service.

Perhaps the most distressing passage in *The Information Film* is that in which Miss Waldron appears to impugn this distinctive attribute of documentary film makers—integrity. She speaks thus of propaganda in documentaries:

A good many prominent citizens, especially businessmen and legislators, have long looked with skepticism on adult documentary-information films, because they fear that the articulate makers and users of these films are, consciously or unconsciously, propagandists of one sort or another. Many of them are. *Many of them do not hesitate to manipulate the screen in the service of their own ideologies even when the film is not intended, by subject or purpose, to do so.* (Author's italics.)

This undocumented charge is the more sinister for seeming to bespeak that theory of the artist as the handyman of other people's ideologies, which appears to have such currency today. All art is propaganda. Art and propaganda are salutary as long as they are free. Art becomes dead and propaganda deadly when prescribed by self-appointed arbiters of what are safe and dangerous thoughts.

But if the scope for documentary films is, at this moment, somewhat restricted, if also, as Miss Waldron points out, the means for their distribution are uncoordinated, prospects are far less gloomy than the reader of her book might be led to suppose. Considering their short history, considering the odds against them, and in particular the dominance of Hollywood and the general practice of all mass media to standardize mass appetites, what is remarkable is current evidence of a growing hunger for the kind of experience which documentaries provide. The growth of film councils and film societies, while still laggard, appears to be sturdy and expansive. The belated recognition of the value of films in the classroom also gives ground for hope.

Even adults need not be despaired of. Interest in films *à la* Hollywood is a teen-age preoccupation. There are more people over thirty who rarely go to the movies than those who regularly attend Hollywood's grade-labeled products. Hollywood itself is now expressing astonishment at the increasing business being done at the so-called art theatres. Community groups are year by year availing themselves increasingly of films of a documentary character.

Extrapolate the present trend only a little distance and the documentary may come into its own. Those who make them have insured their own future by seeking, not wealth or public acclaim, but modest opportunity for self-expression without surrender of integrity. From a social point of view the significance of the documentary film makers is not merely or even, perhaps, primarily the films that they produce but rather the stand they have made for the integrity of art and the true role of the artist in our society. They above all others who deal in filmcraft have seen that our sensibilities are refined and our social insights sharpened by the clothing of living facts with that significance which it is the artist's peculiar prerogative to bring to our own foreshortened and distracted view of things.

Charles A. Siepmann is chairman of the Department of Communications and director of the Film Library at New York University. He is the author of Radio, Television and Society, *Oxford Press.*

two movie books
Cecile Starr

TWO important film books have been published for the first time in this country—*A Grammar of the Film* * and *The Film Till Now.*† Both have appeared on nearly every list of recommended books about the motion picture since their original publication in England in 1930 and 1933 respectively. And since there has always been a scarcity of critical and serious reading matter about films in this land of the double feature, they are welcome and valuable additions to libraries here.

Raymond Spottiswoode was a bare twenty years old when he wrote *A Grammar of the Film.* He was, as he states in the preface to this first American edition, "unembarrassed by any actual contact with film." His aim was to create some order among the confusion of the things he had read and heard about motion pictures, as well as the things he had seen and heard in them. Except for the addition of a new short and amusing preface, in which Spottiswoode makes merry comments about the motives and methods, shortcomings and values of the work of the "young author," the book is unchanged since its original publication in 1933.

Subtitled *An Analysis of Film Technique*, it is a minute probing into the esthetic and technical causes and effects in motion pic-

* A GRAMMAR OF THE FILM. By Raymond Spottiswoode. Berkeley: University of California Press. 328 pp. $3.75.
† THE FILM TILL NOW. By Paul Rotha, in collaboration with Richard Griffith. New York: Funk & Wagnalls. 755 pp. $12.

tures. Particular analytical consideration is given to *Deserter*,
Pudovkin's first sound film, which like many other important films
of its vintage is not available today for screening by late-comers.
A Grammar of the Film purports to elaborate upon a highly complex chart designed by the young author to include, somehow or
other, every facet of film-making and thinking.

For those who already have done a fair amount of reading and
thinking about the motion picture, and especially for students interested in its structural aspects, *A Grammar of the Film* is a reference book of lasting value. In its precise and outspoken, serious and
amusing way, it reflects the wide-eyed adolescence of both the
young author and the youngest of the arts.

If Spottiswoode's book arose "out of the ashes of long-forgotten
controversies," and if his approach was often precious and polished,
Rotha's *The Film Till Now* is almost its antithesis. Subtitled *A
Survey of World Cinema*, it is as much a study of the essential ex-
ternals of the film as Spottiswoode's book is of the vital internals.
Rotha is concerned with white-hot controversies not likely ever to
be forgotten in the motion-picture world, and he attacks them with
a heavy hammer.

A new [1949] fifty-page introduction by the author bitterly reflects Hollywood's industrial stranglehold on motion-picture production, generating new waves of "drama" on the screen instead of
better moving pictures: ". . . if you look at the outstanding work
of the cinema," Rotha writes in the preface, "it is mainly the films
which are wholly original in conception that have created film history: *Intolerance, Caligari, Nanook, Potemkin, The Last Laugh, A
Nous la Liberté, Kameradschaft, The Public Enemy*,"—none was
a transcription from another medium. Despite his genuine horror
of Hollywood, U.S.A., Rotha doesn't fail to lament the many failures in other countries to recapture and reestablish the motion picture as a special creative art.

Almost every important film is at least mentioned in this mammoth volume; many are given a paragraph or a page of discussion.
The careers of producers, directors, and writers are traced in outline. Rotha's attitude to the "star" and to those who make their
extravagant livings clustering around him can be summed up by
the following "typical story" he relates, in which "an American
woman journalist, Louella Parsons," is quoted as having written:
". . . his work as Lord Nelson in *The Divine Lady* proved what
a really fine artist he is. With an arm missing and blind in one eye,
he still manages to have sex appeal."

Richard Griffith's long contribution to the book brings it up to date—a separate section several hundred pages long entitled "The Film Since Then." Less vitriolic than Rotha, less excited about his material, Griffith writes best about the people he loves most, as his sections on Chaplin and Flaherty testify.

In a book of this scope and breadth (it is literally giant-sized, with nearly two hundred still photographs) there are the inevitable number of factual errors, misplaced captions, and disputable matters of opinion. However, a new generation of movie-goers will find *The Film Till Now* an exciting introduction to films they have never been able to see, as well as a challenging criticism of Hollywood and the entire motion-picture world.

To *Ideas on Film* readers these works are more than two important textbooks of the film. They throw light upon the entire documentary movement and upon non-theatrical distribution. No one seriously entertains the idea that the 16mm. documentary is a threat to the motion-picture industry—but its special values are underwritten throughout these two volumes. Both of them are serious attempts to expand the significance and influence of the film, to help make it an adult art and entertainment, growing under the guidance of the film artist instead of staggering under the domination of the film financier. The unhappy part is that so few worthwhile books have come along in the past decade to challenge and surpass these. Lewis Jacobs's *Rise of the American Film* is one noteworthy exception.

That both Rotha and Spottiswoode should have become active in John Grierson's social documentary circle is no surprise, despite the differences in their approach to the film. Both writers were looking for a place to work out new ideas and they found it with Grierson. The real relationship between film experimentation and what Grierson himself has unhesitatingly called the propaganda film is complex; yet this much appears true: the realist-film school in England was always so concerned with presenting its ideas and its material to the public that it gladly opened its mind and heart to many kinds of exploration in new film forms and techniques to assist in an increasingly effective presentation. In contrast, Hollywood is almost exclusively concerned with keeping a firm grasp on proven "box-office" film forms.

True, the documentarians no longer use the same kind of approach to social problems. If we can agree on a definition of documentary—that it is primarily real material, as distinguished from fictional, set down and interpreted on film—we can see two new kinds of documentary films now being evolved. On one hand there is the personal document of experience (*The Quiet One, The Feeling of Rejection*, etc.), and on the other hand, the art documentary (*1848, The Loon's Necklace, The Titan*, etc.)

In both types of films new technique problems are being worked out. The personal documentaries in the fields of mental health, child care, and the like are based on new information supplied by psychiatrists and psychologists; they require dialog and "story" in a real-life setting with real people; they present completely new problems of writing, directing, and editing. The art films, in interpreting and revitalizing motionless objects, retreat to the most basic film principles. Eisenstein may have used the most violent human emotions and actions in his films, but he brought them to a complete standstill by isolating frame from frame, so that he could put these still pictures together again at a pace and in a sequence which produced the effects he wanted. Since the motion-picture industry does not indulge in the task of experimenting and testing new film ideas and values, where else can the work be done except in the "little film"?

Non-theatrical distribution becomes more significant, too, after reading Rotha and Spottiswoode, for there is a vast audience apparently intentionally deprived of the kind of films it wants to see. Rotha quotes at length from an editorial in the *Motion Picture Herald*, which identifies the best movie customer as "a person of nineteen years" and states that it would be "most unprofitable for the motion picture to seek out the genuinely mature instincts. . . ." With this as the film-exhibitor's dictum, it is no wonder that the creative film maker not only must produce his films away from the large studios, but also must turn to ready-made audiences outside the theatre—in clubs, museums, colleges, and so on—and welcome the growing audiences in film societies and such groups as Cinema 16 in New York.

Whether making films, showing them, or writing them, the explorer is seldom to be envied. But without him no new roads would be built. Spottiswoode and Rotha, in their separate film studies, help make the pathways, the highways, and even the dead-ends, more meaningful.

face to face

Julien Bryan

SEVERAL years ago in Warsaw I was asked to show a documentary film before a group of twelve- and fourteen-year-old boys in the Central YMCA. It was a dramatic setting—a devastated city, a badly damaged building, and more than one hundred youngsters who had somehow survived the war.

These youngsters, living as they did behind the Iron Curtain, had some curious ideas about the United States, in spite of the fact that they were YMCA members.

I spoke briefly to them, and then showed them a twenty-minute documentary which I had made several years ago. It pictured an average day in an elementary school in Mt. Vernon, Ohio.

The boys sat transfixed throughout the picture. After the lights were turned on, there was a question period. I supposed they would be very curious about American games and about a school play which had been photographed as part of the film. But nothing of the sort. Out came the first question: "Mr. Bryan, in your pictures you showed boys and girls just like us. Is it really true that boys and girls in America are good children just like us?"

The discussion flowed on for a good half hour. It was in no way political. But a profound new idea had just penetrated the Iron Curtain and the minds and hearts of one hundred small Polish boys: The idea that children in America were like *them*—were good children and could be their friends. They had, in fact, been transported to America by means of films, and they had been eyewitnesses to what went on in an American school.

This was something that lectures and reading had been unable to do for them. They had read plenty of stories about the United States and had heard any number of lectures, but they had also heard plenty of criticism of the United States—criticism which had influenced them to the point where they honestly believed that almost all American boys were bad boys. In a few minutes a film had dramatically shattered a false belief.

Naturally, I am not suggesting that the mere showing of a film will always cause a conversion to the point of view it expresses, but even in the face of powerful prejudices a film can raise questions in the mind of a spectator. For example, a few years ago in Russia, while I was working with an UNRRA mission, I showed another American film called *The County Agent*, made several years ago for the State Department for their use abroad. A high Russian official was fascinated by the film, especially by its photography and music. But the thing that impressed him most was the portrayal of living conditions on American farms: The farms were large, and the farmers lived in comfortable houses, and every farmer owned his own car. This last idea particularly seemed to stump the Russian official. After the showing he took me aside privately and said, "It's a good film, but those farmers' cars now . . . you *lent* them to the men just for the picture, didn't you?" It was too much for him to believe.

Obviously, the film could not change this man into a believer in democracy, any more than my words and arguments could have, but it did make a deep impression on him. In spite of himself and his party-line training, he had become an eyewitness to the American scene. His party had told him how the American farmer had been exploited and oppressed, but this simple documentary film showed him without fanfare or propaganda a side of life in the United States of which he had never heard. His mind, I think, wanted to believe it. His Communist party training made him doubt.

But if this high Communist official believed even a little of my film, imagine the eagerness with which such documentaries would be seized upon and believed by non-Communists in Eastern Europe.

For instance, some time ago I arranged to show several films on American education before a group of teachers and educators in Prague. It was a cold day and the building unheated. To my amazement, more than two hundred Czechs turned out, and all of them were deeply interested in the films. A lecture on American education at such a meeting would have been of some value, but, thanks to film, these Czech educators had paid a visit to a classroom in an American elementary school. For a moment they had been able to identify themselves closely with American teachers and their work.

When the lights went on I could see that they had been emotionally stirred—not by any words of mine but by the things they had seen on film.

Months later I was again in Prague. President Benes had just died, and the country was in deep mourning. The Czech people seemed to know that this was a great turning point in their history. Tens of thousands of them stood for eight or ten hours in line, waiting for their turn to view the body of Benes—old men, soldiers, women, workmen, little children stood silently weeping. Whatever these people were, they were not Communists. Thousands of patriotic Czechs were clearly as sincere and devoted believers in democracy as any of us in America.

I was deeply moved as I watched this spectacle of widespread national grief for a man who was not only a beloved leader but a symbol of democracy to a freedom-loving people. I wanted other Americans to see this historic event as I saw it and felt it then, and so I took pictures of it—with a 16mm. camera.

Later, a group of wealthy and influential men met for dinner at the Waldorf. They called themselves the Circumnavigators' Club and were holding a formal banquet in honor of Juan Trippe. Toward the end of the evening I showed them the Benes pictures. They were deeply moved as they watched it, as I had been at the time of the event itself. For the moment, they, too, were there at Benes's funeral. They, too, were weeping with the Czechs. They, too, were seeing the death of a democracy. But the film had not only moved them. It had made these smart, able businessmen identify themselves with the Czech people. National, geographical, and social barriers were forgotten. They saw the Czechs as human beings like themselves.

The eyewitness and identification appeal of the 16mm. film makes it of tremendous importance as a tool in the promotion of international understanding, and, unlike the Hollywood or theatrical type of film shown in commercial theatres, it can be courageous and controversial. Hollywood still deliberately avoids most controversial issues. It has a long list of taboos. It is brave after an issue has long been decided or after it has become "safe." It never dared to touch Hitler and the Nazis until 1938, although 16mm. films were doing it without fear. Today 16mm. films can still take courageous stands on a hundred controversial subjects: religion, sex education, Russia, and displaced persons. These are subjects which Hollywood cannot or will not touch.

Through the use of this kind of film television can become alive and vital and exciting, for example, a forum type of program can become an hour in which twenty minutes are allotted to the showing of films that will furnish eyewitness material as a background for intelligent discussion. It will become more exciting than a mere radio broadcast of four voices debating an issue, and it will not be an unimaginative telecast of four faces talking monotonously on a television screen.

But wherever 16mm. film is shown, whether on television screens or on the small screens of school, library, and church, it can perform one of its greatest services in creating better international understanding of people and their problems. I see this as a kind of two-way understanding: films about us and our life going out to the screens of the world, and films about other countries, including Russia and her satellites, being shown here.

Films can go even further in promotion of international understanding, however, in interpreting to us the work of our United Nations. I refer here not to the newsreel shots of Vishinsky attacking the democratic way of life or of ourselves defending it, but rather to the positive and unfortunately little-known work that the United Nations has already done and is trying to do in many countries of the world today; the work of the committees on health, on human welfare, on agricultural problems and flood control, and on all the other problems that face us not only as individual nations but as one world.

Eyewitness accounts on film of these activities would be absorbing in themselves. Moreover, they could help create in ourselves and in our neighbor nations the atmosphere of faith which is necessary if the only organization we have that can prevent wars is to survive and do its job.

Julien Bryan is a well-known explorer and lecturer with film, who was graduated from Princeton and Union Theological Seminary, then decided to make social work his career. As a result, his journeyings across the world have brought back much more than the usual traveler's tales; his primary interest has always been in how people work and live. Director since 1945 of the International Film Foundation, founded by a grant from the Davella Mills Foundation, Mr. Bryan still finds time for travel.

our talking pictures

Cecile Starr

IT'S getting so that the movies talk your arm off. This constant yammering is to be expected in Hollywood films which follow, for the most part, the theatre tradition; but it makes itself heard now as a new and serious problem in documentary and educational films as well. Those of us who ardently support the "little" film can no longer overlook the present noisy state of things, much as we might prefer only to remember the films which spoke when they had something significant to say.

For a short period back in the early Thirties motion pictures were colloquially called the "talkies." But, consciously or not, the public soon dropped the word from its vocabulary, indicating that the advent of the recorded word had limited significance beyond the momentary thrill of its discovery. But talk in the movies quickly gained its fullest momentum, giving occasion to the longest jagged line of dulness yet devised.

It was, therefore, something of a relief to stumble upon the documentary films of the middle and late Thirties, perhaps because they were impersonal and disinclined to while away the world's hours in nervous small talk. They commented, but first of all they showed. And the words were used primarily to augment the visual images. When John Grierson made *Granton Trawler* (p. 154) in 1934 he began his experiments on the functional use of sound in film by employing no commentary at all. Even the "live" conversation was mostly inaudible. That was just as well, for the spectator could easily follow the situations as they developed on the screen. Other documentaries, like *Song of Ceylon*, *The Plow That Broke the Plains*, *And So They Live*, *High Over the Border*, and *A Child Went Forth*, earned their makers a silent tribute for notable economy with words—careful, precise, meaningful, and sparing.

But things are changing for the worse. The sound track in to-day's documentary and educational films runs over from one scene to the next. There aren't pictures and time enough to say all that the film makers (or the sponsors?) feel must be said. This com-pulsion to talk, really to preach, may well toll the bell for film as a truly pictorial material. But even if it doesn't prove fatal, it is doubtless a disease. Someone who sat next to me at a screening of the 16mm. film *Productivity, Key to Plenty* used a phrase that diag-noses it aptly—"diarrhea of the sound track."

The movies aren't alone in their guilt. We all talk too much. This is a talking age. Apparently when we don't know what else to do we talk. As individuals, groups, nations, we fire words at one an-other with submachine-gun rapidity. In many ways this craze re-sembles the kind of anxiety that American radio broadcasting suf-fers from—in which more than one moment of silence means that someone will pay with his job!

Of course, the world is full of problems and we want to know an-swers. The movies, like every other means of communication, should help us find them. But all this talk, these words, communi-cation in general, require the equal concept of action. They cannot be accepted as a substitute for action. The most abstract artist, scientist, or philosopher would surely not dispute this. And in the movies, because of the very nature of the medium, mere words are not enough. We need not ask that silences be *imposed* upon the movies, but we can hope to see them used constructively along with constructive picturization. Silence, after all, gives the audience a chance to make its own observations and reflections, to develop *with* the film, not merely to witness the film's development.

However, the pace of dialog and comment in movies today is so fast that there isn't time to hear, much less to reflect. And the pub-lic itself has become thoroughly victimized by this endless barrage of words. Not long ago I attended a theatre showing of some silent Chaplin two-reelers where some of the spectators turned around and indignantly *shushed* others who were laughing out loud. Yet there was nothing to hear from the screen.

Happily, a few good films like *Farrebique* and *The Quiet One* and the new theatrical release *The Bicycle Thief* are pointing out a better reconciliation between the two extremes of sound and si-lence. But there remain the others. What can we do about our talking films? We can't turn off the sound track entirely for fear of missing something essential. We can plead with the film makers to try to weigh their words. And it might help if some serious students of the movies would take a dozen or more of the wordier documentary and educational films, get copies of the spoken commentaries, and make an exercise of cutting the words down by about one-half. It might help even more if they would then submit their final versions to the original film makers for perusal.

Can we hope to put a silencer upon the movies by pointing our trigger finger at them and threatening in the typical Hollywood-gangster way—"You talk too much!"?

looking forward

Cecile Starr

ONCE each year the film reviewer is expected to sit down with a list of the currently released films and select his favorite ten, the outstanding "films of the year." But those of us who are concerned with non-theatrical films (we call a film non-theatrical when it is being shown outside a commercial movie theatre for whatever reason) can enjoy a more relaxed attitude in looking back over the past year. We see, for example, that one of the most popular, most often screened, and certainly best films of the past year, among 16mm. films, was Alexander Hammid's *Hymn of the Nations* (p. 149), the OWI release with Arturo Toscanini. And this is a film that was first released nearly five years ago. That makes it the best film of what year?

The best thing about a really good film is that it lives. Not only has it a distinct quality of aliveness and excitement on the screen, but it also survives over an extended period of time. Without having to rely exclusively upon the stringent principles of theatrical ticket sellers, films which are available for non-theatrical use have more of a life of their own.

The kind of 16mm. films I would include on my list of current "bests"—*The Quiet One, The Loon's Necklace, Farrebique, 1848, Feeling All Right, Nomads of the Jungle*—cannot properly be classified as films of any particular year. (I am reminded of the statement a child psychologist made about parents who speak of their children as being in the third grade as if it were an actual place.) Most of these films were planned and worked on over a period of several years, and the chances are that during the next few years they will be even more successful in terms of showings and popularity and critical acclaim. They are all films which have only begun to live.

And so from this point of view, even more exciting than the number of good films which have been released on 16mm. during the past year is the feeling that groundwork has been laid for more and better films next year and in future years, and for larger, more alert audiences.

Following is a list of the kind of achievements during 1949 which, in this reviewer's opinion, point to better films to come:

1. The Mental Health Film Board, providing an almost model plan for the production and distribution of a series of motion pictures on a variety of important subjects.

2. The Text-Film Division of McGraw-Hill, demonstrating that there is a need for intelligent, adult educational films, and proving beyond reasonable doubt that book publishers *can* sponsor films.

3. The Southern Educational Film Production Service, continuing its exciting program of film-making to meet specific regional needs.

4. The more than one hundred film councils in cities and towns throughout the country, indicating that there is more than passive interest in broadening the usefulness of films and increasing their audiences.

5. The eighty-four public libraries in the country which now circulate films as well as books to their patrons, establishing a basic network for non-commercial 16mm. distribution. (Cooperative film activities among groups of public libraries are spreading so as to include small communities which otherwise could not afford to purchase and use 16mm. films. Experimental operations were begun in the State of Missouri and in the Cleveland area, and plans for similar programs are being made in Tennessee, Louisiana, and Michigan.)

6. Film societies and clubs, many centered around college and university campuses, whose number has grown by leaps and bounds during the past year, meeting increasing success in bringing a variety of unusual films to minority film audiences.

7. Newly established cinema guilds in Port Arthur and Beau-

mont, Texas, guaranteeing audiences a series of foreign films which the group itself has selected for local theatrical (35mm.) showings.

8. National organizations which are looking to films to help them carry on their own work, creating specialized audiences and better standards for special-interest films. (At annual conventions and other meetings it is not surprising to find a theatre of special films being operated on a continuous basis. Recently at a meeting of public-health workers in New York, some seventy-four short films were shown over a five-day period.)

9. Those independent theatre operators who are booking 35mm. prints of interesting documentary films for regular theatrical runs, evoking the applause of audience after audience who are not used to finding intelligent film selection in theatres.

10. And, finally, television program planners are seeing the potential value of films, helping to provide a higher quality of broadcast entertainment for the American public.

The ten best films of the year, or the best hundred—it hardly is important. But it does matter that everyone has an opportunity to see the films he wants to see, that film makers be confident that there will be larger and more varied audiences, and that films become a more integrated part of recreation and of work in as many different kinds of situations as is possible.

II. PRODUCTION AND SPONSORSHIP

the director on location
Willard Van Dyke

THOSE of us who were associated with the pioneer documentary films in this country have been pleased and amazed at the growth of the medium since Pare Lorentz's films *The Plow That Broke the Plains* and *The River* were released in 1936 and 1937. One of the interesting aspects of this growth has been the entry of Mc-Graw-Hill Book Company, with their Text-Film Department under the direction of Albert Rosenberg, into the business of producing films for classroom use.

Early in 1949 Affiliated Film Producers, Inc., was asked by Mc-Graw-Hill to make a series of five films covering certain aspects of courtship and marriage to be used in connection with the college textbook *Marriage for Moderns*, by Henry A. Bowman. Irving Jacoby produced and supervised the writing of the films, and Alexander Hammid and I each directed two of them. (A fifth film was subsequently produced, see p. 189.)

The first four scripts were produced in Columbia, Missouri. They dealt with basic personality types, competition in marriage, adjustment, and problems of courtship. Columbia was chosen as the location because it offered a rich source of young people for acting and because Dr. Bowman conducts his famous course on marriage and the family at Stephens College. The University of Missouri, also located in Columbia, could provide young men for our male roles. Students and faculty members of both institutions, as well as a few townspeople, were used in the films.

There were certain experimental aspects of the project that interested Hammid and me. They also caused us a certain amount of concern. Documentary films began as silent films with a musical background and a neutral narrator. The "actors" were ordinary people performing their daily tasks in front of the camera. Naturally this called for no particular talent and the documentary film director chose his cast for physical appearance and ability to concentrate on the job at hand while forgetting the presence of the camera and crew. Our films, however, called for a large amount of dialog, and it was a question whether relatively untrained people could carry the roles convincingly. The old rule for a documentary director was to set up a situation with which his actor was familiar and then let him react naturally within that situation while the camera recorded his actions. He was rarely asked to speak. Now we were asking students and faculty members to create characters and speak lines in a way that would make those characters believable for an audience.

The natural question is why we didn't use professional actors. We believe that non-professionals, with their untrained spontaneity, can often approach truth more closely than any except the most proficient professionals. Our first important job, therefore, was casting. In this as in every other phase our guide, quite naturally, was the script. A careful breakdown of its needs had given us a knowledge of the number of actors required, but, more importantly, we had by now arrived at a conception of each character in the four films. Hammid and I discussed these people as if they were alive, analyzing their motives, placing them in situations outside the script, watching them react under many circumstances.

Together we began to interview literally hundreds of prospects. Each of us made separate evaluations of the candidates and by consultation arrived at our final casts. In every case, before a final choice was made, each prospective actor was seen under as many circumstances as possible. We were casting for personality traits as well as for physical appearance, and it would help us, and the actors, if the real person was psychologically close to the role he was to portray.

After ten hectic days the casting was complete and the crew arrived. The members of a documentary film crew are usually very different from the technicians who make Hollywood films. Most of our men are in films because they like them; because they feel they are an important means of communication. They have spent years learning their crafts and are technicians of the highest caliber. Most of the seven members of the crew knew each other and had worked together many times. Some of them had been drawn to films from other fields. Our unit manager had studied art at Harvard and had spent a year learning about acting at the American Academy of Dramatic Arts. The cameraman had come to films from music; he had conducted a successful music school. He had photographed many outstanding documentaries including *Valley of the Tennessee, Library of Congress,* and *Toscanini: Hymn of the Nations.* Our electrician had been stage manager for many Broadway productions. These individuals, each doing an important job, were welded into a smoothly operating team.

The function of the director of documentary films is to direct the creative abilities of the cast and crew toward the realization of the script. We were sure of our crew; what about our cast? Would our plan of using non-professionals to carry important speaking parts work? We could no longer rely upon the old method of recording the activities of a man or woman performing familiar tasks in their own environment; we must help our actors to create truth on the screen with unfamiliar words spoken in unfamiliar situations. A superficial understanding of the meaning of the lines is not sufficient; they must be deeply felt and emotionally experienced. This meant that as directors we must know our cast as people, understanding what makes up their personalities.

In achieving this, Stephens College was a great help. They gave us a beautiful house to live in, where we spent our free time, crew and cast together, learning many things about each other, building mutual understanding and respect. The long evenings were filled with discussion and with looking at other documentary films. In this way we learned many things which helped us during shooting. As much of a documentary film director's work is done while he is relaxing as when he is under the pressure of the actual filming; it is during his free time that he gets to know the people with whom he is working. When he knows them well he can help them to find the things within themselves which can be used to create the feeling of truth so essential to the film.

If an actor needed to portray a moment of triumph and was having trouble with it, the director could take him to one side and help him to recall how he felt when he had overcome a particularly difficult problem in his daily life. By now the director knew a great many such stories about the actor. He might know that the girl who was playing her first love scene had never kissed a boy until she had gone home for her Christmas vacation that year. He could caution the crew against kidding her and he could sympathize with, and use (if it fitted the script), her flushed embarrassment after she had kissed the handsome young man who played the scene with her. The director, taking advantage of his knowledge of the people with whom he was working, might sometimes change the script so that it came closer to an actual life experience for his actors, if the change did not alter the original intention of the writer.

When the job is going well, the director knows it by many signs. He awakens in the morning anxious to get to work. He has to be told that if he shoots another scene that day the crew will be on overtime pay. He feels the results of his direction in the smooth coordination of many personalities working toward the single goal of dramatizing the written words of the script for the audience. He and his cast and crew are relaxed and happy, and they work hard. This was such a job.

Willard Van Dyke was a cameraman on The River *and has directed such outstanding documentary films as* The City, Valley Town, *and* Journey Into Medicine. *He is a partner in Affiliated Film Producers, Inc.*

film in the university

Kenneth Macgowan

THE medieval guilds of scholars, which called themselves universities, would be a bit upset at the idea that the higher learning could include the study of how to make motion pictures. They would be quite as upset, of course, over bookbinding, nursing, horticulture, business administration, forestry, gymnastics, social welfare, stenography, public health, mineralogy, folk-dancing, camp leadership, golf, and abnormal psychology. Inevitably, the medieval scholar would be as hostile to making the celluloid book—which is a film—and studying and using the incandescent printing press—which is the motion-picture projector—as monkish copyists of the Renaissance were to the cheap, debased, mechanical imitations of manuscripts turned out by Gutenberg.

But the same impulse that put engineering into the curricula of Harvard and Yale a hundred years ago has slowly forced the motion picture into higher education. The first step was the study and testing and use of educational films. The second was the setting up of producing units in universities, usually in extension divisions. The third and last has been the creation of courses and departments where the skills as well as the theories of film-making are taught on the undergraduate level.

Quite a number of educational institutions maintain production units—at least thirty—but [in 1949] only four universities and one school of adult learning teach film-making. The four are New York University, the City College of New York, the University of Southern California, and the University of California at Los Angeles. The fifth is the New School for Social Research in New York (now the Dramatic Workshop). In all but one, the motion picture has its own department or its own independent curriculum. In one—UCLA—it is integrated into a department which includes theatre, radio, and television.

Here I am dealing only with UCLA, partly because I am more familiar with its set-up and philosophy, and partly because I believe that in its pattern there may be important educational values.

At UCLA the motion picture and radio are treated as off-shoots of theatre. Teaching and learning begin with the study of theatre through the first two years. Only in the junior and senior years does the student specialize in more theatre or in motion pictures or in radio. The value of this, it seems to me, lies in educational morale and in educational method. The student who is enamored of the golden gawds of Hollywood studios and broadcasting stations is forced back to the fine traditions and values of the ancient and creative theatre. His vision of a Beverly Hills swimming pool as the quick and easy end of film study is dimmed a bit by two years of hard work in theatre history, acting fundamentals, scene building and painting, and workshop production of plays, and a course which gives him a lively sense of the social responsibilities of the man who deals with the minds and emotions of millions of his fellow beings.

In terms of pedagogy, it seems practicable to give the student of film a grounding in the acting, directing, and production of plays, and then teach him the modifications that must be made in terms of film. Thus, the study of theatre—a moral gain—is not an academic waste. Later, he must learn, of course, the special and unique skills, such as photography, editing, animation, writing, and design, which apply only to the motion picture.

Another feature of the UCLA curriculum is not unique. This is moving the student forward from courses in theory to courses in practice. The department gives two motion-picture workshop courses during the regular semesters, and what amounts to two more workshops during the summer session. In these workshops— particularly in the last two—the students go through all the practical experiences of film-making. The end-product is not only learning. It is, also, production. The students, guided and implemented by the staff, turn out actual films.

What promise does the work of the University of California and of the other schools where film is taught hold for the future?

Manpower is the first problem, which means teacher-power. The two universities in Los Angeles can and do draw on Hollywood craftsmen for lecturers who give single courses. As the five active schools progress in terms of time and increased efficiency, they will send out—particularly where they have graduate work—men and women who can teach them in new departments.

The producing of teaching films as projects in workshop courses should have a slow but perhaps important effect on the future of visual education. Such films should do something to break the vicious circle that restricts the growth of the motion picture as a vital teaching medium. At present there are not enough projectors in our schools because there are not enough good films to show, and there are not enough good films because there are not enough projectors to make the producing of more films sufficiently profitable. As the universities and their students make more films that can be sold or rented to other schools, they will help—slowly, very slowly, to be sure—to break the circle.

The commercial producers of teaching films may be tempted to look on the producing activities of the universities as unfair competition based on the utilization of free student labor. Instead, they should welcome it as a means of developing a larger market for their own profit. The universities, on the other hand, must be conscious of the future dangers that lie in such competition. As the market for commercial production becomes larger, the universities must channel their efforts towards the making of teaching films that serve special needs. They should turn out films for which there is a limited market, films that are of vital importance, perhaps, but films that could not return their production costs if made in the ordinary way of commerce.

The teaching of film skills in the university is not merely another facet of vocational training; for the making of educational films by its students—in or out of college—can mean a definite contribution to the teaching process in the universities, the high schools, and the elementary schools of our nation.

Kenneth Macgowan, chairman of the Department of Theatre Art at the University of California at Los Angeles, is the producer of a number of outstanding Hollywood pictures, including Young Mr. Lincoln, Man Hunt, *and* Lifeboat. *Professor Macgowan was for six years editor of* Theatre Arts *magazine and has published a number of works on the history and the future of the drama.*

more seeing, less selling

Mary Losey

IT is the most frightening fact of our time that scientific discovery has so far outrun understanding and social organization that the very progress it brings threatens the total destruction of humanity. Every now and then a new dramatic development brings us up short before the fearful realization that we are daily creating the alternative possibilities of a brave new life or a final and hideous finish to it all.

In this medium of the motion picture we have one such invention. Film is a technique for the communication of ideas. I do not include here the Hollywood film, which by choice and necessity has eliminated itself from the discussion of ideas. (It is concerned with marihuana—in one form or another.)

But the documentary film, that is, the film which is intended to say something to somebody for some reason and not necessarily just to earn a direct monetary return, *is* concerned with ideas. And it will depend to some considerable extent upon what ideas it deals with and how it deals with them whether or not documentary film serves the purposes of human survival and human progress.

A few generations ago the visual arts were practiced by individual artists who observed the elements of their world to select and make meaningful what they saw for the enrichment and pleasure of their fellow men. Frequently the artist was sponsored, and the freedom to ponder and create works of art was bestowed upon him by enlightened individuals who could see the society around them but who were unable to give it meaning and interpretation. But Maecenas is obsolete. For all we invoke the freedom of the individual, nothing is created—poetry and painting aside—but through the combined and corporate and cooperative efforts of many members of society. It is therefore to the great industrial enterprises, to governments and public institutions, and private endowments that one looks for sponsorship of the films that may in the years to come light the distance between know-how and understanding which now lies so darkly before us.

Robert J. Flaherty, an intemperate believer in the powers of the motion-picture camera to observe the real world, has shown the way once again to enlightened sponsorship of documentary films. It was nearly thirty years ago that Flaherty first persuaded the Revillon Frères, famous French furriers, that they could well afford to invest in what has since come to be regarded as the first documentary film. The result of that persuasion was a film known to most film-goers of the last generation, and currently being shown again in Europe and England and the North and South American theatres, as *Nanook of the North* (p. 173). But it is not the revival of *Nanook* that proves the point of what wise sponsorship can do to support fine films and at the same time give honor and prestige to the sponsor. It is the fact that Flaherty's most recent film, *Louisiana Story*, released to audiences here in the United States and abroad, is sponsored by one of the most colossal of all industrial empires, Standard Oil of New Jersey. And again, and this time in the face of all the customary press-agentry and selling

now common to sponsored films, he has produced a poetic vision
and lasting human document which will bring pleasure and understanding to audiences for years to come. This time the sponsor
has gone so far as to forego even the customary credits on the film
and seems satisfied to allow the film and the film maker to deal
in their own way and on their own terms with the basic story of
the impact of a vital modern industry upon a simple and even
backward people. Many will ask, "What does it do for the sponsor?" Well, it doesn't tell you to buy oil, or use more oil, or that
oil will win the war or save the peace, or that industry will grind
to a screeching stop without oil, or that this is the oil age. No;
it simply says there is a technology involved in getting oil from
the earth, particularly oil from beneath the waters of a swampy
Louisiana bayou. It says it is not easy and that the men who do it
are hard-working, intelligent, industrial craftsmen, decent and
productive. It makes you wish the men in this particular derrick
could do their job with less trouble, and it shows how a small
boy, whose only previous contact with modern technology has
been his rusty rifle and an occasional glimpse of a motor boat
passing his father's shack, learns that there is another kind of life
beyond his bayou which is a wonderland in itself. It blessedly
leaves the audience to decide whether the commodity oil is of any
importance whatsoever.

We in the United States, however, have yet to find a single
instance of a planned and sustained sponsorship on long-term
public-information lines. There are, however, many chinks in the
wall. Perhaps the insurance companies lead in their sponsorship
of films on health and safety and, perhaps, their interest in human
longevity is the secret to their vision. But cold-blooded as it may
be, the point is that sponsors are making films which are beginning to serve the audiences for whom they are made instead of
the vanity of their sponsors.

Another equation yet to be balanced is the patent concern of
most American industries with a prosperous and active foreign
trade. To date only foundations and governments have seen the
point of making films which help people to see that the healthy
exchange of goods between people and nations is the circulatory
system of their economic life. What with ECA pouring its bil-
lions into reviving European economies, it is hard to believe that
there is no broad-visioned industry in this country which will not
see the advantage of explaining the whole international trade com-

plex to the world's citizens instead of insisting upon marketing rubber gloves to half a billion Hottentots.*

Or take the current uproar over the world shortages of resources of soil and forests and basic minerals. Hundreds of industries base their entire economic existence on these resources. Surely one or several of them will soon see the logic of beginning the slow, careful process of public education that will be necessary to halt this disastrous trend toward the physical depletion of the very bases of human existence.

The list has no end or—for that matter—very little beginning. Do not entirely blame the sponsors for this lack of vision. There are many film makers who are not really concerned with the communication of ideas at all but are merely manufacturers whose motto is "Give the Customer What He Wants." There is also the educator, who is, perforce, a careful type. There are always school boards and parents and curricula and the elders of the community, and the educator must walk deftly around them all on little cat's feet. On the rare occasion when he has the opportunity to breathe life into the dry body of the teaching film, after one brief thrill of hope he usually retreats into committee and comes out with the composite opinion of one hundred carefully selected representatives of opposing points of view, plus one hundred precautions against offending existing custom, dulling every sharp idea, and producing a piece of neutered pedantry that offends nothing but the lively imagination and the hungry mind of the child it was intended to educate. Governments have a way, too, of standing over the camera's shoulder and fogging the lens with their breath. In fact the only party to the whole affair who can plead not guilty is the poor put-upon audience.

But the opportunity resides with the men and women who have consciously and seriously learned to command this new and exciting technique of communication. The whole job still lies ahead. This is a cooperative job between the sponsor and the documentary-film technician and among film makers themselves. All that is needed is to find the patterns of our society which need the lucid revelation of the camera's bright eyes. I believe the people want it.

Mary Losey has been active in many phases of documentary film promotion and production. Currently she heads the film program of the World Health Organization in Geneva.

* Since this article was written in 1948, the ECA itself has produced a number of films on its work in Europe. These films are available free of charge from A. F. Films, 1600 Broadway, New York 19, N. Y.—Ed.

labor and the film

Albert Hemsing

LABOR'S meager efforts to use the film pale beside the achievements of industry and agriculture. Literally thousands of films have been sponsored by business interests. In the last ten years the NAM alone has screened its views on the American social scene before 173 million people.

How does labor get in on all this? It points with pride to *Brotherhood of Man* (p. 216), made by the United Automobile Workers (CIO), and with less than pride to *Deadline for Action* (p. 199), by the United Electrical Workers. But until recently at least, most labor leaders, when they thought about film at all, did so with an attitude that was amazingly horse-and-buggy.

There is a very real danger that the non-theatrical screens of America will become exclusively the spokesman of big business. Labor has made no effort to publicize its views on economics, "Americanism," or any issues of the day with equal effectiveness. Nor can we expect stimulus to independent thought from the timid hedgings of the "social-studies" films produced by educational and commercial film companies. Those who know the spread and effectiveness of films *outside* the theatre and who feel that a free marketplace of ideas is essential to democracy must look to labor to establish a balance.

Of course, nobody needs labor on the screen like labor. Time was when union loyalties were dearly held because they were dearly bought. A worker was most often educated in the precepts of unionism by the business end of a nightstick. Presumably those days are gone for good. Along with them went many of the personal bonds between union and worker. Now we have the true child of his time—the automatic union member, loyal but indifferent, brother to the passive citizen and the Sunday church-member.

The task of educating and inspiring its fifteen million members has become fully as important to the unions as organizing or collective bargaining—and it happens to be a task film is especially equipped to do.

It is customary in articles of this kind to survey what is being done in the field and, with pious hope, to predict a glowing future. In this case there seems to be reason for hope. Film has taken hold in a good number of local union halls and is making a place for itself from the ground up, as it were. It begins to look as if labor's leaders will *have* to rise to the occasion.

There are now three fair-sized nuclei of film users in the CIO. During the last war the auto workers organized a Film Division in their Education Department in Detroit, which makes theirs the oldest and largest labor-film library going. The newest center is the library of the Textile Workers and Amalgamated Clothing Workers in New York, a unique arrangement jointly maintained by these two separate unions. Film source for most other unions in the CIO is the Film Division of the National CIO in Washington. All in all, these three libraries service an average of 275 requests a month—a figure that blushes to be told, considering the CIO's potential audience of five million.

With the AFL the story is briefer—and bleaker. Of the 1,000 projectors scattered over the country in union halls the AFL (with a membership of 8,000,000) accounts for a bare 200, with 800 belonging to the CIO. Much of the credit for the CIO's edge over the AFL in film use belongs to George Guernsey, associate director of the CIO Education Department. Ex-schoolteacher and confirmed film enthusiast, Guernsey not only helped to organize the CIO Film Division in 1947 but since has pushed and pulled scores of locals into using films as a regular part of their program.

While a number of AFL unions occasionally circulate films to their locals, they have no formally constituted film library. So it is encouraging that, after years of urging by union educators like Mark Starr, the AFL Workers Education Bureau is soon to provide a film information service, perhaps even a central AFL library.

The films that do get shown through these channels are essentially fringe films like *Don't Be a Sucker, The City, The House I Live In, The Roosevelt Story*—movies the union can integrate into its education work.

Further growth of film use waits upon the production of a core of films specifically designed to meet union problems. There is no such core at present. Search all the lists and you come up with no more than thirty union-sponsored films. Here is a sampling, roughly classified by content: labor history—*Marching On, The Strange Case of Tom Mooney*; strike stories—*Poverty in the Valley of Plenty, United Action, Conspiracy, The Oakland Story, The Redwood Story*; union education—*The Campus Comes to the Steelworker, Brother John*; political action—*They Said Labor Didn't Count, The Case of the Fishermen, Deadline for Action, They Met at the Fair*; foreign policy—*Rome Divided, Eyewitness in Athens*; institutional portraits—*This is Our Brotherhood, Our Union, The Carpenters' Home, Our Union—Story of Local 91, Look for the Union Label, A Bounty Unpurchasable*.

It could very well be said of the unions which made the films listed above: "Their attitude has been, with few exceptions narrowly parochial or naively propagandist. With funds and organization fully available for the making of inspiring films which would be of direct service to the community, they have tended to spend their money on movies devoted to celebrating centenaries and past triumphs, or to preaching to the converted." These are the words of Basil Wright speaking of the British trades unions. How applicable to the United States!

At least two recent labor films are conceived in a new spirit. Highest praise for *With These Hands*, labor's full-length feature, should go to David Dubinsky. By all accounts, the lively leader of the International Ladies Garment Workers Union threw his unbounded enthusiasm behind its production and has since become labor's most active partisan of the film medium. Though given only a lukewarm reception at its Broadway opening (by critics who ought to be able to distinguish between a historical documentary in dramatic dress and the standard entertainment product), *With These Hands* rates as a fine public-relations effort and far and away the best film ever produced by labor. Of course, Dubinsky's problem is only half-solved. The other half consists of getting the movie shown to the members—and ILGWU locals have neither 16mm. projectors nor a distribution set-up. Taking the members to the theatres is, at best, a one-time outing. In terms of a permanent solution it begs the question.

Union at Work (p. 212), not slick and not expensive (in fact, cheaper than any film has a right to be), bears the stamp of the Textile Workers' experienced education director, Lawrence Rogin, who wanted an honest educational tool. In making the film he was motivated by a clear-cut purpose—to explain a union to its members by dramatizing its services. Members will see it at regular meetings in their own halls because a network of active 16mm. projectors was painstakingly established for two years beforehand. Results to date would seem to bear out the confidence that Textile's President, Emil Rieve, had in the project.

Whether these two so different, but equally purposeful, films mark the beginning of a new era of expanded film activity by the unions remains to be seen. That is a decision which will have to be taken at top levels in the AFL and CIO, and one which should no longer be put off.

Were labor's indecision a question of money alone it could be shown that no major union fails to spend upwards of $100,000 a year on its newspaper. Yet, audience for audience, properly distributed films are cheaper and more effective than printed matter. And since union reserves total in the millions, there need be no question of a choice between the two.

The answer to labor's sporadic and ineffectual film efforts lies in cooperation and planning for both production and distribution. Logically, a coordinating agency similar to the Mental Health Film Board is demanded. A labor film board might even transcend the AFL-CIO split on a well-defined program of priority films on which all the unions can agree. It could make possible what some see as labor's most immediate need: a monthly, ten-minute news-reel.

Labor has to come to grips with creating a program of film use and film-making that is planned and effective, sooner better than later. What it finally does with film will be a test of the maturity of its leadership and its capacity to contribute to democracy.

Mr. Hemsing was in charge of 16mm. distribution for OWI Overseas during the war and later was sent to Great Britain to evaluate the State Department's film services there. He is now director of the film division of two different unions—Textile Workers and Amalgamated Clothing Workers.

for health and happiness
Cecile Starr

(Editor's Note: This editorial and the following article were written in September 1949 to announce the Mental Health Film Board and its plans to produce, for the first time in this country, a series of 16mm. films on mental-health problems. A number of these films are now available for distribution; further information is available from the Board, at 164 East 38th Street, New York 16, N. Y.)

IT'S good news to hear of the planned production of a continuing series of non-theatrical films for adult use, but it's even better to learn that these films will deal with problems of mental health. There are many ways in which films can serve us well, but none is so important, in a sense so unique, as this one.

Every film which has anything to do with people must also to some extent show how people behave. The uniqueness of this series lies in the fact that the films will present behavior problems in the light of established scientific knowledge. Scientists for a long time have been studying human behavior, and they have learned a remarkable amount about it. In his presidential address before the American Psychiatric Association, Dr. William C. Menninger stated the case clearly. "Whether we wish it or not, we cannot avoid the responsibility of helping the public to understand psychiatry," he said. "We can supply the scientific facts on personality development and function; we have some very definite data on the effect of environment, including the influence of social forces. We have some knowledge of the unconscious dynamics which appear so mysterious to the layman. This understanding, if we made it available, undoubtedly could be helpful in alleviating social distress."*

* *American Journal of Psychiatry,* July 1949.

One thing should be emphasized from the start: The films will not be concerned with psychiatry. This is to say that we don't all have to understand psychiatry in order to be healthy and happy. Through its many complicated and tedious research practices, science often comes up with information which we, as non-specialists, never really understand. We are surrounded by apparatuses in our daily lives which we use without a background of special knowledge about them. For example, we take advantage of the exhaustive scientific knowledge about electricity by having our homes properly lit, by listening to our radio, using electric irons, and so forth. Yet we are not all electricians, and few of us aspire to be. We accept a practical explanation of how these appliances function, and we use them as wisely as we can, calling for an electrician when things get really out of hand. Our interest in electricity is not in how it works, but in how it works for us.

The situation with information about mental health is somewhat the same. However, knowledge about mental health cannot be manufactured and marketed in the usual sense. It can be translated from purely scientific applications into terms and situations which we can understand and profit by. This translating job the film can do with amazing facility.

A certain amount of groundwork has already been laid for this new film program. First of all there was the British picture *Psychiatry in Action,* a sixty-minute film produced in 1943, showing various kinds of therapy in a psychiatric hospital in England during the war. The film is distributed in this country by the British Information Services to professional psychiatric workers for their use with medical and lay groups. Then John Huston's *Let There Be Light,* produced by the United States Army Signal Corps, showed similar methods of hospital treatment for soldiers in this country; this film has not been made available for general distribution. A second Army film entitled *Shades of Gray,* purportedly made to replace *Let There Be Light* for some sort of general distribution, likewise has been withheld. Both the Army and Navy produced special series of films on combat neuroses and related problems—but these too were not released generally. Perhaps it is just as well. It was inevitable that mental-health films should be released for public use, and it is preferable that they come from a civilian rather than a military source.

The most popular films in this field are the three productions of the National Film Board of Canada—*The Feeling of Rejection* (p. 183), *The Feeling of Hostility,* and *Over-dependency* (p. 192).

The idea was to produce films which might prove of value for professional use in group therapy. But the wide acceptance the first film received, especially in the United States, showed that the public wanted to find out all it could about this important subject of human behavior. The three films, produced and directed by Robert Anderson (who was the first film officer of the Mental Health Film Board), established a new set of experiences for both producers and audiences, which will certainly be of invaluable help in planning and filming this new series.

In this country several noteworthy beginnings have been made in films relating to mental health. McGraw-Hill's *Emotional Health* and Coronet's *Attitudes and Health* (p. 179) have explained some basic factors in emotional and physical disturbances. Hollywood produced *The Snake Pit*, which won critical and box-office acclaim for a vivid dramatization of mental illness and its ramifications. And the surprise film of many years dealt sensitively with the problems of a young boy in a hostile environment and his chance for a return to a healthy life. That film was *The Quiet One* (p. 175). Irving Jacoby, past chairman of the New York Film Council, who has written and/or produced such outstanding films as *The Pale Horseman*, *Journey Into Medicine*, and the Affiliated Film production *Marriage for Moderns*, has been film consultant to the National Institute of Mental Health of the U. S. Public Health Service. Out of this work and Film Council activity, plans for the Mental Health Film Board began.

The setting is just about perfect. Everyone—professional workers and laymen—has indicated that the time to start learning about ourselves and our relations with other people is right now. The Mental Health Film Board, in producing not merely seven films, but as many as it can on a continuing basis, indicates that it is designed to go as far into the future as will be possible. This program potentially carries the greatest value that has yet been imagined in the relatively young field of 16mm. films. We can only hope that it will be successful to the fullest.

NOTE: *As we go to press the Mental Health Film Board has announced that its first two films,* Angry Boy *and* Steps of Age *are being distributed by International Film Bureau, 6 North Michigan Ave., Chicago 2, Illinois.* Angry Boy *deals with a schoolboy's psychiatric treatment at a child guidance clinic;* Steps of Age *is concerned with problems of growing old.*

scenario for psychiatry

Irving Jacoby and Robert Anderson

THE formation of the Mental Health Film Board, a motion-picture unit that is unique in both its scope and its organization, has been publicly announced in the past week. If it succeeds in its general purpose, to produce and distribute superior educational films in a field where they are badly needed, the Board may well set a precedent for other fields where disorganization and economic chaos have kept such activity on a sporadic, desultory, and ineffectual level.

Mental health is a subject that can only be understood in terms of mental illness, yet the Board, composed almost entirely of M. D.'s, will probably not make a single medical picture out of the considerable resources with which it begins its existence. Mental health expresses itself in the community in human terms, in marriages that work, in labor relations that are reasonable, in children who grow up into happy adults, in a lively cultural life, in people who reach old age with a growing sense of personal peace, in a reduction of crime and juvenile delinquency, in an absence of hate between the different groups that make up the community. And the mental-health film program will be carried out along similar human-interest lines. They will differ from other pictures on similar subjects in only two major ways: (1) They will have an over-all goal of preventing the more serious aspects of mental illness that now constitute America's costliest medical problem, and (2) they will attack these human problems with the information and insight that have been developed through the years by psychologists and psychiatrists working behind the closed doors of laboratories, clinics, and consulting rooms. Mental health is the business of parents, teachers, ministers, doctors, lawyers, businessmen, statesmen, and every other individual in the community who has anything at all to do with inter-personal relationships. The scope of the Mental Health Film Board is to try to help these people to understand their day-to-day problems in terms of the so-called human element that usually contributes ninety-nine percent of the problem, and to increase the productivity of the community by reducing the hidden forces that tend to make its members defeat their own purposes.

The new Film Board is composed of the following psychiatrists: Dr. Leo H. Bartemeier, president of the International Psycho-analytic Society; Dr. Kenneth E. Appel, chief of the Neuro-Psychiatric Clinic of Pennsylvania Hospital; Dr. M. Ralph Kaufman, president of the American Psychoanalytic Association; Dr. Carl Binger, editor of *Psychosomatic Medicine*; Dr. Leon Saul, head of the Department of Preventive Psychiatry of the University of Pennsylvania School of Medicine; Dr. Thomas A. C. Rennie, of Cornell University Medical College and New York Hospital, and Dr. Howard Rome, of the Mayo Clinic. Representing various aspects of public health on the Film Board are Dr. Leona Baumgartner, of the Children's Bureau of the Federal Security Agency; and Dr. Joseph Bobbitt, clinical psychologist of the National Institute of Mental Health. Mrs. Alberta Altman, of the National Institute of Mental Health, who is largely responsible for bringing the Board into existence, and Nina Ridenour, educational director of the National Committee for Mental Hygiene, are to be executive consultants. The Board is also appointing an Advisory Council of anthropologists, sociologists, educators, film producers and distributors, and leaders of lay groups interested in mental health. The Advisory Council, in addition to providing a cross reference to community problems, is designed to link the Board's program to the practical needs of film users throughout the country.

The Board is primarily a policy-making body. It will decide the specific directions toward which the program will work, it will devise a long-range master plan of specific films, it will set up a priority list for subjects, it will set up evaluation projects to consider the films already available in the field. In other words, it will become a center and clearing house for films on mental health. But it will, at the same time, supervise the production and distribution of a number of pictures that it considers of top priority and importance. It is planning to produce the first seven films from funds supplied by the mental-health authorities of thirteen states. The actual picture-making and distribution are to be carried out under contract by various existing firms at the direction of the Board's present film officer, Robert Anderson, one of the authors of this piece. What goes into the films, and even the way in which the films are designed to affect the members of the audience, will be determined in large part by the Board. Unlike some of their colleagues who have been "technical advisors" to Hollywood picture makers, the psychiatrists in this case will be the producers who will use film people as technical advisors. And unlike Hollywood, which has for the most part used psychiatric knowledge to entertain, to scare, and to thrill, the Board hopes to use it to help people live richer lives, to allay their personal anxieties, and to make them happier, more productive citizens.

Early in the development of this project fears were expressed that the notorious differences of opinion between schools and systems of psychiatry would soon lead to serious troubles in deciding the content of the films or even their goals. To be sure, the differences exist, but more and more, as discussions of the plan evoked response from many different quarters of the profession, it became apparent that there exists a great body of thought that is no longer the object of serious doubt or uncertainty.

How this particular body of thought is to be translated to a general audience raises more interesting possibilities than are usually inherent in an educational film project. Psychiatrists, from scientific experience, know that the basic attitudes of people cannot be changed by giving them facts; film makers, from artistic experience, are aware of the same truth. As film makers, we have always tried to exploit, in the best sense of that word, the emotional aspects of our material. However, in the productions of the new Film Board the emotions themselves will constitute a large part of the material. Artistically that should mean good movies, that is, exciting, stimulating, colorful, gripping movies. On the other hand, the unresolved stimulation of certain emotions can result in the production of anxieties and fears that defeat the very purpose of these pictures. The only way to avoid the pitfall will be the development of an interesting partnership between the scientist and the creative person so that, working closely together throughout the entire production process, they will end up with what is both good art and good medicine.

These films, under such conditions, cannot turn into the how-to-do-it, pat-answer pictures that clutter up so many of the educational film catalogs, since no one can make formulas on how to live life. On the other hand, no one will try to turn the seats of theatres and 16mm. auditoriums into psychoanalytical couches. This is simply a project for mass education which is being tackled with the classic documentary film approach that still is, as it was in the days when John Grierson first expressed it, the use of realism to change patterns of thought and feeling on a community level. That's exactly what the psychiatrists, in their learned professional papers, are saying has to be done if we are to get anywhere in preventing mental illness in our time.

experimental films

Arthur Knight

A MOST interesting film phenomenon in postwar America has been the mounting tide of experimental work being carried on outside the Hollywood studios, indeed rejecting completely the standards and aims of the Hollywood film. For these are pictures produced con *amore*, generally privately financed, by young people who seek self-expression in the art that is closest to them, the art they grew up with.

This is not new, this wave of experimental work we now are witnessing. It has happened before, notably in Europe after the First World War and again in this country during the early Thirties. In both instances the films bespoke a profound, personal discontent with motion pictures as they were. Their creators saw artistic problems and potentialities in the medium that the studios had ignored. But where the early *avant-garde* films were seen only by a few of the initiate in small and special halls, today the audience for these pictures seems to be steadily growing. Every art requires an audience but it is an inherent peculiarity of the film that it should be seen by a great number of people at any one time.

Unquestionably the real spark of this American movement has been the tireless Maya Deren. With her program of half a dozen frankly strange-seeming pictures she organized showings in large

cities, visited and lectured at colleges and universities, pamphlet-
eered and publicized until she created an awareness of something
new that she had done. Completely personal in both idiom and
construction, her pictures have probably repelled as many as they
fascinated. But no one has seen a Deren film without being stimulated by the freshness of its imagery and its sheer technical vir-
tuosity. No one has left a Deren performance without sensing the
fact that she had opened new fields for cinema—or, more correctly,
had reopened a field that had lain fallow for almost twenty years.

In any case, Miss Deren fought for an audience and won one.
Her showings in New York's Provincetown Playhouse became
invariable sellouts and were followed shortly by the formation of
Cinema 16, the first organized attempt anywhere to build a mass
audience for experimental films. The original Cinema 16 showings
were held right there in the Provincetown Playhouse (seating
capacity two hundred). But in the past three years Cinema 16 has
grown from a handful of the curious, seeing an occasional program
at the Playhouse, to a substantial throng requiring five repetitions
of each program in two large uptown theatres. Attendance now is
by subscription only: Audiences sign up for a series of eight programs, seeing a complete new show each month.

The surprising thing is that today there are so many experimental pictures around that the Cinema 16 people can pick and
choose—and even reject—in building their programs. This has
come about largely through the enthusiastic support and assistance of the lively San Francisco Museum of Art. The success of
the Deren pictures suggested to a group of young San Franciscans
the possibility of an entire series of such films for their Museum.
Late in 1946 they offered Art in Cinema, a series of ten programs.
Only two of them, however, included any contemporary experi-
mentals. For the main, Art in Cinema explored origins, trends,
and techniques.

At the present moment [May 1950] the Museum is preparing
its sixth Art in Cinema series. Many of the pictures this time will
come from native talent—from James Broughton, Sidney Peterson,
Jordan Belson, Frank Stauffacher, Leonard Tregillus, Hal McCor-
mick. More will come from Hollywood, where another earnest and
able experimental group has sprung up around Curtis Harrington,
Kenneth Anger, and the Whitney brothers. The two groups keep
close contact with each other, exchanging films, ideas, and criticism.

Now, just what are these experimental films? What are they like and what differentiates them from the Hollywood product? Perhaps the most important difference—more important than any camera trickery or Freudian symbol—is the fact that each of these pictures is a completely personal expression by the artist who made it. Whether a projection of his dream world or a working out of his theory of abstract art, it is the creation of an individual, the product of a single mind. Inevitably, there is a certain unevenness about these pictures. Not all are of equal merit, either structurally, thematically, or technically. There is even an important reservation about the term experimental in the minds of the people who make these films: Some hold to the literal meaning of the word and frankly offer their pictures as examples of work in progress, experimental in the sense of working out a problem. Others, like Maya Deren and James Broughton, present their films as complete works of art, with experimental used to describe their general nature. Their audiences must be prepared to share the special interests of the film makers themselves—interests that range through abstract design and music, psychology, psychoses, and, perhaps above all else, the problems of interpreting these interests through the motion-picture camera.

Actually, experimental films take many forms but it might be convenient to divide them simply into the abstract or non-objective film and the subjective film. This admittedly arbitrary differentiation serves a double function by describing both their content and their purposes. Historically, the non-objective films came first with Hans Richter's *Rhythmus 21* (1921), a study in the dynamic rhythms and patterns of rectangles and squares in constant countermotion. Throughout the Twenties Walter Ruttmann, Man Ray, Fernand Léger, and Oskar Fischinger all carried on abstract experiments in a number of different forms, from Léger's piecing together the dissected motion of people and machines into a *Ballet Mécanique*, to Fischinger's laborious frame-on-frame drawings of geometric forms synchronized to music.

Fischinger, working now in Hollywood (but not in the studios), has become a sort of living link between the European antecedents of the non-objective film and the current creators in this form. Perhaps foremost in this group today are the Whitney brothers, winners of two Guggenheim grants. Working with mathematical precision on equipment of their own devising, they have created a series of brief abstract films in which strange, luminous forms flash to a weird and unearthly accompaniment of synthetic sound, with an occasional moment of perfect congruence that is immensely satisfying. In *Dime Store*, Dorsey Alexander has created still another ballet mécanique by moving ten-cent-store objects in gay, humorous patterns to the music of Offenbach; he has also done a couple of black-and-white abstract improvisations that somehow, in their rhythm and delicacy, suggest the expressive line of a Paul Klee print. In Martin Metal's *Color*, oil paints and water colors ooze through prepared screen backgrounds for moments of striking, if adventitious, beauty. Frank Stauffacher's *Zigzag* is composed from the night patterns of neon signs, the shots cut rhythmically to Stravinsky's *Ebony Concerto*.

In the East, Douglass Crockwell, a successful commercial artist, began to search around for media that would lend themselves readily to individual self-expression on film. He has worked out techniques using thick, manipulative paints on glass and molded wax forms that move against strong, colorful backgrounds. The pictures that have come out of his experiments—*Glens Falls Sequence, Fantasmagoria, The Long Bodies*—are at once humorous, winningly naive, and provocative in their use of materials. Francis Lee, a young photographer-painter, has worked out yet another technique for himself, combining moving cut-outs with painted backgrounds that shift and change from frame to frame as new colors and forms are added. Lee, also a Guggenheim Fellow, has completed three short films, *Le Bijou, The Idyll,* and *1941.* In *Light Reflections* and *Paintings and Plastics,* Jim Davis, whose medium is plastics, plays colored lights upon his mobile creations and photographs the handsome, shifting patterns that result.

In all of these—and there are many more—it is immediately apparent that the artist is at least as much concerned with the technical processes of creation as with the artistic impact of the creation itself. In the subjective films, on the other hand, while technique still counts high, the emphasis is rather on shaping an expressive whole. Drawing from such precedents as the Dali-Bunel surrealist classic *Un Chien Andalou* and René Clair's ballet fantasy *Entr'Acte,* the present-day makers of these films follow the same line of dream symbol and free association in the creative process. When Sidney Peterson and James Broughton made *The Potted Psalm,* for example, they worked originally from a script, but then, shooting completed, shuffled and reshuffled their strips of film into a pattern that was visually and psychologically satisfying to them. In *The Cage* Peterson resorts to obvious camera trickery—slow motion, rapid motion, reverse motion, superimposition—but to a completely serious end. In a series of sharply visual sequences, heightened by the very strangeness of the camera work, he depicts the artist's flight from authoritarian influences. In quite another vein, *Odd Fellow's Hall*, a satire on murder mysteries by Denver Sutton and Leonard Tregillus, exploits these same irrational potentialities of the camera.

On the other hand, while employing a more routine camera technique, such films as Curtis Harrington's *Fragment of Seeking*, Joseph Vogel's *House of Cards*, and James Broughton's *Mother's Day* all manage to create lingering, haunting impressions through striking compositions of symbol-laden objects (a framed picture of Father, a derby hat, an umbrella, a knife) within the frame. Even Gregory Markopoulos's *Psyche*, based on Pierre Louys' novel and telling a formal story, narrates on the subconscious level, employing dream imagery throughout.

What comes out of all this are pictures that can be felt rather than understood. Their meanings would be impenetrable on the level of consciousness unless one resorted to a psychoanalytic technique, charting them as you would a case history. They are tied together by a continuity of mood and feeling rather than by any formal story line. Frequently they are shocking—sometimes merely by their strangeness, more often as a deliberate attempt to jolt the audience to a greater intensity of awareness.

Obviously, the degree of participation is a personal thing, dependent on each spectator's own equipment and background. But, inevitably, after the first rush of enthusiasm and interest a sifting process does begin. Once the special idiom of these films has been mastered, once the initial strangeness has passed, it becomes possible to separate the talented from the phony, the sincere from the precious, the creative artist from the merely ambitious. Fortunately since virtually all experimental work in this country is done on the relatively cheap, relatively accessible 16mm. film stock, organizations and even individuals anywhere can rent and study these pictures easily.

Arthur Knight is former chairman of the Film Department of the Dramatic Workshop in New York and film commentator on radio station WFDR. At present he is on the staff of the Institute of Film Techniques at College of the City of New York, and a regular contributor to "S R L Goes to the Movies."

film sources

All the experimental films mentioned in this article—and many more—may be rented from the sources listed below. Write for complete catalogues and prices:

A. F. Films, Inc.
1600 Broadway
New York 19, N. Y.

Cinema 16
59 Park Ave.
New York 16, N. Y.

Creative Film Assoc.
6215 Franklin Ave.
Hollywood 28, Calif.

Maya Deren
61 Morton St.
New York 14, N. Y.

Oskar Fischinger
1010 Hammond St.
Hollywood, Calif.

San Francisco Museum of Art
Civic Center
San Francisco 2, Calif.

Renting to organizations only:
Museum of Modern Art Film
   Library
11 W. 53rd St., New York 19, N. Y.

III. ADULT AUDIENCES

films with a purpose

Cecile Starr

TRY to please everyone and chances are that you won't please anyone very much. This is one of the lessons yet to be learned in the field of mass communications, and it is particularly valid for the documentary film. Dealing primarily with facts and points of view, the documentary film *must* have a purpose, a direction. It must say something special to some special audience. Too many film makers and sponsors, however, are afraid of a direct approach. And too many audiences, as a result, are leaving the screening room asking themselves, "What on earth was that film about?"

It has been refreshing to watch the careers of films which started out with a selected purpose and subsequently found themselves successful on other levels as well. Many of the McGraw-Hill Text-Films, for example, have proved useful in high schools and in a variety of adult non-classroom situations, although they are specifically aimed at the college classroom for use with specific textbooks. Other dramatic documentary films, like *Valley Town* and *And So They Live*, have been highly recommended for use in adult discussion programs, although the producers were aiming primarily at another kind of use for them. Much of the success of the British and Canadian documentaries in this country is due to their straightforwardness.

Of recent films with a purpose few have had so dramatic a history as *Feeling All Right* (p. 183). Its purpose was to get facts and ideas about syphilis across to the Negro population of a portion of the Mississippi delta region. On the following pages Hodding Carter tells of the concentrated and effective use to which this film was put. As he points out, *Feeling All Right* has stood one major test: It has met with the definite approval of the people for whom it was intended. It is important that the film has been received with strong emotions in other sections of the country and in other parts of the world. It is important that it has won awards at several international film festivals. But what is most important is that the people for whom the film was made recognize its inherent honesty and accept it for what it has to say. How many employees can say the same of the industrial and labor films they see?

Credit for the success of *Feeling All Right* goes to the producers at the Southern Educational Film Production Service in Athens, Georgia. Serving agencies of nine Southern states, this organization is in a position to know its audiences and to find out what they need to know. Though only a year old [the film was produced in 1948], *Feeling All Right*, which is S.E.F.P.S.'s outstanding production thus far, has a history to be proud of. John N. Popham, writing in The New York *Times*, estimates that the two-reel film, which cost only $30,000 to produce, has been seen by more than a million persons. General distribution has been taken over by the Columbia University Press's Communications Materials Center under Erik Barnouw, who has produced a number of outstanding nationwide radio shows on the subject of venereal disease.

Feeling All Right is being used in many states and cities outside the South, mainly for Negro audiences. There have been some disturbances about the film, too. For one thing, the New York State Board of Censors refused to license it for public, that is, theatrical, showing. While we cannot support film, or any other, censorship, it does seem reasonable that such a film is not acceptable at this time. An appeal is being made, however, by the Columbia University Press.

There have been conscientious objections to showing the film to white or mixed audiences on the grounds that they may infer that only Negroes have syphilis, since only Negroes have syphilis in the film. Using the same kind of logic we might object to the dozens of other venereal-disease films concerned exclusively with non-Negroes. Nor can we support the cry that *Feeling All Right* furthers, or at least accepts, Jim Crow in the South. As a film it attempts only to deal realistically and sympathetically with things as they are. With obvious concern for all the problems contained in the situation, the producers have singled out one specific problem for dramatization. As it turned out, the film does honor both to the people who made it and the people about whom it was made.

This much is apparent: It is a fine film. It has some shortcomings, without doubt; but it has succeeded in the specific job it set out to do, and nothing can destroy that success. Moreover it can be shown successfully for any other purposes which are as honest and intelligent as its original one. It will fail in situations which, for one reason or another, are fraudulent. That is surely an enviable achievement for any film.

In contrast we see how less direct and honest films backfire on their producers and sponsors. The three Harding College films, dealing with what is vaguely and somewhat unrealistically called "the American way of life," are good examples. One of them, *Make Mine Freedom*, was awarded second prize of $750 and a medal at the first annual Freedoms Foundation ceremonies at Valley Forge, presided over by General Dwight D. Eisenhower. But we have yet to hear *anyone* say of the film, "This film is important to me. It gave me a better understanding of the meaning of freedom." And it is interesting to learn, from someone who has made special inquiries, that the three films are being used extensively as an illustration of the kind of economic thinking prevalent in Europe a hundred or more years ago. To that extent, at least, the films have backfired. Like soapbox orators, throwing their words to the winds, they hope to reach the world at large, and they only briefly attract the accidental passers-by. Although it is always easier to make films which deal in vague and important-sounding generalities, the great number of people are seldom impressed by them.

The S.E.F.P.S. and the Mississippi Board of Health, as well as the other organizations and individuals that took part in the planned production and use of *Feeling All Right*, have shown how to make a film for a purpose. They have not presented things as they are not, but as they are. No matter how much we may wish to improve the world or this country or even the State of Mississippi, we must first see things as they actually exist. Purposeful films cannot do otherwise.

mississippi movie

Hodding Carter

IN a state that ranks with the lowest in so many of the indices of civilization the Mississippi State Board of Health is a conspicuous example of the reverse. Headed by Dr. Felix Underwood, the department has won many citations for its outstanding public-health work. And one phase of this work has been its syphilis control program. In the spring of 1949 the department of health inaugurated a program which it was hoped would greatly step up the number of persons coming to treatment. In each of eight counties during the winter of 1948-49 some five thousand persons were given Wasserman tests by Mobile Blood Testing units sent out from state headquarters at Jackson. Publicity as to where these units with their staff of doctors and nurses would be located was run in local newspapers, placed on radio programs, and advertised by posters and handbills. While these campaigns were considered successes, it was hoped that in Washington County, where the work was begun in March 1949, and where the population was greater than in any one of the eight, some twenty thousand would volunteer for tests. While all other publicity methods previously tried would be used again, one new device would be used—a motion picture.

Mississippi is nearly half Negro. And this half is coincident, in great part, with the lower half, economically speaking, of the population. Further, due to educational disadvantages, many of these people do not recognize the danger inherent in syphilis. For this reason the syphilis rate among Mississippi Negroes is still one in ten, a good gain over the one in five of ten years ago, but still not good enough. Anything that would bring home to the Negroes, especially, the importance of getting the proper treatment would be attacking the problem among the group where the rate was highest. Such was the reasoning of Dr. A. L. Gray, director of Preventable Disease Control.

The upshot of this reasoning was the motion picture *Feeling All Right* (p. 183), made in Washington County, using Washington and Sunflower county Negro educators as actors in a script that was filmed against a background of the life the Southern Negro, and especially the Yazoo-Mississippi Delta Negro, is most familiar with. The original script was prepared by Nicholas C. Read, then director of the Southern Education Film Production Service, with the aid of Dr. W. A. Mason, director of Health Education for Colored in the State of Georgia.

In Washington County, with its two-to-one Negro over white population, *Feeling All Right* was given its first showings. Negro educators and the Negro press, Dr. S. A. Pridgen, the county health doctor, the county's only daily, the *Delta Democrat-Times* at Greenville, and the two local radio stations all spread the word. Handbills announced the sixty places the picture would be shown. From Palmetto School on the Pearson plantation to Mt. Zion Church at Darlove to the Casablanca Lounge at Greenville, the showings were scheduled.

At first the film was offered with the added attraction of a Lena Horne boogie-woogie to bring in the audience. But when it began to play, people came in such crowds there had to be two and three showings a night, and there wasn't time for Lena Horne. The audience had come to see *Feeling All Right*.

Following each showing the representative of the Mobile Testing Unit would tell the audience where the unit would be in that neighborhood within the next thirty-six hours. As they walked out the audience talked about the picture, how good Eldred Marshall was in the lead and Blanche Parks as Irma. They also talked about themselves. There was nothing to be ashamed of. Having a test wouldn't even mean you thought you had the bad blood. It was just smart to know—like Roy in the picture.

And they saw for themselves what it was like to go to one of the state's rapid-treatment centers for venereal disease, where free cures were given in six days. To provide for the wage-earner's family during his hospitalization the whole family is invited to come and enjoy the food and recreation at the centers during his stay. There is no stigma attached to syphilis, and they saw that the trip to the center was a pleasant vacation at state expense.

The upshot of the Washington County campaign was some 15,000 tests given at 138 stations, with more than 700 cases brought to treatment during the drive. The final figure of cases treated was 1,765.

Since those five weeks in March and April 1949, *Feeling All Right* has been shown [in the period to April 8, 1950, when this article appeared in the *Saturday Review of Literature*] to 1,531 audiences in Mississippi with a total attendance of 235,173. Of this total number of showings there have been forty-two in public theatres throughout the state. The first of these was at the Bridges, Negro-owned theatre in Greenville, during the campaign. Approximately ninety percent to ninety-five percent of the total audiences have been colored. Wherever it has been shown to white audiences it has been received enthusiastically. But its primary purpose was to reach the Negro population.

Careful scientist and able administrator that he is, Dr. Underwood will not attribute all of the Washington County campaign's success to the motion picture, nor the success of the campaign in the subsequent counties where it was used. But he does say: "Where the film has been used along with the special case-finding project, it has boosted the number of people volunteering for blood tests. Even though the results cannot be measured immediately, we feel that it has great educational value which will project itself many years hence."

But in appealing to a large number of people what could be more effective than a story filmed in terms of their own lives?

Hodding Carter, author of Southern Legacy, *is the Pulitzer Prize-winning editor of the Greenville (Miss.) Delta Democrat-Times.*

film councils at work
Glen Burch

IN the fall of 1948, in Spokane, Washington, the young, community-minded director of audio-visual education of a local university became concerned over the haphazard manner in which community groups obtained and used 16mm. sound films in their programs. Casual inquiry revealed that few program planners had ever heard of the better educational and informational films now available. Most of them, he found, were totally unfamiliar with local film sources, and had little training or experience in the effective use of films and film equipment. He talked informally with some interested friends—the local public librarian, the program director of the YMCA, a local school principal. They decided that some kind of a cooperative effort was indicated to improve the accessibility and use of good films in their city. More people were called in, and the result was the formation of the Spokane Film Council —a coordinating body that now embraces representatives of more than sixty local agencies and organizations. In the first six months of its existence, the Council helped set up a card catalog of the more than two thousand titles now available in the Spokane area, which is kept in the Public Library. It conducted monthly film screenings and put on demonstrations. In April 1949, it brought its first year of activity to a fitting climax by holding a film festival featuring twenty carefully chosen non-theatrical films.

Spokane is just one of more than 170 communities (in thirty-eight states and the Territory of Hawaii) where the film-council idea is being put to work by representative local groups. Autonomous in character, organizationally fashioned to fit the individual needs, resources, and interests of their respective communities, these local film councils are primarily concerned with encouraging the use of films and filmstrips as tools for learning and understanding. Convinced that films have a unique and potent usefulness in the advancement of the education of young and old, their members are working to coordinate film information, improve local film-distribution facilities, provide opportunities for film previews and for training in film evaluation and use.

Now a little over four years old, the film-council movement is largely an outgrowth of community experience with 16mm. films during World War II. Under the leadership of a National 16mm. Advisory Committee, thousands of volunteer groups were organized all over the country to show films relating to the war effort. When this program was completed in 1946 many community leaders said in effect: Since films have proved so useful in wartime in helping us to work together, clarify our common objectives, and acquire needed new skills, we should use them to help tackle the many problems that face us in the postwar period. Organized cooperation, *at the local level*, seemed the best way to begin—and the community film council was on its way.

Like any genuine grass-roots movement, initial local film-council leadership varied widely from community to community. In the little town of Allegan, Michigan, a minister was the prime mover. In Lompoc, California, a recreation director provided the spark. The research director for the local Council of Social Agencies and the audio-visual director in the public schools teamed up to get the Rochester, New York, Film Council on its feet. A club woman rallied support for the idea in Upper Darby, Pennsylvania, and a Parent-Teacher's Association chairman put it to work in Colton, Oregon. Impetus came from a librarian in Kalamazoo, Michigan; an industrial engineer helped set up a council in Cleveland.

Individual film-council programs reflect a wide range of interests—as well as no small amount of ingenuity and energy. The Film Council of Atlanta—one of the first to be formed—has a particularly distinguished record of achievement. During 1949-50 this Council conducted more than forty weekly meetings and programs, and climaxed a full year's work with the sponsorship of an Audio-Visual Workshop for community leaders and teachers. In Delaware County, Pennsylvania, the local film council has just completed a series of eight demonstration film forums on current topics. (It spent a good part of its first year of existence raising funds for a projector.) At Gary, Indiana, the film council's monthly meetings are planned around films on specific community problems—sex education, mental hygiene, traffic safety, etc.—and a special effort is made to bring in the leaders of groups and agencies for whom these problems are a matter of special concern.

Recognizing that many groups are discouraged in their use of films because of the improper or inept way in which they are projected, many local councils have instituted training programs designed to improve the quality of showmanship in volunteer operators. In at least one small community, plagued by a high incidence of film damage, the establishment of a certification committee within the local film council to test and issue certificates to volunteer operators, had salutary results. In another—Houston, Texas—members of the local film council are encouraging high-school students to become expert projectionists and serve community groups by presenting Certificates of Award, with appropriate ceremonies, to those who can pass certain prescribed tests.

In the fall of 1950 the Des Moines Film Council cooperated with Station WOI-TV at Iowa State College in the planning of a series of televised film forums. So far as is known, this is one of the first attempts to use television to demonstrate a film based on discussion technique, and if successful it may forecast a widespread use of this new medium for that purpose.

In the average community today, most club or organization program planners have had no real experience with the better 16mm. films now available, out of which they can make satisfactory judgments of their own particular program purposes. How many of the readers of the *Saturday Review of Literature*'s "Film Forum," for example, have an opportunity to preview any of the films reviewed in it before using them? Local film councils, particularly those in smaller communities, are meeting a real community need by providing, cooperatively, regular screenings of important new films. In this connection an increasing number are finding in the community film festival a dramatic and effective device. The Chicago Film Council is generally given credit for originating the idea in 1947, when it presented on seven successive evenings an ambitious Films of the World Festival, featuring important documentary and educational films—both 35mm. and 16mm.—produced in this country and abroad. A year later the Cleveland Council took up the idea, and using only films that could be procured locally, sponsored a one-day festival, which aroused city-wide enthusiasm and has been made an annual event. One of the most successful of recent festivals was conducted in the town of Stamford, Connecticut. For this event seven committees previewed 87 films, 43 of which were shown to a group of 344 community leaders representing some 77 local organizations. Categories included in the festival were: Your Home, Your School, Your Faith, Your Health, Your Job, Your Government, and The Arts.

In some of the smaller places—Casper, Wyoming, and Greenville, North Carolina,—film councils have been instrumental in establishing community film libraries, and in larger cities—Rochester, New York, is a good example—they have occasionally played an important role in helping the local public library to broaden its services to include films.

One of the most useful and also the most obvious functions these local film councils perform is that of keeping their members in communication with one another. Through monthly meetings, and through regular bulletins members are kept informed of new films, given program suggestions, etc. The Newark, New Jersey, Council has done a particularly good job in this respect, issuing a monthly *Film Council Notes*, which contains film reviews.

Local film councils keep in touch with one another's activities through the Film Council of America, a non-profit, educational organization, which sponsors the movement in this country and serves as a clearinghouse of information about it. The Film Council of America, which in 1948 and 1950 received grants from the Carnegie Corporation in support of its activities, publishes a monthly newsletter on local council activities, gets out occasional film lists and program aids. In 1948 it issued a series of pamphlets —based on local council experience to date—on such subjects as film forums, festivals, film workshops, film evaluation, the establishment of information centers, and the conduct of community surveys. It recently inaugurated a drive to identify and help establish community film information centers throughout the country and published a Preliminary Directory, listing 845 centers, in July 1950.

The great strength of the film-council movement lies in the fact that it is community based. The men and women who are working in it share two common faiths. They believe that films and other audio-visual materials have an enormously important role to play in increasing the individual's understanding of the world around him, and in helping him to make those adjustments in himself and in his human relationships which will enable him to live a socially useful and personally satisfying life in a rapidly changing world. But they also believe that individuals, and the groups with which they are associated, can and must learn to choose for themselves, from among all the films available, those best suited to their individual needs and interests.

The film-council movement might be defined as a growing and determined effort on the part of the people of this country to (1) make good films and other useful audio-visual materials readily accessible where they live, and (2) learn how to select them wisely and use them effectively in programs for the common good. In so far as progress is made toward these goals the ever-present danger that films will become increasingly a medium for mass exploitation and indoctrination will be greatly diminished. And films will begin really to come into their own as the unique instruments of popular enlightenment.

For more than two years Glen Burch has been executive director of the Film Council of America. Formerly he was assistant director of the American Association for Adult Education.

the film society

Amos Vogel

THE experiences I have had since helping to found an organization in New York called Cinema 16 prove, it seems to me, that with ingenuity, perseverance, knowledge of films, and luck, anyone can operate a film society. A non-profit membership organization presenting unusual documentary and experimental films, Cinema 16 acquired more than three thousand yearly members in the first three years after its founding in 1947, making it the largest film society in the country. Started by people with enough confidence in the non-fiction film to believe that there must be a larger potential audience for them than those consisting of school children, members of women's clubs, and hospital inmates, it aims at the glorification of the fact film. Its programs read like a *Who's Who* of many of the best fact and *avant-garde* films, contemporary as well as classic, and its activities have been reported locally and nationally in major newspapers and magazines, and on the air. Members are drawn from seven states, and include teachers, artists, workers, program directors, film producers, and businessmen. Sponsors include Robert Flaherty, Richard Griffith, Paul Rotha, Jean Benoit-Levy, Dr. Siegfried Kracauer, Arthur Knight, Mary Losey, Hans Richter, John Huston, and Jean Renoir.

Activity of any kind is impossible without the committing of errors. Nevertheless, if you are determined to run a local film society—and go ahead you should—here is some information to help you avoid obvious mistakes.

It is a catastrophic fallacy to assume that running a film society involves nothing more than an idealistic concern with good films, coupled with their lackadaisical presentation to willing audiences. On the contrary, the individual brave enough to venture into this troublesome field, must be—no matter what the size of the society

—an organizer, promoter, publicist and copywriter, businessman, public speaker, and artist; a conscientious, if not pedantic, person versed in mass psychology. He must have roots in his community. And he must know a good film when he sees it.

Thus you need film sources and film evaluation. The two are distinct. More often than not, you will have neither time nor money to preview films. Distributors' catalogs are not always objective guides. Many catalogs overlap, rental rates vary with various distributors. It is therefore best first to get the two basic master catalogs available: "The Educational Film Guide" (H. W. Wilson Co., 950 University Avenue, New York); and "The Blue Book of 16mm. Films" (Educational Screen, 64 East Lake Street, Chicago). Both list practically all presently available 16mm. films and their sources, from whom you may obtain further catalogs. "The Educational Film Guide" features more detailed evaluations. "The Educator's Guide to Free Films" (Educators Progress Service, Randolph, Wisconsin) lists a great number of free films. New York's Museum of Modern Art Circulating Film Library (11 West 53rd Street, New York) has the finest and most comprehensive collection for film societies, with use of their films restricted to bona-fide membership and non-profit organizations. Scientific films (restricted to special groups) are obtainable from the Psychological Cinema Register (Pennsylvania State College, State College, Pennsylvania); experimental and *avant-garde* films from Cinema 16 (59 Park Avenue, New York).

For information and reviews of new releases you will find it important to subscribe to leading 16mm. magazines, such as *Film World* (6047 Hollywood Boulevard, Los Angeles, California); *Film News* (112 West 48th Street, New York); *Educational Screen* (64 East Lake Street, Chicago, Illinois). Get back numbers of the *Film Forum Review* (Institute of Adult Education, Teachers College, Columbia University, New York) which—together with the *Saturday Review of Literature*—has presented the most mature evaluations of 16mm. films.

Do not think it easy to get an audience just because you have a film that you alone know to be good; you must let your fellow man know that it is worth his while to see it. Neither must you assume that an audience of twenty is your maximum. Publicize your shows in local newspapers by sending them announcements and news stories. Fire your local movie critic with the importance of your project. Give storekeepers a pass and they will display your window cards. Send program announcements to all organizations, schools, and clubs for display on their bulletin boards. If you show a film on Greece, for example, send special announcement and block tickets to local Greek organizations. Do the same with your parent-teacher groups when you have a film on child education. Contact your radio or television station; they will help if you can show that you are performing a community service.

Names and addresses are your greatest asset. Get names from clubs, camera clubs, women's, parent-teacher, YMCA, and labor groups. Mail copies of your program to them. Build up your own mailing list. Never let anyone see a show without getting his name. Hand out interest blanks or offer a special incentive so you will get the names. If your budget allows it, run a neatly designed small ad in your paper with a coupon for name and address.

After you have found an audience, you must learn to hold it by proper programming. This is where you are on your own. If you haven't the feel for balanced programs, you will fail. The science of programming cannot be taught; it requires psychological insight into the likes of other people and continuing contact with your specific audience to permit you to correct yourself as you go along. Five excellent and serious social documentaries may produce one very bad program. You must lighten programs by humorous shorts, dance or music films, or cartoons. A color short brightens any program, and if presented at the end, often provides a much-needed fillip. A variety of films is usually preferable to an entire evening of one subject. If yours is a functional program, centered around documentaries on, say, atomic energy, variety can be introduced by a cartoon (*One World or None*). Never overpower your audience with too many or too heavy films; moderation and variety will make them come back for more the next time.

Carelessness and amateurishness are the bane of the 16mm. industry. Portable equipment and low film rentals have enabled unqualified individuals to slap together a program, present it one night—and set back 16mm. in the particular community for another five years. It is an error to assume that a good film will "go across" no matter how it is presented. Showmanship is one of the first prerequisites of a successful film society.

Before your show, test your auditorium for acoustics, comfortable heating arrangements, proper electrical connections. Check or provide shades to keep all light from entering. If possible, use curtains or black fabric to mask off the screen to prevent the usual naked 16mm. screen, complete with tripod, from impressing your audience with the amateurishness of the performance. If there is no booth, place the projector above the heads of the audience where its noise will be least audible. If you have a booth, arrange for a fifty-cent buzzer-and-code system to communicate with the projectionist who is almost as important to your show as a good film. Check and clean your prints; if possible, splice them onto larger reels to reduce work at the performance and lend it greater professional flavor. Test your projector. If you rent one, and have no time to check it, don't run your show. You will still keep more good-will than by exposing your audience to the horrors of an improperly working machine, while damaging prints at the same time.

During the show, keep all doors closed. Ask the projectionist to move around quietly and, if he has brought his family to watch him, to wait to discuss personal matters until after the show. Check and correct your sound constantly (sound level varies greatly on 16mm.); watch for focusing and framing, and dirt in the aperture. Be sure not to flash the leader on the screen.

In general, remember that you are a missionary for a wider use of 16mm. films and that you should try approximating professional theatre standards, with the possible exception of providing popcorn or exhibiting insipid films. For further information, get "The Projectionist's Manual" (Educational Film Library Association, 1600 Broadway, New York) or "Projecting Motion Pictures in the Class Room" (American Council on Education, 744 Jackson Place, Washington, D. C.).

Legal matters are often important. Consult a lawyer; ask him to serve on your board if you have no money to pay him. Find out about fire regulations, licenses, possible censorship regulations.

Whatever you do, be prepared for much work, unexpected and recurrent headaches, no remuneration—except the deep satisfaction that comes from accomplishing a very much needed job: that of bringing socially purposeful and artistically significant films to more and more people.

Amos Vogel did creative and critical film work in his native Vienna, where the Nazis' skilful manipulation of the screen convinced him of need for greater production and exhibition of films to present facts. He escaped to the United States after the German invasion, studied at several American universities, and made an extensive survey of the documentary and experimental film field. With wife Marcia he formed Cinema 16 in 1947.

european film festival

Kurtz Myers

FOR the film-minded tourist fortunate enough to be in Edinburgh between August 20 and September 10 last year [1950], and sufficiently indifferent to other arts to turn his back on the many attractions of the concurrent music and drama festival, there was a rich cinematic mine to work. In the course of forty scheduled programs he could have viewed nearly two hundred films, carefully selected and presented. These would have been films in the generally serious tradition of the documentary film, relieved by occasional examples of Gallic irreverence (*Transports Urbains*) or American impudence (*Muscle Beach*). He would still have had time for such supplementary attractions as the military tattoo, staged nightly on the Castle esplanade; Sir Thomas Beecham's fireworks; and the exhibition of paisley shawls.

Actually the tourist makes a very small contribution to the success and the unique quality of the Edinburgh film festival. Capacity and overflow crowds are not testimonials to the enterprise of Cook's or the American Express but rather to the widespread interest in the film as a medium and in film-making which has been developed in Britain over a period of years. Queues in Britain are a fact of life which Americans quickly accept; but queues waiting for admittance to programs of documentary films are a phenomenon worth pondering.

They are in a way the symbol of the years of experience and the careful planning which have resulted in Edinburgh in a film festival unique in scope and quality. There are other international film festivals; at least a half-dozen major ones are offered to the Continental tourists. But these other festivals rely heavily on feature films, on the attendance of film celebrities, on the pleasantness of the resort-town life which goes on about them. Edin-

burgh operates in, and creates, a different climate. It limits its
scope to films which can be encompassed by three qualifying words
—realist, documentary, experimental. It is governed by a policy of
film selection and a tradition of film appreciation which is mature
and serious. Informed audiences are as much a part of its distinction as are the films themselves and the intelligent administration.

In a sense Scotland is the spiritual home of the documentary,
a circumstance which has little bearing on the amount of film
production which is carried on there. Scotland's alliance with the
documentary film is exemplified today by the Scottish names active
in documentary film production, by the twenty-one year career of
the Edinburgh Film Guild, by the documentary film literature
which issues from Edinburgh and Glasgow presses, by the year-
round activity of the Federation of Scottish Film Societies (chron-
icled in its monthly magazine, *Film Forum*), and by the considerable, but cautious, progress of Scottish teachers in their adoption
of films for teaching purposes.

Compared with Edinburgh, the Continental festivals, with their
overtones of *tourisme* and *chi-chi*, seem almost irreverent. Even at
Venice, where during the first ten days only non-theatrical films
are shown, this contrast is felt. The Venice authorities obviously
strive for international representation. Having received entries from
all over the world they seek to organize them into rough subject
categories. If there are other standards of organization and selection in operation there, they are not apparent. Films of quality
there were at Venice in 1950 but to one viewer at least, it seemed
at times that they had slipped in by accident. Contributing to the
poor impression created at Venice were the crowded programs
which frequently continued past one in the morning and which
often offered a whole series of films whose method and quality
could have been adequately conveyed by one or two examples.
This latter criticism applies particularly to American television
and *avant-garde* films so generously represented on the programs.

The Italian festival operates under the further handicap of too
pleasurable a setting. Close by are the beach and the casino. Even
the ten or fifteen minutes consumed in crossing the Grand Canal
is an inappropriate prelude to four hours of unbroken film inspection. Edinburgh, with a raw wind blowing or a Scottish Sunday
setting in, is undoubtedly the more suitable setting for the contemplation of films in the realist tradition.

The advantages of attending such international film festivals
would seem to be three. There is the chance to view films of many

types, to get an over-view of world film production. This is particularly valuable to Americans, who are inclined to have highly specialized film interests, relating to job or avocation, and who see few films outside their own field. In the second place, there is the opportunity to meet other film enthusiasts, film producers, and film consumers. At Edinburgh this is managed very well through the club facilities of Film House. Finally, there is the opportunity to compare national styles in film-making and to indulge in the kind of speculation about cultural patterns which was encouraged this year at Edinburgh by the presentation of all-Danish and all-French programs, and the appearance of *Our India,* an evening-long saga of India's past and present, incorporating a wealth of Indian and Western concepts.

One is tempted to make generalizations. One declares that this film could have been made nowhere else. One sees patterns of film-making developed in Britain being taken up elsewhere—in Denmark, on the Gold Coast, in Malaya. One becomes conscious that the Canadians can treat any subject more attractively if they are allowed to photograph it against the British Columbian outdoors, as in a film on social case work titled *Friend at the Door.* One becomes aware of the infatuation of the Italians for nocturnal studies of their cities and for the volcanic islands (the films shown at Edinburgh preceded, and inspired, the Bergman and Magnani *opera*). One is immensely attracted by the lyric, humorous feeling for the countryside revealed in the Danish films. One cannot forget the wit and polish and individuality of such French films as this year's *Les Charmes de l'Existence, Paris Plein Ciel* and the uproarious *Transports Urbains,* which lampooned the documentary approach as well as the Versailles tramway system.

These special qualities are the more evident when one can observe identical subject matter treated by film makers of different countries. A number of such comparisons were possible at Edinburgh this year. Two of the longer films dealt with prison life of soldiers during World War II. The British entry, *The Wooden Horse,* was given the honor of opening the festival, an honor which in the previous three years had been accorded to *Farrebique, Louisiana Story,* and *Berliner Ballade.* Subsequently *The Red Flower,* a major effort of the seven-year-old Yugoslavian film industry, was offered. The British film was criticized for slighting the psychological factors and concentrating on the drama of the escape; the Yugoslavs were taken to task for trying to tell so many stories of divided loyalties, although the considerable technical achievement of the film was recognized.

Another marked contrast was afforded by two films on the rehabilitation of veterans, both intended to prepare civilian audiences, particularly families, for the adjustments which must occur when men finally leave the hospital. Both films, incidentally, demonstrate techniques of treatment and give a generalized picture of the administration of the veterans program. The American film *Time Out* is a much more direct assault on the emotions, with a frank use of patient's stream of consciousness narration, of trickling tears and of vibrato strings. It shows the impressive physical equipment of the hospital, and it shows the high-powered council of specialists whose knowledge is at the patient's service. It is an expert film and just how much more can be said is not evident until one has seen *The Undefeated*, the outstanding British film of the 1950 festival. Here the attitude is that the patient must be prepared in the hospital for the difficulties of life outside. We see the fittings of the artificial legs and hear the jokes which the other patients repeat; we hear the cruel sympathy of some of the ward visitors; we see the falls and accidents which occur while a man is trying to learn to use his legs again. We hear the bitter comments of the bureaucrats about the veterans who have left the hospital but still have not learned to sign their importunate letters with more details than a J. Smith. The audience's sympathies are stacked as much in the central figure's favor in the British film as in the American. But how much greater is the final impression deriving from the indirection and the understatement. And how important is the realistic milieu of the British film and the extraordinarily sensitive performance by Gerald Pearson, a young officer in the Parachute Regiment who lost both his legs in the war. Not even a snapperoo ending could spoil this one.

The great popular success of the festival was without question *Kon-Tiki* [currently released to theatres in the United States]. Though almost wholly devoid of the photographic excellencies of other films shown at Edinburgh, it was superb evidence of the fact that unique subject material can triumph over crude technique. Not for a moment does one question the crew's wisdom in packing the camera away when things got really tough, and one readily accepts the use of poor still photos if they are needed to piece out the thrilling story. Heyerdahl's narration is excellent, enhanced by his accent and the well-practiced humor which had been tested in numerous lecture dates.

Nearly as appealing as *Kon-Tiki* was Disney's *Seal Island*, already well known and admired at home. A dozen other American films were exhibited. These included one film several years old, *Brotherhood of Man*, and one originally produced in Switzerland but subsequently re-edited in New York, *The Titan*. Unfortunately a number were scheduled for the specialized evening showings at Film House (perhaps because only 16mm. prints were available). It is regrettable that larger audiences could not have seen *Grandma Moses* and *Palmour Street*. Two films which did reach the larger audiences were *Muscle Beach*, a dark-horse entry, and *The Tanglewood Story*, widely touted as this year's outstanding American contribution. *Muscle Beach* is a ten-minute satire on the pursuit of physical culture on the Santa Monica Beach. Its special distinction is in its imaginative use of the sound track. Earl Robinson sings, in folk-song style, the praises of that poise and sense of well-being which can be acquired by the cultivation of the body. His commentary is perfectly integrated with, but at all times contradicts, the frenzied physical exertions on the screen. *Tanglewood Story* suffered because too much was expected. It is a handsome picture of the youthful, shirtsleeved approach to serious music-making at Tanglewood. It dispenses with narration and makes maximum use of its rare musical opportunities. Because it was commissioned by the State Department for its Overseas Information Program it was apparently expected to carry a much more obvious ideological load than it was prepared to deliver.

Other films worthy of comment must here be slighted—such as the film tribute to W. B. Yeats, Ludwig Berger's feature-length dance film, and *Domenico d'Agosto*, a lusty, thickly populated film about Sunday at a Roman beach, produced by Luciano Emmer, until now considered a specialist in filming such other matters as the art product of Giotto and Goya.

But final comment must be reserved for *La Vie Commence Demain*, the altogether original film by France's woman director, Nicole Védrès. Produced with the collaboration of UNESCO and the active aid of the American and British information services, this film was finished only two days before its scheduled showing on the festival's final day. Reduced to its simplest elements *La Vie Commence Demain* is a series of interviews with half a dozen leading figures in the intellectual life of France. Each of them talks about the promise which tomorrow holds. The interviews are held together by the device of having a young provincial on holiday (Jean-Pierre Aumont) meet a Parisian journalist (André

Labarthe) who ridicules the younger man's absorption in history and sets out to convince him, by introducing him to Sartre, Le Corbusier, Jean Rostand and the others, that the future is infinitely more exciting. As the authorities talk, their remarks are illustrated by a considerable amount of scientific footage which will be new to lay audiences.

The penultimate sequence is an apocalyptic one, indicating what the future holds if such a scientific triumph as atomic energy is misused. The final sequence outlines the positive application of the same resources. Though somewhat uneven in interest (the sections on biology and physics tend to overwhelm the rest) *La Vie Commence Demain* is an exceptionally expert, original and challenging film. It strikes an interesting balance between the attractiveness of strongly developed personalities (how photogenic these French authorities!) and the large issues which completely transcend personalities, and it is gratifying to see at last a film which relates directly to the program of UNESCO fulfilling the urgent plea made in Cleveland two years ago by Dr. Torres-Bodet for films of this kind.

Such a film as *La Vie Commence Demain* gives hope that the documentary film makers have not lost the sense of social responsibility which was once their distinguishing characteristic. At Venice and at Edinburgh one listened in vain for the questioning voice. Where once through film we posed social issues we now document accomplishment, explain services, re-create creation (as in the art films of recent years), memorialize the deceased, record the experiment. May we hope for more challenging films at Edinburgh in its next years?

Kurtz Myers has been chief of the audio-visual department of the Detroit Public Library since 1946. His report on the 1950 film festivals in Europe emphasizes the isolation of the United States in relation to world-wide documentary production and underscores the need for an international exchange of 16mm. films in some systematic and meaningful way.

IV. FILMS FOR CHILDREN

kid stuff

Cecile Starr

WHENEVER the subject of children's entertainment comes up it inevitably turns into a heated discussion about television. For the sake of avoiding argument, and saving space, we can begin here with the conclusion that children's television and radio programs, with their violent action, monotone excitement, and habit-forming nonsense, have set a new high in entertainment which deadens the spirit and the intellect. And we may as well add that very few adults can put up a good fight against these household opiates which keep their youngsters quietly hypnotized for hours at a time. The children who have been "boarded out" in this way —to sponsors and entertainers whose motives are easily recognized as ulterior—can hardly be expected to develop a vivacious interest in creative entertainment. Thus the circle is made—and everyone is sitting in it. Let us hope that there is a way out.

It would be fine to be able to say that the answer to these entertainment problems can all be found in 16mm. programs. The truth is that there are some wonderful films for children on 16mm. film, but there are also some awfully poor ones. However, the pattern in 16mm. production has not yet been set, and there is still room for optimism. By putting the good films to the best possible use, adults not only will provide good entertainment for their youngsters, but they also will be sponsoring more and better film production.

The occasions and places for children's recreational film programs are almost limitless. Schools and churches, Y's and scout groups, libraries and museums are all likely to own and use 16mm. projectors for a part of their regular work. Why not use them also for unqualified fun? Recently I visited a program at the Public Library in Westport, Connecticut, and I could hardly have been more favorably impressed. One hundred and twenty children sat in motionless outline in the dark, while on a large screen in front of them an Indian legend was being reenacted, telling the story of how the loon got its necklace. The applause at the end of the film was not the usual self-conscious kind of noise-making, but individual, spontaneous clapping of hands—as if the children themselves were surprised and delighted that they had enjoyed the film so much.

Film programs like this one are given every second Friday at the Westport Library from fall through spring. They were started two years ago under the sponsorship of the Friends of the Westport Library, of which Mrs. Lewis Welch is currently the president. It was organized and sparked by a group of mothers eager to bring in creative film entertainment for the children in the community. A 16mm. sound projector was donated to the library by a local citizen, and since the work is all done by volunteer mothers, expenses are minimal. This year the Friends of the Library have budgeted $250 for eighteen different programs, amounting to less than $14 a program. This covers film rental, transportation costs, and occasional repairs and replacements for the projector. Each program is about forty minutes long, and is shown twice in the library, at 3:15 and 4:00 P.M.—both times to capacity audiences of 120 children between the ages of seven and twelve. In addition, the same films are shown to two different groups of hospitalized children in the area. This means that the average cost a showing is about $3.50, something like a nickel a child. "We make no pretense of formality," says Mrs. Edwin Thayer, chairman of the children's film-program committee. "A corps of volunteer mothers hands out newspapers as the kids come in, and they squat on them on the floor, gathering the papers up at the end of the show. We've had no 'keeping-order' problem, despite predictions: the children seem to like the good-natured handling we give them, and they are absorbed enough in the films to give them their complete attention. . . . We have the backing of the schools, which let us keep up permanent posters on which we change the billing from week to week. . . . The most rewarding feature to us is that in a town where many families have television sets the same children reappear week after week, and they seem wonderfully enthusiastic about the movies we bring. This, we like to think, is because our choices are right on the button for their age level and open all kinds of new worlds to them." Among the films that have been shown are such diverse subjects as *Ski Safari, Apache Indians, Here Comes the Circus, Learn to Sail, Eskimo Hunters, Story of the Bees, Nomads of the Jungle, Brotherhood of Man,* and *Party Lines.*

This year the Westport film programs have become a real community project. The local women's club is providing plastic material for permanent "sit-upons," to replace the newspapers, and the Girl Scouts are sewing them. Mrs. Thayer and the Friends of the Library, the volunteer mothers, the library staff, and the other groups have brought a big nickel's worth of entertainment to the children of their town. It is important that the films are all hand-picked to interest the children of Westport. But equally important is the adult cooperation and activity which make the film shows possible. The children may not realize it, but this is entertainment that is different—and in more ways than one. It seems a model all energetic parents would wish to consider.

In selecting films for the shows Mrs. Thayer has discovered that the most perplexing problem is that of finding acceptable cartoons. In a forty-minute program she finds that one ten-minute cartoon is a must, but thus far they have been far below the high quality of the other films. There are some old Mickey Mouse cartoons, but despite the miraculous impact of the name, the shorts are nothing to rave about. The other cartoons—Andy Panda, Woody Woodpecker, and so on—are definitely third-rate entertainment. Youngsters inevitably like them, though, probably because of the wild tempo, and until someone comes along to employ these techniques with more palatable subject-matter, these will have to do when cartoons are scheduled. A few miscellaneous cartoons merit special merit: Coronet's *Visit from St. Nicholas* * is the only

* For address of all distributors mentioned here, see list of National Distributors. All films are between ten and fifteen minutes long, unless otherwise stated. See page 125 for this list.

Christmas cartoon I have found at all pleasant. The McLaren animated films, with their brilliant colors and strange patterns, ought to be hits with most age groups. These delightful films are about three minutes long and available from the National Film Board of Canada. A different, but equally delightful kind of color cartoon, produced by the Canadian Film Board and distributed here by Encyclopaedia Britannica Films, is *Teeth Are to Keep*. It's clever and rambunctious, and even though it is about dental care there is no reason why it can't be shown for good fun as well as for good health.

A number of fairy tales have been filmed and released during the past year, none of which tickled my fancy. But I must admit that I am not easily pleased along these lines, and I leave it to the young people themselves to decide how good the films really are. My guess is that they are best suited to preschool children. Sterling Films has a series of twelve ten-minute shorts which includes such titles as *Sleeping Beauty, Cinderella, Hansel and Gretel, Rumpelstiltskin*, and so on. They are acted out by real people, with simple stage props and settings—not much one way or another according to my sampling. Coronet Films has released some puppet fairy tales, including *King Midas, Pied Piper, Jack and the Beanstalk*, etc., and they are available in color or in black-and-white. Encyclopaedia Britannica Films has *Little Red Riding Hood*, done with hand-puppets in color, with some traces of humor and originality to recommend it. That organization's *Three Fox Fables* and *Hare and Tortoise* are the Aesop stories with real animals. None of these in my opinion really succeeds as a film. And, according to Mrs. Thayer, the Westport children have been disappointed in the fairy tales they have seen. Perhaps we are better off without make-believe on film until someone comes along to create a new Méliès-like magic especially for children and especially for the movies.

Some good make-believe situations can be found in industrially sponsored films made especially for children. Mrs. Thayer points out such films as American Telephone and Telegraph's *Party Lines* and the National Biscuit Company's *King Who Came to Breakfast*, were color puppet films that her group has enjoyed. The youngsters have also liked some of the industrial how-to-do-it films —showing, for example, how ice-cream is made or how to make soap sculptures. All these sponsored films are distributed free of charge; usually you pay transportation costs. Many are available direct from the sponsors, while others are distributed by commercial film dealers like Association Films, Princeton Film Center,

Modern Talking Picture Service, and the like. Since they all are primarily for advertising purposes, you are at the mercy of the sponsor. If he can see farther than the end of his nose, his films ought to be interesting and fun. But there is no way of knowing in advance. You have to see the film for yourself in order to know what you are getting.

But even without going into the business of make-believe, there is a wealth of exciting material for children's films. Animals, domestic and wild, always delight and interest small fry. Sports and skills of all kinds, as well as adventures of life and people in other lands, keep young eyes glued to the screen. And we should not forget that children are just as interested in the adult world as we are, if not more so. There is hardly a limit to the subjects: nature, aviation, science, and all the tricks and gadgets of our society. In selecting films for children, with all these subjects to choose from, it would seem wise to check with your own group to find out what their special interests are.

I'll run through the lists of films I have seen recently, to cover as much as possible in a limited amount of space. For young children animal films are always a hit. The March of Time Forum has just released a color production from the New York Zoo, *Andy's Animal Alphabet,* which is just right for the smallest tots. Sterling's *Who's Who in the Bronx Zoo,* Young America's *Curious Coati, Adventuring Pups, Baby Animals, Let's Look at Animals, Life in an Aquarium,* and Encyclopaedia Britannica's *Live Teddy Bears, Animals Growing Up, Common Animals of the Woods, Circus Day in Our Town,* and *Insect Zoo* are other good examples of the numerous supply of animal films.

Arctic Dog Team and *How to Build an Igloo,* productions of the National Film Board of Canada, are in color and may be rented or purchased from the Film Board's office. *Grey Owl's Little Brother* and *Grey Owl's Strange Guests* aren't about owls at all, but an Indian who has made friends with the beavers. *New Homes for Beavers* show how the animals are being moved to northern areas of Canada to build their dams and help control floods. *Bronco Busters* is the kind of cowboy thriller that older children should enjoy. These last four films are fairly old, but a limited number of prints is available for free loan outside the school. Then A. F. Films' *African Big Game* (twenty minutes), and Pictorial's *Adventures of Chico* (fifty minutes), are excellent animal adventures for older and more daring children.

For some pleasant glimpses of life in other countries Julien Bryan's films about the people of the Orient are first rate. *Sampan Family, Japanese Family,* and *Pacific Island* are all handsomely photographed, distinctly pleasing, and intelligent. The films show children at work and at play in their own ways, some strangely different and some strangely similar to our own. Produced and sold by the International Film Foundation, the films are about twenty minutes each. The Bryan films are easy to recommend for youngsters and for any of their parents who care to attend.

Another fine series, "The Earth and Its Peoples," offers *Eskimo Hunters, Highlands of the Andes, Horsemen of the Pampas, Farmers of India, On Mediterranean Shores,* and others. In these films the photography is seldom less than startlingly beautiful, and in each there is adventure as well as information. There are thirty-six films in all, each about twenty minutes long, available for sale or rental from United World Films. The best of the lot is still Victor Jurgens's *Nomads of the Jungle.*

Children's Concerts, a forty-minute film produced by the Canadian Film Board and distributed here by Encyclopaedia Britannica, not only explains the rudiments of formal music but also presents an informal introduction to rhythm and melody and harmony in a lively and entertaining way. Eugene Kash, the personable Canadian conductor who originated and conducted the weekly children's concerts in Ottawa, is the musical host in the film. An older film, still unique and wonderful, and perhaps better suited to bigger children, is the British Information Services's *Instruments of the Orchestra* (twenty minutes). Brandon Films has two American folk-music items: *Tall Tales* (ten minutes) and *To Hear Your Banjo Play* (twenty minutes).

In sports films the supply is almost without bounds. There are how-to-do-its and highlights-from-great-games covering every field from A to Z. *Sport's Golden Age* (sixteen minutes) is an RKO release distributed by McGraw-Hill Text-Films surveying several generations of champions. The March of Time's *Fight Game* (eighteen minutes) should be a favorite with boys and their dads. Official Films and Castle Division of United World Films list other titles by the dozen; none of them are outstanding film productions, but that doesn't seem to bother anyone.

For teen-agers learning to drive there are a number of helpful instructional films, but the two I like best are more humorous than serious. RKO's *Highway Mania* (seventeen minutes), distributed by McGraw-Hill, and the British Information Services's

Worth the Risk (ten minutes) are as clever as they are true. I think a lot of youngsters will appreciate the absence of sermons, and at the same time they will learn a lot about the importance of careful driving.

Budding botanists will be interested in John Ott's films on plant life. *Time Lapse Photography* shows Mr. Ott's intricate studio of cameras, clocks, and machines which photograph plant growth in slowest motion (an iris plant, for example, grows before your eyes at a rate ten thousand times faster than normal). *Spring Blossoms* (nineteen minutes) shows flowers of all kinds from all parts of the country—azaleas and camellias, crab-apple blossoms and jack-in-the-pulpits, shooting stars, daffodils, and buttercups—a life cycle completed in less than a minute. *Plant Oddities* gives a more sinister picture of the plant world—pitcher plants, which intoxicate insects to catch them, sensitive plants which can be anesthetized by ether like human beings. The three films are in color and like all time-lapse films are fascinating, though not up to the high quality of the British "Secrets of Nature" series, which, unfortunately, has no counterpart in this country.

Maps and Pioneers (twenty-two minutes), a historical film in color about the settling of Virginia, is available from the Film Production Service, Department of Education, Richmond, Virginia. Other films about Captain John Smith, Thomas Jefferson, and Patrick Henry are also available for rental and sale. The Idaho State Department of Aeronautics, Capitol Building, Boise, has made a forty-minute color film entitled *The Air Age*, which is just about all-inclusive on the subject of peacetime aviation. Prints are for sale from that office, and a few are available for loan.

And all this is only the beginning. There are enough good films to last for the lifetime of the child, and then, of course, enough good films to see him through adulthood. Every year approximately one thousand new films are released. They deal with the earth: its mountains, rivers, cities, farms, factories; and with the air over the earth and the mysteries under it. They cover the peoples of the world: in Alaska, Peru, Holland, China, Africa, Australia, and every place where intercommunications have been set up. They cover the arts and crafts: pottery-making, finger-painting, choral singing, primitive dances, and puppets. Wild flowers, weather, birds, deserts, volcanoes, good health, safety, camping, boxing, fishing, winter sports, and so on. To the adults who read this article I leave the question in your hands: How does this kind of entertain-

ment compare with Howdy Doody and the Lone Ranger and Hop-
along Cassidy? Your children will be influenced by *your* answer,
not by mine.

films for neighbors

Pearl S. Buck

*(Editor's Note: Pearl S. Buck, distinguished author, Nobel Prize
winner, and president of the East and West Association, is doubt-
ful that the family film group she writes about below can properly
be called a film council; however that may be, it certainly can be
called a delightful film experience for the community. This article
appeared first in the* Saturday Review of Literature; *copyright
1950, by Pearl S. Buck, and reprinted here by permission of the
author's agent, David Lloyd, New York, N. Y.)*

OUR Green Hills Farm Film Council consists of the family. Indeed, the whole thing began with the children. It grew, as I remember, out of the wistful parental hope that by getting a good sound
motion-picture projector we could stave off the television set that
we knew was looming in the dreams of the youngest members. We
bought the projector. Later, it is true, with some resentment, we
were also compelled under pressure to buy the television set. The
two do not conflict. The television is every day, the film shows fort-
nightly. The real joy to be found in the film projector is the power
to choose programs and thereby restrain murderers, cheapskates,
thieves, racketeers, Wild West show-offs, and the like, from coming right into the living room.

The children, somewhat to their own surprise, enjoyed the films,
too. Then it seemed a pity not to show them to more persons.
School friends were invited and were so enthusiastic that the Green
Hills children felt reenforced. Parents, we found, were brave
enough to drive miles to encourage their young to see good pictures.

The Green Hills main house is blessed with a fine and roomy old barn, which has been made into a place of enjoyment for all ages. It seats a hundred people easily. We invested in folding chairs and started to give regular programs every second Friday during the season, when it is dark enough at 7:30. Last spring we kept on a little too long, and the setting sun, streaming in through the barn windows, spoiled our last show. On the Monday before each program we send out postcards to the children's friends and to everybody around who might like to come.

They come quite regularly, people from neighboring villages, the families of the farmers, and boys and girls from the local 4-H Club, whose regular meeting place anyway is our barn. Our audiences usually number well over fifty and sometimes nearer to a hundred. They are of all ages, from Mr. Hamill in his seventies to the farmers' babies. David, our two-year-old Indian-American boy at Welcome House, is an extremely active and articulate member and makes audible comments on items of interest in the pictures. The other Welcome House babies, Leon, who is Chinese-American, and Sumie, who is Japanese-American, will join when older.

Not long ago all the children in the first grade of a school in Doylestown, our county seat, were brought by their teacher and some of the mothers. They sat on cushions on the floor up front and added much to the occasion by their spontaneous laughter, squeals, and applause.

Our pictures are carefully chosen. The Princeton Film Center does an excellent job of advising us and accepting our suggestions and then of getting the films to us on time. The rural delivery postman is generous about taking them away the morning after so that they can get to the next place on time. Since we have an audience so mixed in ages and interests our pictures must not be too special, and we have not yet come to the point of having discussions about the films except in the family and with those who linger after the show.

We believe in knowing more about everybody, and so each program must have a good film about another country, as well as one about our own country. We can take some propaganda but not too much. Soil erosion, race relations, the importance of good roads must be skilfully treated and not at too great length. A good comic is an essential on every program. Perhaps we need laughter more than we need sermons. Prejudice is not very prevalent in our partly Quaker, partly Mennonite community, and the county agent is very efficient in talking us out of soil erosion. But a good laugh makes anything go. Much as we love Mickey Mouse, we need far more really good humorous pictures, not necessarily cartoons.

The younger generation now runs our show. John and Edgar alternate on the sound projector and on the little old one on which we run silent shorts to keep the very young quiet while the sound films are being changed. So we have a continuous performance. Jean takes charge of turning the lights off and on. Richard arranges ahead of time a program of music on the automatic record player, which he runs while the people gather, or in any interval caused by our now rare breakdowns. We parents are nearby merely for advice. Occasionally the operator of the small machine gets so interested in the sound film that he forgets to have his fill-in ready.

Is the Council a success? We here at Green Hills think so. The test is our steady crowd, which comes out even in bad weather. As a by-product, and a valuable one, there is good family education in choosing films, in knowing what films are being made, and in learning how to carry out a community project, in planning the program, setting up equipment and chairs, and making people welcome and comfortable, and putting the barn to rights again after the show.

ADVENTURES OF BUNNY RABBIT

Produced and distributed by Encyclopaedia Britannica Films. (Ten minutes.)

The story is reminiscent of Peter Rabbit and Mr. MacGregor's cabbage patch, with a live bunny in the leading role. Something of the habits and characteristics of the animal are shown; all in all, quite delightful.

(C.S.)

A CIRCUS WAKES UP

Produced by Films Polski. Distributed by Sterling Films. (Ten minutes.)

Before the big show begins, there is a great deal of exciting activity which the ordinary ticket-holder seldom has a chance to see: the elephant gets a bath, the lions are fed, acrobats rehearse, clowns put on their make-up and their outlandish costumes. And the film ends when the real circus begins. (C.S.)

CLEARING THE WAY

Produced and distributed by United Nations Film Division. (Forty minutes.)

Some New York City children find out about the United Nations when their favorite vacant lot is taken over as part of the grounds for the new United Nations headquarters. The film shows how the new buildings were planned, the demolition of the old East Side tenements, and ground-breaking ceremonies for the new buildings. The film is a bit too long, and some of the dialog is stilted; but the story essentially is interesting and worth while. Directed by Hans Burger. (C.S.)

GRAY SQUIRREL

Produced and distributed by Encyclopaedia Britannica Films. (Ten minutes.)

A charming squirrel family, with three little ones who climb around, munch acorns, and perform other everyday squirrel antics that add up to an animal film of considerable appeal.   (c.s.)

HELLO PIRRO
PIRRO AND THE TELEPHONE
PIRRO AND THE PHONOGRAPH

Produced by Alvin and Darley Gordon. Distributed by Official Films. (Approximately ten minutes each.)

Pirro is as delightful a puppet as we've ever seen, with a curiosity which children are sure to delight in. In these three films Pirro discovers himself in a mirror for the first time; he finds out how a telephone is used and is taught how a phonograph works. It's all very constructive for the younger set, and they should enjoy it heartily. Pat Patterson, who created and manipulates the puppet, provides the running commentary, which is warm and pleasant at its best, at worst too nervously repetitive.

Other titles in the series are *Pirro and the Thermometer, Pirro and the Alarm Clock, Pirro and the Lamp, Pirro and the Magnet, Pirro and the Scale, Pirro and the Vacuum Cleaner,* and *Pirro and the Blackboard.* The films were directed by Alvin J. Gordon, visual educational consultant of San Francisco State College.   (c.s.)

THE PRINCESS AND THE DRAGON

Produced by Films Polski. Distributed by Sterling Films. (Ten minutes.)

A puppet fairy tale, excellently executed, with a fire-breathing dragon, a jolly king, his beautiful daughter, and a cobbler hero. Winner of the Cleveland Film Festival award as best children's film for 1949.   (c.s.)

SANDY STEPS OUT

Produced and distributed by Sterling Films. (Ten minutes.)

Sandy, our canine hero, visits a farm and meets rabbits, chickens, sheep, goats, ponies, ducks, etc. Pleasant throughout.   (c.s.)

SING A SONG OF FRIENDSHIP

Produced by New World Productions. Distributed by Official Films. (Two separate reels, each about ten minutes.)

Older children will enjoy these two reels of community singing, with words and music by Irving Caesar (of "Songs of Safety" fame). Each reel has three complete songs, sung by the Ken Darby Chorus, with color-animated pictures to tell the stories of tolerance and understanding. The cleverest of the lot is one entitled "Thomas Jefferski." "A name like Thomas Jefferson in some lands o'er the sea, would not be Thomas Jefferson but Thomas Jefferski. . . ." The point being that "people with the strangest names can be the best of friends." (c.s.)

A VISIT WITH COWBOYS

Produced and distributed by Encyclopaedia Britannica Films. (Ten minutes.)

A city boy visits a ranch, learns about modern cattle-tending, and sees a rousing rodeo. The film was made at an Arizona ranch, and has a pleasant Western musical background— a new and commendable addition to the Encyclopaedia Britannica's films.
                                   (c.s.)

WIND FROM THE WEST

Produced by Arne Sücksdorff. Distributed by Films of the Nations. (Eighteen minutes.)

Ranking among the best children's films of all times, this motion picture will undoubtedly be popular with all its audiences for many years yet. The story: A Swedish schoolboy dozes in his classroom and dreams that he returns to the home of his ancestors in Lapland. Excellent outdoor photography, and a fairy-tale air of drama and adventure. Directed by the noted Swedish documentary producer Arne Sücksdorff.   (c.s.)

WONDERS IN YOUR OWN BACKYARD

Produced and distributed by Churchill-Wexler Films, 137 N. La Brea Ave., Los Angeles 36, Calif. (Ten minutes, color.)

A boy and girl explore their backyard for wildlife and find worms, a common house spider, a millipede, sow bugs, and a snail. The film is well organized—informative, entertaining, and unpatronizing. One remarkable sequence shows a snail walking over a pane of glass, photographed from the underside—as imaginative and fantastic as any fairy tale. The film ends with a suggestion to look around in your own backyard and "you'll be surprised at how many wonderful animals you can find."   (c.s.)

THE ZOO

Produced and distributed by Encyclopaedia Britannica Films. (Ten minutes, color.)

A fine trip to the zoo, in which we meet bears, lions, kangaroos, giraffes, zebras, elephants, and so forth. Vivid color helps make this one of the more pictorially attractive animal films for children.   (c.s.)

V. CLASSROOM FILMS

films for learning

Cecile Starr

MOST educators sincerely believe in audio-visual education, but many of them regard it as something for future, rather than present-day consideration. "We'll use more educational films when more good ones are available," they say. Yet catalogs are full of titles of new non-theatrical films, and the production schedules indicate that the next year will see an even greater increase in their number and variety. How well do these films serve an educational purpose? What do educators want of films? What characterizes a good educational film?

First of all, what characterizes good education? There are two basically different approaches—education by formula and education by experience. And films which would effectively serve one would probably fail miserably to meet the requirements of the other. The educator who is interested in education by formula will want a film which authoritatively gives answers to the questions it raises, demonstrates prescribed techniques, and makes of learning an almost automatic process. In many ways education by formula resembles the older teacher-ruler-blackboard method, but it has a more widely accepted applicability in the advanced teaching of specialized skills in professional training and in the armed forces. And it is still used in many general classrooms where teachers—and parents—prefer the immediate classroom results of authoritarian instruction to the less apparent results of the guidance method.

Educators who teach by formula want films which fit into that pattern of teaching. Almost inevitably they are dissatisfied with every film they see. It doesn't tell enough, or it tells too much. It is too long, or it is too short. The music isn't good, or the music is so pretty it distracts. Film makers who try to meet the demand for films-to-a-formula usually end up in hot water. "This isn't what I meant at all," says the educator; and the film maker mutters to himself, "You don't know what you want."

Some answers to problems of this kind will be found in the final reports of the Instructional Film Research Program, currently being conducted at Pennsylvania State College under sponsorship of the Navy Department. There for several years a series of systematic tests and experiments have been made in an attempt to ascertain the relative effectiveness of such factors as color versus black-and-white, dramatic versus factual presentation, use of authentic sounds, musical background, and some forty-odd other details. Although the final results of these studies haven't yet been published, we cannot anticipate that they will shed much light upon problems outside the rapid, mass-training programs to which they were primarily directed. We cannot expect that films by formula will be any more effective than education by formula.

Even within its own terms, there can be little more than theoretical significance in research material of this kind. For once it has been shown that maximum effectiveness in an educational film is obtained through certain technical and stylistic elements, this is true only in comparable situations.

Education by experience presents problems of an entirely different kind. Here the teacher serves primarily in motivating and guiding the students, with emphasis on their active and somewhat free participation in the learning situation. In education by experience there can be no formula for good films. Judging from past efforts, we can only expect that the man who can make a good film can also make a good educational film, for he knows the best ways to achieve maximum effectiveness in film and understands the particular values of the non-theatrical film.

For example, of the dozen or more films I have seen in the recently produced series entitled "The Earth and Its People," about half were exceptionally fine while the others were definitely disappointing. And nothing can account for the great difference in quality among the films as much as the fact that they were made by different men. It is not merely coincidental that production credits on the outstandingly good films name the same men (Jules Bucher, Victor Jurgens, and John Ferno, for example) who have made fine films for other purposes.

There are only three basic things a good film can do in helping to educate by experience—interest, inform, and arouse. The film must interest first of all, for without holding the active attention of the group it cannot possibly stimulate learning. The film must also inform, to whatever degree the subject and situation demand; this information must be believable as well as authentic. And the film must arouse. A good film will stir the mind and heart of each person in the audience. A good teacher can further capitalize on this arousing quality of the film by directing the students to follow up activities through study, discussion, or experiment.

Just how the film can best meet these three requirements is really the business of the film maker, for there is indeed no formula. Certainly he needs the cooperation of a competent educator to advise on subject-matter problems. He also needs the assistance of skilled cameramen and technicians, writers and artists, to blend the talents which will produce the total film. He needs a reasonable budget and adequate time in which to plan, as well as shoot the film. And, most of all, he needs to be the right person for the job—interested, capable, sincere, understanding, and alert. For time and again the good film maker has shown that he approaches his material not in order to teach but in order to learn. What he sees and hears and learns goes straight-away onto the film to become for the audience a fresh, meaningful, and important experience in education for living.

What, then, can educators expect of a film? No more than they can expect of any other guest in the classroom. The film has literally been exposed to certain experiences, and it reproduces those experiences for the audience. The way in which it does so expresses that film's personality, and the way in which those experiences are assimilated and used makes for education. If we want a film to say what we want it to say, no more and no less, in the exact way we have in mind, we shall have to expect it to be no more exciting than a schoolboy reciting the lesson he has learned by heart. If we want a film to tell us what it knows, we shall have to permit it to do so in its own way. And whatever the case, we should remember that a good film is a good educational film, just as a good experience is a good educational experience—in or outside the classroom.

if you want to get across an idea . . .

B. Lamar Johnson and
Robert de Kieffer

"IF you want to get across an idea . . ." epitomizes not only a central emphasis in the teaching of communications at Stephens College, it comes close to epitomizing the educational philosophy of the college: if learning is to be significant it must be planned in terms of the needs to be served—both in the lives of individual students and in the society in which they live.

With this philosophy as the basis for building a college curriculum, Dr. W. W. Charters some twenty-five years ago made a study of the activities of women. In this study and in additional investigations since then, the college staff has identified ten areas of need common to all women: communication, citizenship, appreciation of the beautiful, physical health, mental health, consumer problems, philosophy of life, occupational planning, knowledge of the world of science, and home and family life.

In each of these areas Stephens has developed a program of instruction planned in terms of the life needs of women. Such a program must, of course, make sense not only in terms of what is taught but also in terms of how it is taught. With this in mind, the faculty uses, for example, discussion, conference, laboratory methods, and experiments, with such teaching materials as books, recordings, radio, wire and tape recorders, models, slides, and films.

Among these materials the faculty is giving a place of high importance to films. In 1948, for example, 6,553 reels of motion pictures (representing 659 different titles) were shown. The important factor is not, however, the number of reels shown but the *quality* of use; that is, the *relevance* and *effectiveness* of the film as used in a particular learning situation.

In the teaching of *communication skills* (writing, speaking, reading, and listening), films which have been found helpful include *Speeding Your Reading,* an introduction to correct habits of silent reading; *The New Voice of Mr. X.,* the voice mechanism and the production of speech, and *Telephone Techniques.* For students having particular difficulty with the mechanics of writing, film strips such as *The Comma* and *Subject and Predicate* are used.

Although films are used primarily in group situations, students upon occasion take advantage of the fact that film catalogs and films are available for individual use. Jane, who was writing an investigative paper on "Progressive Education," found the March of Time film on that subject to be one of her most helpful sources. In our future library we shall have individual projection rooms where students may project films for their own individual use—just as they now may listen to recordings in our listening rooms.

Among other aids to the teaching of communication skills are the wire, tape, and disc recorder to encourage individual and group self-criticism of speech, voice, and discussion. The opaque projector is used for projecting student written work on a screen for study and criticism by an entire class.

In the area of *citizenship,* and particularly in our basic social problems course, emphasis is placed upon the citizen's responsibility to identify and study important political, economic, and social values and problems. Two films are used to introduce students to democracy and its competitors: *Democracy,* with its emphasis on human rights and responsibility, and *Despotism,* with its contrasting stress on restrictions of freedom. During their consideration of public opinion and political parties, students see how a corrupt political machine operates when the film *You the People* is used as a springboard for study and discussion. *John Doe, Citizen,* on the other hand, demonstrates how an aroused citizenry working together can achieve an effective town government. By viewing *One World or None,* students are aided in becoming aware of the devastating power of the atomic bomb and its consequent requirement of world unity. Where motion is not necessary film strips may be used—as, for example, in describing the organization of one effort toward world unity, the United Nations.

In the area of *appreciation of the beautiful* the more than eight hundred students in the introduction to humanities course have wide opportunity to experience the materials of art, literature, and music. As an aid to understanding art, classes study art objects—originals when available—but more often slides and colored reproductions. The motion picture is used in this area to demonstrate the creation of a work of art—as in *The Making of a Mural* (Thomas Hart Benton) or *Making an Etching* (Charles J. Martin).

Although the usual approach to literature is through the reading and study of literature itself, recordings (Maurice Evans's *Hamlet* or the poetry recordings of James Weldon Johnson) and films (as, for example, *England, Background of Literature* and the highly successful theatre film *Henry V*) also have their place.

In studying music, students listen to recorded music both in class and at special listening hours. Even in this area, however, there is an important place not only for such films as *The Instruments of the Orchestra* but also for films presenting concert artists, such as Myra Hess playing the first movement of Beethoven's *Sonata Appassionata*.

The value of films in the area of *mental health* is suggested by the psychology professor who reports, "I can elaborate at length on the child's need for recognition, but a motion picture showing a child presenting his art 'masterpiece' to a scoffing or indifferent parent, as in *The Life History of Mary*, makes the point in short order."

Representative of the uses which teachers of psychology make of films are these: *Feeling of Rejection* is used to demonstrate a psychological principle. *The Boss Didn't Say Good Morning* is a somewhat exaggerated presentation of the psychological effect on his employees of a boss's failure to say, "Good Morning." The effect of labeling a child as different from other children is demonstrated by a sequence from *The Devil Is a Sissy*. *The Ape and the Child* helps students visualize an important psychological experiment, and *Study of Johnny and Jimmy* provides a basis for case-study analysis.

The field of *home and family life* is one of the more difficult areas in which to locate teaching films that are functional in terms of the real life problems of home makers. In one unit of the course, the films *Human Reproduction* and *The Birth of a Baby* have been found valuable. For other parts of the course, completely satisfactory films are not available. The faculty in this field is at present, however, working on the possibility of using selected theatre films as aids to teaching. An initial tryout of this plan was made last spring when *I Remember Mama* was shown at a local theatre. Through the courtesy of the director of the film, George Stevens, course instructors were able to preview the film several days prior to its showing for students. Following this preview, teachers prepared questions related to family unity as illustrated in the film and presented them to their classes. Following its showing classes discussed the film, just as they would any educational film. Both instructors and students report that this particular film proved to have real value in their study of family unity. The staff is continuing to explore the possibility of using selected entertainment films as aids to teaching in this area.

And so we might go to other areas of the curriculum such as *physical health* and the use of such films as the *Digestion of Food* and *Story of Menstruation;* and *knowledge of science* and the use of varied films including *The Birth of a Volcano, Atomic Power, The Plow That Broke the Plains, Evolution, Bacteria,* and *Endocrine Glands.*

But perhaps enough has been written to indicate that the faculty of Stephens College is using functional films and other learning aids as it carries forward its self-assigned task of building an educational program designed to fit the life needs of women.

Dr. B. Lamar Johnson is dean of instruction and librarian at Stephens College in Missouri. Dr. Robert de Kieffer, his assistant, is head of Audio-Visual Service of Stephens College, and in 1949 was president of the Film Council of America.

midwest takes the lead

Wesley H. Greene

THERE is much talk today about 16mm. films and how to see them. Sometimes, in fact, there is more talk than action. In one city the organizing group almost talked a proposed film council out of existence in a year of discussions of a constitution. Finally this group set up some film previews and now the city has an active film council. In Chicago no attempt was made to put the organization on paper until the Chicago Film Council had been operating for almost two years. In addition to occasional luncheon meetings the Chicago Film Council has a monthly preview of new films the last Friday of each month. In 1947 this group sponsored the first 16mm. World Film Festival held in the United States. From coast to coast there are over one hundred cities, large and small, which have film councils. In the larger cities the film council serves as a 16mm. professional group as well as an agency for introducing films to community leaders, arranging previews, and making suggestions to local organizations concerning the use of 16mm. films in their programs. In some communities the film council has formulated public demand for better use of films through schools or public libraries.

A film council or film preview group cannot thrive on talk alone. While conventions of people who work with films may well meet to discuss matters of common professional interest, it is important that groups interested in films see films first and talk about them later. Films are an important agency of education in a democracy, but there is more to democracy than technique, and film groups particularly should beware of meetings where time is wasted gracefully and nothing of consequence done according to Hoyle.

At the organization meeting of the Chicago Scientific Film Society in 1946 the group first spent an hour seeing *Spelunking* (cave exploration), *Your Children's Eyes* (British documentary), and a Canadian color film, *Insects.* Seventy laymen and professional workers had assembled—all acting as individuals and not as spokesmen of their organizations. In ten minutes those present endorsed the idea of a film society to hold monthly showings, authorized the temporary chairman to enlarge the organizing committee to seven, and asked the committee to bring a slate of officers to the next film showing. The meeting was concluded by showing Shell Oil Company's *Hydraulics* and Coronet's color film *Sulphur and its Compounds.*

In many schools and colleges throughout the country students see films in classrooms and lecture halls. On college campuses, even where films are not often used in classes, students have set up showings of foreign and documentary films. About 1935 three students organized a documentary-film club at the University of Chicago and today this group presents a monthly documentary-film program and a monthly feature. The University of Chicago Chapter of the United World Federalists presents a weekly film program, and more than a dozen other student groups on the campus show films outside the classroom. At the University of Chicago for several years there have been thirty extra-curricular showings a month under student sponsorship.

The general practice in the country is for showings outside the classroom to be self-supporting. Most of the showings mentioned were set up originally in 35mm., but today the large majority of all campus showings are 16mm. This is a matter of convenience and availability of films. A 16mm. sound film showing can be set up almost anywhere—in a room at home or in an auditorium. The film itself is on safety stock, and anyone who can drive a car can learn to operate a 16mm. sound projector in an hour or less.

Campus film showings are also in 16mm. because thousands of films are available only in this size. The annual issue of the "Educational Film Guide," published by H. W. Wilson Company, lists more than five thousand titles and gives brief descriptions of each. Not one percent of these films is available in 35mm. size. In fact, many—particularly the color ones—were produced originally in 16mm. and not in 35mm.

Films, like books, do not have to be funny or thrilling or fictional to be entertaining to those for whom they were produced. And in some communities films, like books, may be borrowed from public libraries. Among the larger film collections in the country are those at the public libraries in Cleveland, Akron, Cincinnati, Toledo, Charlotte, Rochester, Stamford, Detroit, Milwaukee, Louisville, Dallas, Seattle, and Portland. In Wyoming the Weld County Library provides a film as well as book service and in Missouri the State Library makes films available to the public. Many public libraries which have not yet set up film collections are prepared to give out information concerning film sources.

There are hundreds of commercial film rental libraries scattered over the country and some of these rent educational and documentary films as well as features. The film rental structure of the 16mm. industry was set up in the depression years and rates are not much higher today than then. In some areas, however, if children are to have access to the latest and best educational sound films, parents will have to rent the films and show them at home. In the United States we have all kinds of extremes, but the extremes in visual education are among the strangest of all.

Schools draw films from libraries maintained by boards of education, state universities, and, in the case of Ohio, Virginia, and Louisiana, from libraries set up by the state. [Since this article was written (March 1949), Arkansas, Georgia and Oklahoma have

established state film libraries, and other changes in the status of
film programs in the public schools are always underway.—Ed.]
Unfortunately in some areas, particularly in the East, school authorities have been slow to provide for visual education. A few
comparisons will be shocking, but I give them because there is no
point in dodging the facts. Educational-film producers and distributors often meet in hotel rooms at convention time and discuss
the markets for their wares. They tell each other that New England and New York and a few other states are very slow to buy
educational films. They say that more films were sold in the State
of Mississippi in 1947 than in the entire State of New York, that
Oakland bought more films than New York, and Dallas more than
Philadelphia. They mention that every high school in Chicago
now has a library of the most important films and that the Board
of Education there buys as many prints of each film as teachers
require. You hear that Arkansas and Arizona each bought more
films last year than all the schools and colleges and boards of education in the five New England states. There are more prints of
sound-educational films in the rental library maintained by Indiana University than there are in all educational-film libraries from
the District of Columbia to the Canadian border including Pennsylvania, New York, and New England. Over fifty million people
live in the strip of states along the Atlantic stretching from Maine
to Florida, yet only about ten percent of the educational films sold
in the U.S. are delivered to buyers in this area.

Wide use of films in education is made in the Middle West,
where such state universities as Indiana, Michigan, Wisconsin,
Minnesota, Iowa, Missouri, Kansas, and Colorado have long maintained film libraries to serve all film users at nominal rates. Notable
also is the tremendous growth of the visual medium in the schools
and colleges of Washington, Oregon, California, and Texas. In
these states there are close to two hundred film libraries owned and
operated by city- and county-school systems. The rule in California
and Texas is the exception in New England and New York. The
only Atlantic state which compares favorably with California is
Virginia, where a remarkable system of film libraries was set up
under the guidance of the State Department of Education when
Colgate Darden was governor of the state.

It should not be inferred that Eastern cities have no films at
their boards of education. Philadelphia and New York have had
film libraries for many years, but these are stocked principally with
silent films, and almost no provision is made for the purchase of

enough new sound films. Those in charge of the programs of visual education in these two cities have had many years of experience, but cannot be expected to do a job with the inadequate sums put at their disposal. But one of the worst financed cities in the East when it comes to visual education is Washington. The budget set up for both personnel and films is hopelessly inadequate, and no one seems to know how to remedy the situation. While the Board of Education in Baltimore does an admirable job and has money to buy films, children who live in the nation's Capital are virtually deprived of many excellent visual aids.

Fortunately, those who want to see films do not have to wait on administrative decisions of governments. They can acquire a 16mm. projector for little more than the cost of a good radio and share the expense of films with a few neighbors. What has been done by 16mm. film groups on and off campuses can be done by any group of people who wish to see films.

Wesley H. Greene has for more than a dozen years operated his own 16mm. distribution firm, International Film Bureau, Inc., in Chicago. Previous to that he had spent five years at the University of Chicago as teacher in the Laboratory Schools and director of activities at International House. During the war he was coordinator of distribution with the National Film Board of Canada.

VI. GETTING THE FILMS AND SCREENING THEM

mainly mechanical

Raymond Spottiswoode

THAT we are all of us movie-goers today is just as much taken for granted as that we are all of us motorists. And as the very word motorist has thus acquired an old-fashioned sound and an aura of veils, goggles, and dusty roads, so our movie-going has become a weekly commonplace. Most of us have lost interest in whether our autos have their valves in the head or at the side, or whether they can climb such and such a famous grade in high gear. Such talk is twenty years old. Similarly, the day when a movie-goer would say, "The sound wasn't so good on that picture, was it?" or, "Didn't it look a little fuzzy sometimes?" has long faded from memory.

Lapped in the comfort of a resilient chair, his head automatically tilted to the angle of the screen, today's movie-goer is bathed in a melodious current of sound, and basks in the light of the images which flow past his eyes in liquid succession. Nothing disturbs his trancelike state of well-being, his identification with the wonderland which lies beyond the screen.

But what is this? Our friend's dream has been rudely shattered. The seat beneath him has become angular and unyielding, and his nether members tell him that the show has lasted much too long. He finds that he must dodge to and fro past a moving sea of heads to get a full look at the screen—a screen which dimly reflects an image fuzzy at the edges and lacking most of that glossy quality which used to let him feel himself through so easily into the world of film. And it is not only his eyes that are strained. The spoken word must compete with the echoes which chase it from corner to corner of the room; and often it reaches him distorted like the twenty-dollar mantel radio long relegated to junior's playroom.

The film ends, and after a long pause another takes its place. But this one has every appearance of mania, for the characters are standing on their heads and unintelligible jargon comes from their lips. A titter runs round the audience, the projectionist mumbles his apologies, the light goes on again and the film is laboriously rewound.

Yes, you have guessed it. Our friend is at a typical 16mm. screening; that is the explanation for his nightmare. Is it surprising that 16mm. programs almost always seem too long? That people stay away from them in droves, as they did when flickering almost killed the movies fifty years ago? It is as if we were forced to read from torn and crumpled books, piecing each sentence together with infinite care.

If this were the whole 16mm. story, we could as well close up this department and go home. It is true that most 16mm. shows are marred, and many are spoiled, by these irritating defects which are sensed by the audience even when they are not clearly recognized. But what is possible on 16mm.—commercially and not merely in the laboratory—is far beyond what is common practice. One of America's greatest technical authorities on the 16mm. film remarked quizzically the other day, "Why don't you tell your readers that there's no good reason why 16mm. sound should be held down to the poor quality in the theatres?" What he meant was that the Academy standard, laid down long ago to take account of obsolete sound equipment, does in fact fall much below the very best that can be recorded on 16mm.

It is easy to blame this gap between the possible and the actual on the projector manufacturer, whose business it is to create the film image in light and sound. But the manufacturer deserves every sympathy. Each individual picture on his strip of film is half the size of a postage stamp—but it has to stand up to critical scrutiny when enlarged to the size of an El Greco! And this film travels at less than half the speed of its 35mm. theatre counterpart, making the sound more than twice as difficult to record.

Yet the projector which is supposed to make 16mm. film look like 35mm. cannot be heavily built or professionally maintained. It must be light enough for a hundred-pound school teacher to lift, and simple enough for a twelve-year-old to operate. At the same time it may have to stand up to rough jolting in an automobile along country roads as it is moved from one village to another for mobile screenings.

For packing all these capacities into their machines—albeit in very varying degree—the manufacturers deserve the greatest credit. True, the hundred-dollar projector promised during the war is still a mirage. But for the price of a television set, a really good 16mm. projector can be bought which will bring to any club or union local or social group in the smallest village throughout the country a picture of the world and how it lives and what it is thinking. . . .

Raymond Spottiswoode has directed a number of documentary films in Canada, England, and the United States. He is the author of A Grammar of the Film, *and for nearly a year was editor of the 16mm. film column of the* Saturday Review of Literature.

documentary dilemma
Arthur L. Mayer

SOME years ago I wrote a plaintive piece entitled "Is There a Documentary in the House?" The answer was, of course, in the negative. At that time a leading educator could say, "The only picture I ever saw worth my time was one on relativity—and they paid me to see that." A typical small-town exhibitor could decline to play documentaries in his theatre because "folks around here are accustomed to pictures on filum and wouldn't like 'em no other way."

We have escaped from those exclusively escapist days, but except in the urgency of wartime, little water has passed over the documentary dam, although a large body of it has accumulated in a muddy pond above the movie mill. It is muddy with wasted motion, conflicting currents, and periodic upheavals. There is no central, reliable source of information about what pictures are being planned and what pictures are being produced. At one time, for instance, there were seven different pictures being produced by seven different government agencies to make seven different versions of how to swim. There is today no Federal Government film service and it will shortly even be impossible to obtain a current report on the state of Government picture activity. The governments of other countries have no one to whom they can turn for assistance in trying to make contact in the United States with the production, planning, and distribution of fact films. The most shocking omission of all, from the point of view of those who turned to documentary because they recognized its value as a creator of international understanding and good-will, is the fact that the United Nations itself has no methods of conveying its needs to the makers of films or their sponsors, and no way of making use of the American documentary-film movement as a whole.

We find today a plethora of organizations calculated to do everything about documentary films except to get them intelligently planned and financed, competently produced, and effectively distributed. There are available funds from Government sources and big business, as well as civic, philanthropic, and educational groups, but these funds are not now channeled to fertilize the educational and social projects of film planners. There are potential backers of documentaries in every walk of life who want to use the medium and who recognize its potential usefulness but whose actual experiences in their ventures with it have proved frustrating. There are competent producers whose best energies are being dissipated in the futile and unrealistic pursuit of production money when they should be concentrating their creative efforts in the art of film-making. There are nationwide audiences which have far too often been on the receiving end of a disappointing progression of unrelated and often second-rate shows. The continued existence of these audiences, however, is a convincing proof of the extent to which they could grow.

Obviously, what is needed today is an over-all documentary film service conducted on a non-profit basis and financed in its inception by a few of the major foundations. Within a few years it could easily be self-supporting. Such a service would have three basic functions: planning and financing programs, supervising production when required, and rationalizing distribution. It would help to bring into being the hundreds of good films which could be made in this country if any responsible agency existed in which educational authority, sponsorship, and audiences could place confidence. It would be an invaluable asset to the Army Department, which for the third successive year [1948] has been voted an appropriation by Congress of $800,000 for the production of documentary films for the conquered countries. The two previous appropriations have never been utilized, and without wise counsel there is a grave danger that a similar fate may overtake the third. It would in no way conflict with the existing valuable organizations which are already functioning in the documentary field. The Educational Film Library Association speaks for the educational film libraries. But to whom does it speak when it uncovers a need? The Film Council of America is speaking more and more for the general lay audience, the heterogeneous community groups who use films, but where can it turn for stimulation of new production? The American Council on Education Motion Picture Project studies and plans and even writes scripts of films considered educationally desirable, but who takes the scripts in hand and goes out and finds the funds to make them into films? The American Library Association speaks for its thousands of members who are plotting a course in the visual media, but what influence does it wield in the development of new plans for production today?

In the cauldron of chaos there are brewing today films on music, the history and the appreciation of art, inter-cultural relations, foreign trade, child health, and the natural sciences. The United Nations requires films on such a multiplicity of subjects that I hesitate to mention only a few, such as the planning and utilization of resources in a river valley system, impending world shortages of food and fuel, the unification of electrical resources for the nations of Europe. Individual producers are grappling with similar problems. Philip Ragan, for instance, is seeking to produce a film on world government; Julien Bryan plans a series on the peoples of the world, and Robert Flaherty, fresh from the triumph of *Louisiana Story*, dreams another of his heart-warming interpretations of the communion of man and nature. These projects would be facilitated by a central service which would work with them and help to secure the authority and needed funds.

No films must be planned, financed, or produced unless a rational approach can be made to their distribution. Failure to do so is as shortsighted as to build a house equipped with electrical and plumbing facilities one hundred miles from the nearest supply of electric power and running water. Unfortunately, most of the creative enthusiasm for documentaries has come from producers who have little knowledge and even less interest in the how's and why's of distribution. Non-curriculum films dealing with current information, to be effective, must reach their audience and perform their major function in a period of two or three years. New patterns of distribution are beginning to emerge and they must be worked out and worked with.

Ultimately, the public library will be as competent a center of information and service in the visual media as it is now in the printed word. Above all, I believe that under the guidance of a central, responsible non-profit service such as I have suggested, individual producers and sponsors, without sacrificing their artistic or intellectual integrity, can unite in a kind of documentary United Artists for the effective release and exploitation of their product. Documentaries have, as they say, come of age. Now they need what the old Jews used to call a "shatchen" to see that they are properly introduced and profitably affianced to their long expectant and ardent audience.

Arthur Mayer, well known to New Yorkers as the former owner of the Rialto Theatre, served as head of the Army Film Unit in the U.S. Zone of Germany during 1948-49. As supervisor of the Motion Picture Association's "Pilot Project" for educational films, he became interested in 16 mm. distribution. He is now executive vice president of the Council of Motion Picture Organizations, Inc.

films, films, everywhere . . .

Cecile Starr

IN the three years since the "Film Forum" made its first appearance in the *Saturday Review of Literature* several thousand readers have written in to ask, "How can I get to see that film?" Information films have never failed to interest a wide range of people, and in response to their steadily growing interest the current production of important idea films is booming: *Human Beginnings, Challenge: Science Against Cancer, Hyde Park, Marriage for Moderns, A Time for Bach, Maps and Pioneers, Palmour Street—A Study of Family Life,* and on and on.

As worthwhile 16mm. production increases confusion mounts. How to get hold of the film you want when you want it? It is not as easy as it should be.

To add to the confusion, 16mm. films are more easily available today than ever before. But they are not available in any recognizable and predictable pattern. A study recently completed by the Film Council of America shows that about half the total number of prints of fifteen important test films are concentrated in the Middle Atlantic states clustered about New York City and in the Midwest, around Chicago. That leaves the other half for the entire remainder of the country. Film libraries in the South, in New England, and in the Rocky Mountain area have few prints of those films, and in some cases the films were not available at all.

Even in the prominent film-center areas it isn't easy to know where to find a specific film. There are about one thousand film libraries in this country and it is safe to wager that no two are alike. Each has its own distribution policies, its own terms of rental or loan, its own idea of service to the public. In one city the public library has a large and popular film collection for free use by its citizens, while the library in another city of equal size and importance offers no film facilities whatsoever. University extension services often maintain mammoth film libraries for circulation throughout the state (or further) to interested groups at moderate rental fees. But not every state offers this service. School systems usually have their own large film collections; some restrict them to actual classroom use, while others attempt to serve adult needs in the community. The extensive use of 16mm. films in our public schools is reflected in the recent report by Seerley Reid of the United States Office of Education (*Educational Screen*, June 1950) that eighty-four percent (more than 21,000) of all high schools own at least one 16mm. sound projector, and half of them have been acquired since the end of the war.

Some colleges and universities (for example, Teachers College of Columbia University) serve their own campuses with films, while others (Columbia University Educational Film Library) rent and sell films throughout the country. Religious organizations, state and Federal agencies of all kinds, industrial organizations, and labor groups maintain film libraries for the use of their own and affiliated groups; often they lend or rent the films to outsiders. And filling in the last gap between the film producer and the film user is the commercial film library, which makes a business of buying films for the sole purpose of renting or selling them. These commercial film dealers usually also sell and rent projection equipment, as well as other audio-visual materials and supplies.

This being the state of things, it is possible to obtain a print of a two-reel film like *The Feeling of Rejection* (p. 183) from a state health agency or a city public library without any charge, from a university extension library, from the major distributor, or from a commercial dealer at a rental fee varying from $2.50 to $5, depending upon distribution policies. Further variation in price is based on film sponsorship.

To make matters worse, the film user today must rely upon all these distribution sources at once, for not every film library owns a print of every film. Since more than seven thousand films are currently available, the goal would be preposterous. Even more regrettable is the fact that not every good film library owns a print of every good film. Many own only one print, while several prints are needed for simultaneous use in the area served by the library. As a result film users must turn from one source to another, often resorting to the major distribution outlet for a particular film. And since there is no really effective network of 16mm. distribution throughout the country, more and more major sources are being established. The current issue of the *Educational Film Guide* lists more than 750 of them—from the American Automobile Association to the Zachry Institute of Human Development. Some of them handle primary distribution for hundreds of titles, others have only one film to their name. The list is staggering. On one hand, the film companies: Abelard Films, Academy Films, A. F. Films, Africa Films, Agrafilms, Art Films, Association Films, Athena Films, Avis Films, and so on. On the other hand there are organizations which distribute 16mm. films only incidentally: Aetna Life Affiliated Companies, American Library Association, Aluminum Company of America, Allis-Chalmers Manufacturing Co., American & National Leagues of Professional Baseball Clubs, American Bible Society, American Can Company, American Cancer Society, American Telephone and Telegraph Company, American Institute of Baking, American Legion, American Social Hygiene Association, Associated Boys Clubs, Audubon Society—to name a handful.

The distribution dilemma is not likely to be solved in any remarkable way in the near future. Film users are left more or less to their own devices. Two pamphlets help give direction to the bewildered: A *Directory of 897 16mm. Film Libraries*, compiled by Seerley Reid (available from the Superintendent of Documents, U. S. Government Printing Office, Washington 25, D. C.); and *How to Obtain and Screen Films for Community Use*, prepared by this reviewer and available from the Film Council of America, 57 E. Jackson Blvd., Chicago 6, Illinois. Each is sold at fifteen cents a copy. And while 16mm. distribution is being thrashed out, the *Saturday Review of Literature* continues its program of assisting readers in selecting and obtaining special films for program and home use.

Despite the staggering confusion in the distribution field, more films are being seen now than ever before. Film festivals, such as the one recently held in Stamford, Connecticut, make it possible for large audiences to keep up with the new information films. Hotels and resorts are advertising the regular screening of documentary and educational films as an added attraction to vacationers. Special film societies are springing up in large cities and on college campuses (but their growth here can't compare with the phenomenal increase in Britain—from forty-five to more than two hundred in the past five years). In New York City such movie theatres as the Paris, the Park Avenue, and the Art have been consistent in their policy of showing outstanding short subjects like the Norman McLaren animated abstractions, the Louis de Rochemont "Earth and Its Peoples" series, and other special-interest shorts like *Matisse, Maillol,* and *Van Gogh.* (It was unpardonable, in this connection, that the showing of the majestic Michelangelo film *The Titan* was followed in a Washington theatre with the painful staccatoes of Woody Woodpecker.) Television, too, offers new outlets for documentary films, but films which were not made especially for this medium suffer greatly under the handicap of the small screen and poor visual reception.

Sixteen-millimeter films are around us. But the unquenchable question remains: "How can I get to see *that* film?"

films in public libraries
Patricia Blair

SOME people are still surprised at the thought of public libraries circulating 16mm. films along with books and reference materials. In the raised-eyebrow department the questions run something like this: Why? Does it work? What developments do you see in the future?

The why is simple. It is a part of the philosophy of the modern librarian. He believes that the library must become a people's communication center, using all the new as well as the old tools to meet new and complex demands facing us and to give the pleasure which comes with the sharing of experiences and events.

As librarians prepare to meet the needs of today's community which must grapple with the implications of atomic energy, vote with intelligence on matters of world-wide import, and achieve insight and perspective on socio-economic problems which lie painfully close to home, they are finding the use of the informational and documentary film effective and dramatic—a powerful ally with which to reach many thousands in the adult community.

Does it work? The emphatic answer from every community

which has such 16mm. film lending service at its fingertips is yes. During the month of March 1949, the spring test period for which the American Library Association collected film statistics, fifty-six public libraries reported that their films were shown 32,554 times to 1,579,380 people. These fifty-six libraries own 7,292 films and had total budgets of $141,820 with which to purchase new films in 1949 exclusive of gifts, deposits, foundation grants, and appropriations for personnel and equipment.

Statistics at best are cold. What about the films and the people who use them? The collections cover a variety of subjects with emphasis upon the great issues of our day—current affairs, human relations, atomic power, international relations, foreign trade, labor-management relations, and public health. As the growing libraries are able to meet the most pressing demands, they tend to broaden their coverage to include motion pictures on child care and psychology for lay groups; films on music, art, and the crafts; religious and children's films; and travelogs and training pictures.

Almost all of the public library film departments find certain films to be timeless, and great titles like *The River, The City, Boundary Lines,* and the *Brotherhood of Man* appear in nearly every collection. Also, specific interests peculiar to the locale show up in the films on the Northwest and Alaska in the Seattle Public Library, on industrial training and human relations in the Cleveland Film Bureau, and on rural health and safety in the Missouri State Library's traveling circuit of films.

The people who use the films come from all professions and represent many interests. In Missouri an elderly farmer in blue jeans asked the bookmobile librarian to show a film on Russia, because, he said, "How can I be a good farmer unless I know how all the people in the world live?"

In Elyria, Ohio, the police department wrote on their film report for *The Feeling of Rejection:* "Very interesting and educational to the police department. Mental hygiene films are important. Let's have more of them."

The director of a big city's Urban League, the leader of a small Grange, the supervisor of nursing in a hospital—each has a distinct use for specific films and each can give an illuminating comment on the film's use and contribution.

The story of how this business of circulating films on a library card works is as fascinating and varied as are the cities in which such service is available. Many different levels exist. While the Boston Public Library was opening the doors of its new Film Department on April 1, 1949, a veteran staff in Milwaukee was getting out more than four thousand films a month to its churches and clubs. In Nashville the first purchase order for forty prints was placed that month, and in Cincinnati a well-established automatic routine between the library and the social agencies assured careful supervision for all showings of such films as *Meeting Emotional Needs in Childhood* and *The Feeling of Hostility*. In Detroit the library's Audio-Visual Department and the Merrill Palmer School had the film program *To Help You to Understand Your Child* running simultaneously in ten neighborhood branches.

In every one of the public libraries it means careful planning to gear film service to the community's living issues, and it means thoughtful selection and constant promotion through all possible channels.

The latter cannot really be difficult since the reception of such local service into a community is usually accompanied by overwhelming enthusiasm and gratitude. Not only do film users advertise the service by word of mouth, but spontaneous offers of help and financial assistance are often made. Such groups as ministerial associations, the National Conference of Christians and Jews, service clubs like Rotary, local cancer control or anti-tuberculosis units frequently come forward with sums of money or with films to give to the central fund or collection which, through the public library, belong to everyone.

After this service is established any interested citizen may receive assistance in program-planning and advice on selection of the best film for his purpose; and upon presentation of his library card together with the necessary information about proper equipment, he may then draw out a film to take home under his arm along with a play, a biography, or perhaps a recording of his favorite symphony.

It is dangerous to attempt to play the prophet, but some signs are clear. Internal changes in professional training and attitudes are involved. People who are going to select and guide the use of the full scale of informational materials will have to have adequate training to enable them to do this intelligently and with vigor.

For you, the user of film, there is the possibility that within the foreseeable future, local, regional, and/or statewide film distribution networks may be made possible. This involves many things. The population and income levels of the individual library are the two most important factors to consider. As we work toward larger, more adequate units of library service and gain experience in cooperative *regional* service, the opportunities for realizing widespread grass-roots film availability become proportionately greater.

That is why the two experimental film circulation projects in northern Ohio and in the State of Missouri, made possible through grants from the Carnegie Corporation of New York, are so exciting. In them we have a testing ground for the joint purchase and use of films by families of small and medium-sized local libraries clustered around a parent library with a reservoir film collection. One test is being conducted in a highly populated industrial and urban area and another in a rural state where bookmobiles carry the projectors and films across the great rivers into farming country and up into the hills to isolated groups. In the northern Ohio area, where this bringing of documentary and informational films into the adult community sprang to life very quickly within an already existing film framework in Cleveland, the results have been phenomenal. The participating libraries in ten adjacent towns unanimously reported that within the first three or four days of every month the new group of films is booked solid—by the churches, the Y's, the Scouts, settlement houses, men's clubs, parent-teacher associations, public-health nurses, and so on. In such a situation the films do not reach a saturation point in any one place, and each library receives a new selection of films each month.

Greater accessibility is bound to be followed by generally better use. For with the growth of practical experience in the field, backed up by research in the universities, we should see a steady rise both in expert use of films and in taste. Development of a discerning eye, on the part of large groups, for the complex art of the cinema will inevitably result in a demand for better quality. It is not likely that people who have seriously viewed a *Louisiana Story*, a *Loon's Necklace*, and a *Seeds of Destiny*, or who have been consistently exposed to the kinds of films made by such observers and creators as Flaherty, Willard Van Dyke, John Grierson, Julien Bryan, Irving Jacoby, or Raymond Spottiswoode will ever again be really satisfied with pedantic or trite film treatment.

Since we neither live nor work in vacuums, neither does any individual, institution, or agency work alone in the film field. Films are made by groups of people; they are seen and enjoyed by groups of people drawn together through mutual interests or banded together in a community film council or in a film society.

You can use your library's films on your club programs, in your church, in your homes, as part of your civic programs. Ask your library about such service. The librarian in Sandusky, Ohio, said after the first two months of film-lending: "We are all just bursting with enthusiasm over the regional project and how we can use the films effectively. Once more we would like to tell you how lucky we think we are to be a part of this demonstration." Many other public libraries are only waiting for the public interest and financial support which alone can make new services possible. . . .

Patricia Blair was graduated from Western Reserve University School of Library Science in 1940. From 1947 to 1951 she was film advisor for the American Library Association, a position made possible by a special Carnegie grant.

the university extension film
library's role

F. C. Lowry

FROM any viewpoint, it is evident that the state universities, land-grant colleges, and the regional universities, through their university extension divisions, have pioneered in, and proved the worth of, audio-visual aids in the fields of youth and adult education. They have also stimulated the use of the informational film as a measure of general public information. The foresight of the university extension divisions in the organization meeting of the National University Extension Association in 1915 embraced consideration of the use of films as a means of education for all people. At that time they established a visual-aids committee for study and promotion of the new motion picture in education as well as the other types of visual aids already in use.

Throughout the years of the old portable 35mm. projector, using the inflammable film, this committee and its successor, the audio-visual education committee, experimented in the use of films in education. It pressured producers and copyright owners of entertainment films to cut selections and make available to Association members suitable portions for educators. Eventually, after the introduction of the 16mm. film, and its resulting competitive group of 16mm. producers, this committee did secure the formation of a 35mm. producers group to lease and produce, on the 16mm. noninflammable stock, appropriate segments of 35mm. films for education.

Perhaps the greatest advance in film use was stimulated by these universities during the war. During the early years of the war, the National University Extension Association established the Educational Film Library Association, which comprised, along with the universities, other film users and educational-film distributors. The purpose was to form a large enough group to persuade government and the industry to abandon the tight commercial procedures established for government-produced or government-sponsored films to provide a free flow of these films to the public. It succeeded. Again, with its cooperation, the Office of War Information Advisory Committee, which was a loose association of government agencies, the industry, the universities, and other film users and distributors, was set up in Washington for stimulation and proper and wider distribution of government-produced films in the war effort. These divisions of university extension, through their film libraries, were prominent in the war bond drives and all educational phases of the war effort.

In the meantime, other educational agencies had become interested in the use of audio-visual materials in education. The American Library Association discovered that here was a substitute more effective than, or certainly as effective as, books and the pictorial materials, which its members had previously been housing and distributing on loan. The National Education Association established the Department of Audio-Visual Instruction to deal with the problems relating to the use of audio-visual materials in the schools and the American Association for Adult Education was likewise interested in the problem area of this new field of educational effort. So there were a variety of educational agencies directly concerned with "increasing the information and working toward the general welfare of people by fostering, improving, and promoting the production, the distribution, and the effective use of audio-visual materials." The university film libraries, working through committees of the National University Extension Association and its protégé, the Educational Film Library Association, were on the ground floor actually doing the work as well as talking theory.

Acknowledgment must be made here to the splendid wartime cooperative spirit of the new 16mm. industry, then represented through the Allied Non-Theatrical Film Association, the National Association of Visual Education Dealers, and the Visual Equipment Council, in all matters basic to the development of audio-visual film use in education. Fine cooperation was shown, also, by the Hollywood group, through an organization called the Teaching Film Custodians, and by the newsreel producers.

The university extension film libraries are the means of opening for the public the reservoirs of information and educational possibilities inherent in universities. The divisions of university extension are roadways from the universities to their respective public. These roadways are traveled in both directions. The needs of the public move in to the university. The answers go out through these divisions. The first vision of university extension divisions, in 1915, was that here in the visual field, with all its media, were means for correctly and efficiently explaining facts and giving sound impressions to its clientele. University extension has a three-fold purpose: teaching, servicing, and stimulating. University extension film libraries hold within themselves all of these three possibilities. Hence, it has been a prime concern of university extension divisions over the years that they develop these media and the avenues for their intelligent distribution and use to the highest degree.

The success of the universities' work in their respective areas can be well illustrated by the fact that a short time before the war there were not many 16mm. projectors in use in the public schools. A recent survey in Tennessee revealed that there are a thousand times as many projectors in use now in that state's public schools as there were at the beginning of the war. A proportionate increase could be shown in the projectors used by civic clubs, parent-teachers associations, and adult organizations generally. This means that the extension film library in the University of Tennessee has in a remarkable degree stimulated the use of films for both the public school education and mass information. The same sort of stimulation through demonstration has taken place throughout the country.

The people look to their universities to furnish them the best; they expect from them objective information, free from the taint of special interest. The university extension film library has the whole faculty of the university to draw from in evaluating the films which it places in stock for distribution. Moreover, the simple distribution of films, whether free, for a service charge, or for a profit-taking fee, is definitely not the limit of the obligation of an educational film library. The impact of the audio-visual aid is not so simple or so nearly evanescent as that of the printed or spoken word. The effects are about as continuing as those of experience itself. Therefore, no false impression should be left on the recipient, and it is necessary to know how to use each specific film and the films must be evaluated for the purposes for which they are used. Here is importance for film library and university faculty relationships.

There is another function of the university film library. Film users have a right to expect the film library to teach them how to use films to the best advantage, both in securing information for themselves and in the use of these media for the instruction of others. The university extension film libraries can carry these demands in to the university, and the university faculty is the group capable of setting up means of instruction in these particulars. So the university extension film library undoubtedly has also been one of the main elements in impressing the need for courses in audio-visual education on the faculties of their universities.

The university film library is supplementary in all particulars. It will supplement the public libraries' services through block loans and on occasion will assist in film forums, demonstrations, and pageants. It will provide a broad base of documentary and factual films for use of all types of adult groups and will maintain its ability to present well-balanced programs on issues. It will maintain an adequate film information center. It will provide over-all audio-visual news services. It will build some films directly applicable to its physical area alone and will seek others to relate the conditions of its area to the conditions of the world. It is an integral part of the film educational program of the state.

F. C. Lowry is dean of the University Extension of the University of Tennessee and a former president of the National University Extension Association.

commercial film dealers

Lillian Rubin, NAVA

THE National Audio-Visual Association—NAVA—is the trade organization of commercial sellers and makers of audio-visual equipment and materials. It was formed in 1949 through the merger of two ten-year-old associations, the National Association of Visual Education Dealers and the Allied Non-Theatrical Film Association. NAVA (pronounced as in "have a") has a membership of approximately five hundred companies. Of these, about four hundred are specializing dealers in audio-visual equipment and commercial 16mm. film libraries, and the remaining hundred are the film and filmstrip producers and equipment manufacturers. A geographical directory of members of the association is available without cost from NAVA headquarters at 845 Chicago Avenue, Evanston, Illinois.

At this point it might be well to stop and consider just what an audio-visual dealer is and does. Most important, he is a *specialist*. Many dealers are former educators who believed in the future of audio-visual education and went into the field commercially, while others are businessmen who have had long experience in the field, but all are qualified to give advice and assistance to their customers in selecting the right equipment and films for their needs, and all specialize in audio-visual aids. Dealers usually sell all kinds of audio-visual equipment—sound, slide, filmstrip, and opaque projectors, playback units, recorders, public address systems, screens, and the necessary accessories. They also have service departments for the maintenance and repair of equipment. Nearly all dealers have rental libraries of educational, religious and entertainment films and filmstrips, and most of them annually publish catalogs listing these films. Equipment as well as films can be rented from the audio-visual dealer; or a complete show, including equipment, operator and films, can be furnished. The average size of an audio-visual business is three or four persons, although there are a few employing a hundred or more. Audio-visual dealers have the facilities and knowledge not only to sell a piece of equipment, but to help the customer select the right equipment for his needs, to keep it in good condition, and to keep a constant source of materials available so that the customer is able to use his equipment to best advantage.

In 1939 these dealers began to feel the need for a national association, and a small group of them got together during a meeting of the National Education Association and formed the National Association of Visual Education Dealers. At about the same time another group of film libraries and distributors formed the Allied Non-Theatrical Film Association. Both were dedicated toward broad objectives rather than the advancement of any individual members' own immediate interests, and the two organizations operated separately until their increasingly common sphere of operations made a merger desirable. This was completed in 1949, resulting in the present organization. NAVA is a non-profit association, supported entirely by membership dues. A seventeen-man Board of Directors, elected from and by the membership, governs the organization and sets its policies, which are then carried out by a full-time paid staff of four persons who handle the association's various activities, including its publications, from NAVA's national headquarters in Evanston, Illinois.

NAVA's general objectives are to stimulate more widespread use of 16mm. films and audio-visual materials, to improve business practices in the audio-visual field, to collect and furnish information to members, and to work for the improvement of the audio-visual and 16mm. film business in general. In line with these objectives, the organization undertakes a widely varied line of activities. One of NAVA's basic functions is getting people together —in spirit as well as in person. To do this it sponsors the National Audio-Visual Convention and Trade Show, held in Chicago each summer about a month before schools open. In addition to the annual convention, three regional meetings are held each winter for discussions of regional and local problems.

Because of the rapid growth of the audio-visual business, many audio-visual dealers have felt a need for better training for themselves and their employees. For this reason the association established the National Institute for Audio-Visual Selling, an annual one-week training course for NAVA members and their employees, held each summer just before the annual convention in cooperation with the Audio-Visual Center of Indiana University, Bloomington, Indiana. At the Institute courses are given in the latest techniques of using audio-visual teaching tools. Emphasized throughout the Institute program are the ways in which dealers can better serve the users of audio-visual tools.

The association has several publications, chief among which is *NAVA Newsletter,* a condensed bulletin, published every two weeks and designed to keep members up to date on what is happening in the audio-visual field. Other publications include *Current Models of Projection Equipment,* giving specifications on all types of projection equipment; *Used Equipment Price Reports,* and *Confidential Reports,* published as the occasion demands to bring members business suggestions, tax advice, and advance information on developments in the field.

Since many NAVA members have small businesses and cannot afford to keep extensive information files on all the new films and types of equipment which are constantly coming on the market, the association keeps these files for them. In this way film users can go to any NAVA dealer, large or small, with their questions and be confident that if the dealer does not have the information on hand he can procure it quickly from NAVA. The Association also backs up individual members in combating unfair local restrictions on the use of 16 mm. films. An example of this occurred a few years ago when unions in several towns and cities attempted to have laws passed preventing the showing of 16mm. films in any public place (which would include schools, churches, etc.) without use of a fireproof booth and other elaborate installations, claiming that such showings constituted a fire hazard. Since 16mm. films are *not* a fire hazard (although 35mm. theatrical films are), the association collected statements from The Underwriters' Laboratory, Eastman Kodak, Ansco, and other well-known and reliable sources, proving that 16mm. films did not constitute a fire hazard. Folders containing these statements were then sent to members who requested them to fight the passing of such laws. They have succeeded in their purpose so well that today no such laws exist to our knowledge.

Other services of the Association include wide distribution of the NAVA Membership Directory, use of the NAVA Membership Emblem on members' store windows and stationery, representation in Washington (becoming increasingly important), participation in a group film insurance policy, and so on.

At present NAVA is working on two plans to broaden the audio-visual field in general. The first, the Audio-Visual Industry Advertising plan, will utilize a series of advertisements in national publications to bring the audio-visual story to those who are unfamiliar with it. The other, the National Legislative Plan, will attempt to coordinate efforts to obtain larger appropriations for audio-visual education from state, county, and city governments. If successful, this plan will result in schools being able to purchase more equipment and materials and thus make wider use of audio-visual education in teaching.

industrially sponsored films: telephone film distribution

Henry Habley

(Editor's Note: Rounding out the 16mm. distribution scene is the industrially sponsored film, usually circulated free of charge as part of a public relations, and sometimes a direct advertising, program. In the article below Henry Habley, supervisor of Film and Display Distribution at American Telephone and Telegraph, explains how his organization circulates. its films both through its own local offices and many other 16mm. channels.)

THE value of the film as a medium for the transmission of information about the telephone business has long been recognized by the Bell Telephone System. There is now a wide variety of subjects devoted to many facets of the business that have been proved interesting to all types of audiences. Fundamentally the telephone business is a community-centered enterprise. The equipment serving a particular community has been tailored to fit the requirements of the telephone users in that locality. It is natural then that people look to the local telephone office for information about the business. The objective, therefore, is to provide films at the local community level.

Both the production and distribution of films is geared to that end. The selection and production of a film subject presents few problems. Long experience, confirmed by tests of audience re-action, indicates what films to make. The cost of production, too, is minor, compared to the cost of distribution. The major problem is to get films screened before the audiences for whom they are intended. The primary objective is to make it handy to get films quickly and easily at minimum cost.

Most showings are booked through the local telephone business office either by lending films or by a complete telephone company program including projection equipment and an introductory talk. Films are also placed on deposit with other organizations. In this category are the local public library, the commercial film dealer, and university audio-visual bureaus. Often a school system requests some of our films if the subject fits the curriculum, and in one case a specialized film on how to use the telephone was produced, solely at the request of educators, for teaching purposes in elementary schools.

State-wide agencies, including universities, museum, and Government bureaus, serve the smaller communities and towns, often reaching audiences not readily available in other ways. Long established national film distribution agencies have served usefully. Not only do they publicize the films, but many users of films go to those sources as a matter of habit. These national distributors of industry films have a definite place in rounding out the 16mm. distribution activity.

All the channels of distribution mentioned are used to help the local telephone office circulate more films than can be handled through a single office. Care is taken, however, to keep the local telephone office informed of all such activity.

Often telephone subjects are of such wide interest that motion-picture theatres like to include them in their programs. This is especially true of the neighborhood type of house, and demand is heavy for the kind of film that is devoted to presenting an interesting story about a facet of American life as universal as the telephone. Active solicitation of theatre bookings has not been found necessary. The primary requirement is to produce the kind of films wanted and to make their existence known. It is found that good films have a way of bringing additional bookings each time they are shown. They don't gather dust on the shelf. The investment in the film library is proved sound by the simple testimony of the empty film rack.

Most effective distribution of films provides a well-rounded program to reach all possible audiences. It remains true, however, that densely populated areas are more active because there is lack of flexibility in present distribution methods. The awareness of this problem is resulting in a continuing growth, with each year showing a larger demand for telephone films.

As a means of checking the effectiveness of distribution as well as the quality of the films, the member telephone companies of the Bell System pretest new films for audience reaction before general release. Besides knowing the degree of interest in the film, much is learned that is helpful in directing future production. It is, therefore, easier to make the right kinds of pictures available for particular audiences.

national distributors

TO rent or purchase prints of the films reviewed in the following section, consult your local educational or commercial film library first (see page 127). The national distributors listed below can be consulted if the films are not available locally. This list contains the names and addresses of national distributors represented by two or more film reviews. Addresses for those with only one film review in this volume are given in the main credits of the review.

A. F. Films, 1600 Broadway, New York 19, N.Y.

Association Films, 35 West 45th Street, New York 19, N.Y.

Athena Films, 165 West 46th Street, New York 19, N.Y.

Australian News & Information Bureau, 634 Fifth Avenue, New York 20, N.Y.

Brandon Films, 200 West 57th Street, New York 19, N.Y.

British Information Services, 30 Rockefeller Plaza, New York 20, N.Y.

* Castle Films, or Castle Division of United World Films, 1445 Park Avenue, New York 29, N.Y.

Contemporary Films, 13 East 37th Street, New York 3, N.Y.

Cooperative League, 343 S. Dearborn Street, Chicago 4, Illinois

* Coronet Films, Coronet Building, Chicago 1, Illinois

Encyclopaedia Britannica Films, Wilmette, Illinois

Film Program Services, 1173 Avenue of the Americas, New York 19, N.Y.

Film Publishers, 25 Broad Street, New York 4, N.Y.

Films, Inc., 330 West 42nd Street, New York 18, N.Y.

Films of the Nations, 62 West 45th Street, New York 19, N.Y.

French Films and Folklore, Box 2A, 431 Riverside Drive, New York, N.Y.

International Film Bureau, 6 North Michigan Avenue, Chicago 2, Illinois

* International Film Foundation, 1600 Broadway, New York 19, N.Y.

* Library Films, 25 West 45th Street, New York 19, N.Y.

* March of Time Forum, 369 Lexington Avenue, New York 17, N.Y.

* McGraw-Hill Text-Films, 330 West 42nd Street, New York 18, N.Y.

Museum of Modern Art Film Library, 11 West 53rd Street, New York 20, N.Y.

National Education Association, 1201 Sixteenth Street, N.W., Washington, D.C.

National Film Board of Canada, 1270 Avenue of the Americas, New York 20, N.Y.

National Film Distributors, 112 West 48th Street, New York 19, N.Y.

New York University Film Library, 26 Washington Place, New York 3, N.Y.

New York Zoological Society, Education Department, New York 60, N.Y.

* Official Films, Grand and Linden Avenues, Ridgefield, New Jersey

* Pictorial Films, 105 East 106th Street, New York 29, New York

Princeton Film Center, Princeton, New Jersey

RKO Radio Pictures, 16mm. Division, 1270 Avenue of the Americas, New York 20, N.Y.

Religious Film Association, 45 Astor Place, New York 3, N.Y.

* Sterling Films, 316 West 57th Street, New York 20, N.Y.

United Nations Film Distribution Unit, Room 945D, 405 East 42nd Street, New York, N.Y.

United World Films, 1445 Park Avenue, New York 29, N.Y.

* Young America Films, 18 East 41st Street, New York 17, N.Y.

---

* Available for purchase only. In most cases, rental requests will be referred to a library owning the film in question.

a selected list of 16mm. film libraries

Alabama
Montgomery—Photo & Sound Co., 124 Church St.
University—University of Alabama, Box 1991

Arizona
Tucson—University of Arizona, Visual Aids Bureau

Arkansas
Conway—Arkansas State Teachers College, Normal Station
Little Rock—Democrat Printing and Lithographing Co., 114 E. Second St.

California
Glendale—Ambrosch Film Library, 1122 E. Colorado Blvd.
Long Beach—Long Beach Public Library
Los Angeles—Ideal Pictures, 2408 W. 7th St.
Los Angeles Public Library
Methodist Publishing House, 125 E. Sunset Blvd.
William M. Dennis Film Libraries, 2506½ W. Seventh St.
Oakland—Ideal Pictures, 4247 Piedmont Ave.
Redwood City—Sequoia Audio-Visual Service, 1005½ Brewster Ave.
Sacramento—McCurry Foto Co., 731 Eye St.
San Francisco—Association Films, 351 Turk St.

Methodist Publishing House, 85 McAllister St.
Photo & Sound Co., 116 Natoma St.
San Jose—American Film Center, 394 W. San Carlos St.
San Raphael—Marin Motion Picture Service, 8 Francisco Blvd.
Santa Monica—Santa Monica Public Library

Colorado
Boulder—University of Colorado, Bureau of Audio-Visual Instruction
Colorado Springs—Eastin Pictures, Colorado Springs Bank Bldg., P.O. Box 613
Denver—Akin & Bagshaw Film Library, 2023 E. Colfax Ave.
Centennial School Supply Co., 3680-3912 Huron St.
Colorado Visual Aids Supply Co., 1118 Broadway
Dale Deane's Home Movie Sales Agency, 28 E. Ninth Ave.
Ideal Pictures, 714 Eighth St.
Modern Films, 583 S. York St.
Fort Collins—Larimer County Library, Fort Collins Public Library

Connecticut
Greenwich—Pix Film Service, 34 E. Putnam Ave.
Hartford—Harrison Harries, 110 High St.
Middletown—Russell Library

NOTE: Public libraries supply films *only* to their own communities.

New London—SerCon, 160 State St.

Stamford—Ferguson Library

Torrington—Flieg & Newbury, 45 Water St.

Waterbury—Eastern Film Libraries, 148 Grand St.

Wethersfield—Taylor Films & Equipment Co., 42 Wells Road

District of Columbia

Washington, D.C.—Public Library The Film Center, 915 Twelfth St., N.W.

Florida

Miami—Ideal Pictures, 1348 N. Miami

Stevens Pictures, 9536 N.E. Second Ave.

Tampa—Southern Photo & News, 608 E. Lafayette St.

Georgia

Athens—University of Georgia, Old College.

Atlanta—The Distributor's Group, 756 W. Peachtree St., N.W.

Ideal Pictures, 52 Auburn Ave., N.E.

Idaho

Boise—Boise Junior College, Educational Film Library

Illinois

Blue Island—Coronet Films, 13039 S. Western Ave.

Carbondale—Southern Illinois University, Audio-Visual Aids Service

Champaign—University of Illinois, Visual Aids Service

Chicago—American Film Registry, 24 E. Eighth St.

Association Films, 206 So. Michigan Ave.

Chicago Public Library

Ideal Pictures, 65 E. South Water St.

International Film Bureau, 6 N. Michigan Ave.

Methodist Publishing House, 740 Rush St.

Evanston—Evanston Public Library

Oak Park—Stinson Projector Sales, 521 S. Lombard Ave.

Peoria—Peoria Public Library

Springfield—E. L. O'Hair Film Service, 1443 N. Third St.

Urbana—Shick Film Service, 404 N. Goodwin Ave.

Winnetka—John Ott Film Library, 730 Elm St.

Indiana

Bloomington—Indiana University, Audio-Visual Center

Gary—Gary Public Library

Indianapolis—Ideal Pictures, 815 N. Pennsylvania St.

South Bend—Burke's Motion Picture Co., 434 Lincoln Way West

Wabash—Dennis Film Bureau, 29 E. Maple St.

Iowa

Ames—Iowa State College, Visual Instruction Service

Cedar Rapids—Pratt Sound Films, 720 Third Ave., S.E.

Davenport—Eastin Pictures, 711 Putnam Bldg. P.O. Box 598

Des Moines—J. G. Kretschmer Co., 316 Royal Union Bldg.

Ideal Pictures, 1108 High St.

Midwest Visual Education Service, 1120 High St.

Kansas

Salina—Leftingwell's Audio-Visual Service, 232-A South Santa Fe

Wichita—Frank Bangs Co., 315 N. Emporia

Lawrence Camera Shop, 149 N. Broadway

Kentucky

Louisville—D. T. Davis Co., 528 S. Fifth St.

Hadden Films, Inc., 423 W. Liberty St.

NOTE: Public libraries supply films *only* to their own communities.

Louisville Free Public Library
Office Equipment Co., 119 S. Fourth St.

Louisiana
New Orleans—Ideal Pictures, 3218 Tulane Ave.

Maine
Orono—University of Maine, Audio-Visual Service, South Stevens Hall
Portland—D. K. Hammett, Inc., 620 Congress St.

Maryland
Baltimore—Enoch Pratt Free Library
Ideal Pictures, 506 St. Paul
Methodist Publishing House, 516 N. Charles St.

Massachusetts
Boston—Boston Public Library
Ideal Pictures, 40 Melrose St.
Joe Cifre Inc., 44 Winchester St.
New England Film Service, 755 Boylston St.
Stanley - Winthrop's, Inc., 20 Shawmut St.
Wholesome Film Service, 20 Melrose St.
Fitchburg—Fitchburg Public Library
Lynn—Massachusetts Motion Picture Service, 132 Central Ave.
Worcester—Bailey Sound Film Service, 59 Chandler St.

Michigan
Ann Arbor—University of Michigan, Audio-Visual Education Center, 4028 Administration Bldg.
Dearborn—Dearborn Public Library
Detroit—Detroit Public Library
Engleman Visual Education Service, 4754 Woodward Ave.
Ideal Pictures, 7338 Woodward Ave., Rm. 407

Methodist Publishing House, 28 E. Elizabeth St.
UAW-CIO Film Library, 8000 East Jefferson
East Lansing—Capital Film Service, 224 Abbott Rd.
Flint—Jensen, Inc., Hotel Durant Bldg.
Grand Rapids—Middleton's, Inc., 360 Jefferson Ave.
Kalamazoo—Kalamazoo Public Library
Locke Films, 124 W. South St.

Minnesota
Minneapolis—Elliott Film Co., 1110 Nicollet Ave.
Ideal Pictures, 301 West Lake
Midwest Audio-Visual Co., 2216 Nuallet Ave.
Minneapolis Public Library
University of Minnesota, Audio-Visual Extension Service, 230 Northrop Auditorium

Missouri
Columbia—University of Missouri, Visual Education Department, 23 Jesse Hall
Houston—Texas County Library
Jefferson City—Jefferson City and Cole County Libraries
Missouri State Library, State Office Building
Kahoka—Sever Memorial Library
Kansas City—Ideal Pictures, 1020 Oak St.
Methodist Publishing House, 1021 McGhee St.
Select Motion Pictures, 1326A Oak St.
Kennett—Dunklin County Library
St. Louis—Embassy Enterprises, 34 North Brentwood Blvd.
Ideal Pictures, 5154 Delmar Blvd.
Pictosound Movie Service, 4010 Lindell Blvd.
St. Louis Public Library

NOTE: Public libraries supply films *only* to their own communities.

Nebraska
Omaha—Church Film Service, 2595 Manderson St.
Modern Sound Pictures, 1410 Howard St.
University of Omaha, Bureau of Teaching Aids

New Hampshire
Durham — University of New Hampshire, Audio-Visual Center, Hewitt Hall
Manchester—A. H. Rice Co., 78 W. Central St.
Rice Film Co., 123 Pleasant St.

New Jersey
Ridgewood—Art Zeiller Co., 26 Hudson St.

New York
Albany—Hallenbeck and Riley, 558-562 Broadway
Brooklyn—Fisher Studio, 803 Lincoln Place
Reed & Reed Distributors, 7508 Third Ave.
Buffalo — Buchan Pictures, 79 Allen St.
Buffalo Film Library, 1009 E. Lovejoy
Ideal Pictures, 1558 Main St.
New Berlin—Wilber Visual Service, 28 Genesee St.
New York City — Association Films, 35 W. 45th St.
American Museum of Natural History, Audio-Visual Aids Center, 79th St. and Central Park West
Audio Film Center, 45 W. 45th St.
Brandon Films, 200 West 57th St.
City College School of Business, Audio-Visual Extension Service, 430 W. 50th St.
Columbia University Educational Films, Communication Materials Center, 413 W. 117th St.
Contemporary Films, 13 E. 37th St.

Methodist Publishing House, 150 Fifth Ave.
Mogull's, 112 W. 48th St.
New York University Film Library, 26 Washington Place
Rochester—James E. Duncan, Inc., 186 Franklin St.
Rochester Public Library

North Carolina
Chapel Hill—University of North Carolina, Bureau of Visual Instruction, Swain Hall
Charlotte—Public Library of Charlotte and Mecklenburg County
Raleigh—National Film Service, 14 Glenwood Ave.

Ohio
Akron—Akron Public Library
Cincinnati—Cincinnati Public Library
Ideal Pictures, 127 W. 5th St.
Methodist Publishing House, 420 Plum St.
Cleveland—Academy Film Service, 2300 Payne Ave.
Church School Pictures, 1118 Walnut Ave.
Cleveland Public Library
Dayton—Twyman Films, 400 W. First St.
Elyria—Elyria Library
Lorain—Lorain Public Library
James B. Upp Motion Picture Service, 552 Oberlin Ave.
Massillon—M. H. Martin Co., 50 Charles Ave., S.E.
New Philadelphia — Tuscarawas County District Library
Springfield—Warder Public Library
Toledo—Gross Photo Mart, 236 Huron St.
Toledo Public Library
Youngstown—Public Library

Oklahoma
Norman — University of Oklahoma, Extension Division
Oklahoma City—Ideal Pictures, 310 N.W. Second St.
Oklahoma City Libraries

NOTE: Public libraries supply films *only* to their own communities.

Oregon

Corvallis—Oregon State System of Higher Education, Department of Visual Instruction

Portland—Cine Craft Co., 1111 S.W. Stark St.

Ideal Pictures Corp., 915 S.W. Tenth Ave.

Methodist Publishing House, 521 S.W. 11th Ave.

Owens Motion Picture Service, 1014 S.W. Second Ave.

Pennsylvania

Erie—Kelly Studios, 14 E. Tenth St.

Harrisburg—J. P. Lilley & Son, 277 Boas St.

Hawthorn—B. E. George, Audio-Visual Aids

Indiana—Indiana Film Library

Millersville—State Teachers College, Film Library

Pittsburgh—Methodist Publishing House, 642 Smithfield St.

Pennsylvania College for Women, PCW Film Service

Sharpsville—L. C. Vath, Audio-Visual Education Supplies, Box C

State College—Pennsylvania State College, Audio-Visual Aids Library

York—York Film Library, Hartley Bldg.

Rhode Island

Johnston—Avard J. Sloat, Film Library, 640 Greenville Ave.

South Dakota

Brookings—South Dakota State College

Sioux Falls—Harold's Film Library, 308 So. Phillips

Tennessee

Chattanooga—Eastin Pictures, 830 Cherry St.

Memphis—Ideal Pictures, 18 S. Third St.

Southern Visual Films, 686 Shrine Bldg.

Nashville—Methodist Publishing House, 810 Broadway

Tennessee Visual Education Service, 416A Broad St.

Texas

Abilene—Abilene Christian College, West Texas Film Library

Austin—Leistico's, 3808 East Ave.

University of Texas, Visual Instruction Bureau

Commerce—East Texas Audio-Visual Aids Library, State Teachers College

Dallas—Dallas Public Library

Association Films, 1915 Live Oak St.

Ideal Pictures, 4000 Ross Ave.

Methodist Publishing House, 1910 Main St.

Southwest Soundfilms, 423 South St. Paul St.

San Antonio—Donald L. Smith Co., 1110 Main Ave.

Utah

Logan—Utah State Agricultural College, Audio-Visual Education Department

Salt Lake City—Deseret Book Co. Film Library, 1400 Indiana Ave.

Ideal Pictures, 10 Post Office Place

University of Utah, Extension Division

Virginia

Norfolk—Tidewater Audio-Visual Center, 617 W. 35th St.

Richmond—Ideal Pictures Co., 219 E. Main St.

Methodist Publishing House, Fifth and Grace Sts.

National Film Service, 202 E. Cary St.

Washington

Ellenburg—Central Washington College of Education, Office of Visual Education

Note: Public libraries supply films *only* to their own communities.

Pullman—State College of Washington, Audio-Visual Center

Seattle—Rarig Motion Picture Co., 5514 University Way

Religious Visual Aids, 4002 Roosevelt Way

Seattle Public Library

Thompson Film Services, 815 E. Pine St.

University of Washington, Instructional Materials Center

West Virginia

Charleston—United Films, 818 Virginia St., W.

Morgantown—West Virginia University Library, Audio Visual Aids Department

Wisconsin

Fort Atkinson—Dwight Foster Public Library

La Crosse—La Crosse Public Library

Madison—University of Wisconsin, Bureau of Visual Instruction, 1312 W. Johnson St.

Milwaukee—Arkay Film Service, 843 N. 32nd St.

Gallagher Films, 639 N. Seventh St.

Photoart Visual Service, 840-44 N. Plankinton Ave.

Racine—Racine Public Library

Sheboygan—Mead Public Library

Wyoming

Laramie—University of Wyoming, Wyoming Film Library

NOTE: Public libraries supply films *only* to their own communities.

VII. FILM REVIEWS

16mm. film reviews

EDITOR'S NOTE: To make the best use of these reviews, the reader should keep in mind the following facts:

1. These reviews were written at different times, by different people, and appeared first in the *Saturday Review of Literature* and the now defunct *Film Forum Review*. Although they have been shortened where necessary, no attempt has been made to rewrite them to compensate for their differences in length and style.

2. Despite the differences in the reviews, they all share a common purpose, twofold in nature: first, to provide information about films of more than routine interest; second, to help establish some standards for evaluating non-theatrical films.

3. The films reviewed are representative selections from among the many non-theatrical films available and should not be considered as a comprehensive list. Production dates are given for films released prior to 1945.

4. The reviews are arranged alphabetically within subject area groupings.

5. To obtain any of the films for possible loan, rental, or purchase, the reader is urged to consult his nearby 16mm. film libraries.

A list of selected commercial and educational 16mm. libraries is given at the end of section vi on page 127. This list was compiled with the assistance of Lillian Wachtel. Addresses of national distributors appear on page 125.

6. Since this volume includes reviews of a selected and limited number of films, there are a number of national distributors who unfortunately are not represented in this volume. A more complete list of national distributors can be found in the H. W. Wilson *Educational Film Guide.*

7. The initials after each review signify the following:

(RS) — written by Raymond Spottiswoode for the *Saturday Review of Literature* (from September 1948 to May 1949)

(CS) — written by Cecile Starr for the *Saturday Review of Literature* (from June 1949 to January 1951)

(FFR) — written by an editor or staff member of *Film Forum Review*, and based upon a group evaluation (from October 1946 to December 1948)

1. ANIMALS AND ADVENTURE

The Adventures of Chico
African Big Game
Come to the Circus
Daredevils of the Alps
The Falkland Islands
Hermits of the Sky
High Over the Borders
Life on the Western Marshes
Our Animal Neighbors
Realm of the Wild
Spelunking
Stars in Stripes
Sweeney Steps Out
Totems

2. ART, MUSIC, AND FILM

Art
Art Treasures from the Vienna Collections
1848
Fiddle-de-dee
French Tapestries Visit America
Henry Moore
Lascaux: Cradle of Man's Art
The Loon's Necklace
Masterpieces from the Berlin Museums
The Maya Through the Ages
Painting with Sand
Rubens
Van Gogh
What is Modern Art?

Music
Carmen
Hymn of the Nations
Instruments of the Orchestra
Jose Iturbi
Listen to the Prairies (A City Sings)
Music in America
Myra Hess
Paderewski
Story of a Violin
Toronto Symphony #1
Toronto Symphony #2

Film

Animated Cartoons: The Toy That Grew Up [and] Biography of the Motion Picture Camera

Basic Motion Picture Techniques

Facts about Film

Film and You

Film Tactics

How Motion Pictures Move and Talk

March of the Movies

Four British Documentary Classics

Granton Trawler

Lever-Age

Night Mail

Song of Ceylon

3. CHRISTMAS AND RELIGIOUS FILMS

Answer for Anne

Christmas Carols

Christmas Rhapsody

Creation According to Genesis

Holiday Carols

The Life of Christ

The Nativity

One God—The Ways We Worship Him

The Way of Peace

4. EDUCATION

And So They Live

A Better Tomorrow

Cambridge

A Child Went Forth

The Children Must Learn

Does It Matter What You Think?

The Fight for Better Schools

Learning to Understand Children

Lessons From the Air

Princeton

Role Playing in Human Relations Training

The Safest Way

The School

School in Centerville

The School That Learned to Eat

Schoolhouse in the Red

Scottish Universities

Teachers' Crisis

Who Will Teach Your Child?

5. FEATURE FILMS—AMERICAN AND FOREIGN

(See "Available Features" by Cecile Starr)

W. C. Fields: Four Films
The Bank Dick
My Little Chickadee
You Can't Cheat an Honest Man
Never Give a Sucker an Even Break

Great Expectations

The Long Voyage Home

March of the Wooden Soldiers

The Mikado

Miracle on 34th Street

Nanook of the North

The Overlanders

The Quiet One

The Titan

The True Glory

Zéro de Conduite

6. HEALTH—PHYSICAL AND EMOTIONAL (Including Child Care and Psychology, Sex Education, the Physically Handicapped, and Psychiatry)

Alcohol and the Human Body

Attitudes and Health

Careers and Cradles

Challenge: Science Against Cancer

Children Growing Up With Others

Children of the City

Clean Waters

The Eternal Fight

Feeling All Right

The Feeling of Hostility

The Feeling of Rejection

First as a Child

First Steps

Fitness is a Family Affair

Highland Doctor

Human Beginnings

Human Growth

Human Reproduction

Invisible Armour

Journey Into Medicine

Know Your Baby

Life With Baby

Life With Junior
"Marriage for Moderns" Series
  This Charming Couple
  Marriage Today
  Choosing for Happiness
  It Takes All Kinds
  Who's Boss?
Meeting Emotional Needs in
  Childhood
A Message to Women
A Modern Guide to Health
Nobody's Children
Over-Dependency
Pay Attention
Problem Children
Problem Drinkers
Small Fry
Starting Line
Unconscious Motivation
The Walking Machine
Your Children and You
Your Children's Ears
Your Children's Eyes
Your Children's Meals
Your Children's Sleep
Your Children's Teeth

7. LIFE IN THE U.S. (Including
Minority Problems, Housing, La-
bor and Management, Natural
Resources, etc.)

The City
The Color of a Man
Crossroads for America
The Cummington Story
Deadline for Action
Florida, Wealth or Waste
For Some Must Watch
Funny Business
Highway Mania
The House I Live In
In Balance
Library of Congress
Make Mine Freedom
Make Way for Youth
Men of Gloucester; Pueblo Boy;
  Southern Highlanders
A Place to Live
Power and the Land
Radio Broadcasting Today
The River
The Roosevelt Story; FDR—The
  Life of Roosevelt

Seminoles of the Everglades
Swedes in America
There Were Three Men
Union at Work
Valley of the Tennessee
Valley Town
Whoever You Are

8. PEOPLES AND PLACES

a. *Mutual Problems*
  Atomic Power
  Boundary Lines
  Brotherhood of Man
  One World or None
  The Pale Horseman
  The People's Charter
  Picture in Your Mind
  Round Trip
  The Story of Money
  Stuff for Stuff
  A Tale of Two Cities

b. *Africa*
  Achimota
  Daybreak in Udi
  New Ways for Old Morocco
  Rhythm of Africa

c. *Asia*
  Farmers of India
  India, Asia's New Voice
  Mother
  Nomads of the Jungle (Malaya)
  Peiping Family
  Tropical Mountain Land (Java)

d. *Australia and the Pacific*
  Highway to Hawaii
  In the South Seas
  Men and Mobs
  Namatjira the Painter
  Pacific Terminal
  The Philippine Republic

e. *Canada*
  Family Outing
  Introduction to Gaspé
  The Rising Tide
  Rocky Mountain Trout
  Ski Holiday

f. *Europe*
  Bread and Wine
  Farmer-Fisherman (Norway)
  Majestic Norway
  New Earth
  Picturesque Denmark

Picturesque Sweden
Wings to Ireland
g. *Europe's Children*
   The Children's Republic
   A Penny's Worth of Happiness
   Tomorrow's a Wonderful Day
h. *Films in French*
   Autour d'un Clocher
   Le Moulin Enchanté
   Profil de la France
   La Rose et le Reseda
i. *Latin America*
   The Amazon Awakens

Americans All
The Bridge
Cross-Section of Central America (Guatemala)
Horsemen of the Pampas (Argentina)
Tomorrow's Mexico
Wings Over Latin America
Wings to Cuba and the Caribbean
Wings to Mexico and Guatemala

1. animals and adventure
(See also "Films for Children," page 73)

THE ADVENTURES OF CHICO

Produced and directed by Stacey and Horace Woodard. 1937. Distributed by Pictorial Films. (Sixty-five minutes.)

In the ten or twelve years since this film was made, there probably hasn't been one audience that didn't think it ranked with the best they ever saw. It is a simple story of a Mexican boy's adventures with the animals that inhabit the land he lives in. There are some strange types among them, but except for a not very convincing encounter with a deadly rattler, Chico has a way with them all.

This is a feature-length film, just the right length for a party of youngsters or their parents. Language teachers may be interested in knowing that the film is also available with a Spanish sound-track.

(c.s.)

AFRICAN BIG GAME

Produced and distributed by A. F. Films. (Twenty minutes.)

The camera takes us into the Chad region of French Equatorial Africa, where the hunt is on. And the game is varied—crocodiles, ostriches, leopards, buffalo, antelopes, and more. Through salt beds an elephant herd is trailed and a six-ton mammoth with tusks a yard long is killed. It means food for the natives, trophies for the hunters.

The natural sounds and spontaneous actions of men and animals in the film help make it a real eye-witness experience for the audience. Photography is again above par. *African Big Game*, like nearly all the other A. F. releases, makes adventure meaningful and succeds in making learning the exciting adventure that it should be for old and young alike.

(c.s.)

COME TO THE CIRCUS

Produced and distributed by Library Films. (Twenty-six minutes.)

This isn't the colossal, gigantic, stupendous show that could be called the greatest on earth, but a typically European one, in which circus artistry has priority over noise and confusion. The film provides close-range views of a number of interesting animal acts: sixteen trained horses, an elephant that stands on one leg, ten very amusing polar bears performing on a slide with unamused expressions on their dead-white faces, and tigers jumping through hoops. In addition, an expert tight-rope walker does some amazing acrobatics, and later displays her skills atop a fifty-foot swaypole. The Fratellini clown troup ends the film with a surprisingly good laugh.

Camera work in the film is static and dull, but there's enough action in front of it to keep most audiences amused. Young or old, if you can take your circuses minus peanuts and popcorn, you'll enjoy this one. (c.s.)

DAREDEVILS OF THE ALPS

Produced and distributed by A. F. Films. (Twenty minutes.)

This film concerns an expedition to the tops of five straight-walled peaks of the Devil's Needles near Mont Blanc in the Alps—as dangerous and daring an adventure as any of us could want to stay home from. It suffers from some unnecessary repetition, but on the whole is much superior to the usual outdoor adventure film. (c.s.)

THE FALKLAND ISLANDS

Produced and distributed by the British Information Services. (Eleven minutes.)

A matter-of-fact account of life and work at the British meteorological station in Antarctica, where important weather data are radioed out to ships at sea and the surroundings are, to say the least, unusual. (c.s.)

HERMITS OF THE SKY

Produced and distributed by A. F. Films. (Ten minutes.)

Life at one of the most unusual observatories in the world, where four volunteer astronomy workers spend nine snow-bound months out of the year in a scientific "castle" in the Alps. (c.s.)

HIGH OVER THE BORDERS

Produced by the National Film Board of Canada. Distributed by the New York Zoological Society. Written and directed by Irving Jacoby; edited by John Ferno. (Eighteen minutes.)

This is a film on the migration of the birds of North and South America. Starting with the simple tale of an American farm boy who sees his swallows have left their nest as winter approaches, the film unfolds a comprehensive view of bird travels over both American continents. Later we see the same swallows in their Latin American summer homes where another young boy eventually watches them depart to "los Estados Unidos."

The film touches on a great many aspects of bird life as they affect bird migration. The factors of diet, plumage, sex life, physical abilities are all introduced. Many different birds are identified and some of their characteristics enumerated.

Some attention is given to the program of the United States Bureau of Wild Life and the assistance it receives from hunters and bird lovers in all countries. At the end, the film concludes with some of the reasons for the bird's seasonal migrations, and returns to its central thesis that the bird's flight is an example of ability to penetrate and overcome distance and the restraints of national boundaries. . . . The technique and artistry of the production are on a high level. . . . (F.F.R.)

LIFE ON THE WESTERN MARSHES

Produced and distributed by the National Film Board of Canada. (Thirteen minutes, color.)

Most of this film is concerned with the work of Ducks Unlimited in preserving wild fowl in Northern Canada. The thousands of broods of ducks and geese which settle in Canada each summer have been dying out because of floods, dried-up marshes, and stagnant water. With only three out of ten new-born fowl surviving, it was necessary to start special construction projects in the marshlands to make it possible for the birds to live and multiply.

Other Canadian animals needing similar protection are shown in the last part of the film—the moose, beaver, musquash, and cedar waxwing. There is a natural kind of charm in this film, and the color photography is excellent. (C.S.)

OUR ANIMAL NEIGHBORS

Produced and distributed by Coronet Films. (Eleven minutes, color.)

A pleasantly informative film about many kinds of small animals which children may watch in the country— among them, squirrels, chipmunks, moles, shrews, field mice, and bats. A really remarkable amount of information is compressed into a single reel without hurrying, and the presentation and color photography are excellent. With its gay and cheerful picture of the woods and their inhabitants, this makes an excellent entertainment film. (R.S.)

REALM OF THE WILD

Produced by the U. S. Dept. of Agriculture. Distributed by Castle Division of United World Films. (Twenty-eight minutes, color.)

As a documentary film, *Realm of the Wild* has relatively modest aims. It is little more than a tour through our nation's forests with a simple plea for conservation of wild life as its message. But it is one of the most handsome and exciting outdoor color films ever made. Audience after audience has felt its distinctive charm and appeal. Those who are quite unfamiliar with the documentary film have responded to it without inhibition or sophistication. "This is the first film I've ever seen that showed wild life in the raw," said the representative of one enthusiastic city audience, "and it's really wonderful." It is difficult to imagine an audience that would disagree. Excellent color photography. (C.S.)

SPELUNKING

Produced and distributed by A. F. Films. (Twenty minutes.)

Something quite new in sport and science is presented in this film about cave exploring, or as it is officially called, speleology. The underworld expedition takes place in the Alps region of France. Equipped with a two-way telephone (one person remains outside the pit to relay important weather information), with head lamps, safety ropes, and other necessary supplies, this group had the additional burden of generators, lighting equipment, and cameras. *Spelunking* is in fact the first film record of its kind.

Legend says that this is a bottomless pit, yet after a perilous descent of 170 feet, the bottom of the cave is reached, and once again scientific accuracy has defeated superstition. Here we see strange beauty, unlike anything on earth yet part of the earth. The film delicately balances its two themes: On the one hand, it provides the direct and simple thrills of adventure; on the other, it indicates man's fear of the unknown, his unending curiosity and restless spirit, which again lead him to knowledge.

Spelunking could hardly be a more interesting and unusual film, nor could its treatment be more intelligently and sensitively devised. The background music is excellent and the photography impressive. It is a film that can be seen several times with enjoyment and interest.

(C.S.)

STARS IN STRIPES

Produced and distributed by the New York Zoological Society. (Ten minutes, color.)

For the first time in fifty years, three captive-born tiger cubs have been successfully raised—and in a New York apartment, of all places. This film shows their development from a babyhood of less than three pounds each to a massive maturity of five hundred pounds or more.

Since tiger mothers kept in cages have the melancholy habit of refusing to feed their young, it was necessary to farm the new-born cubs out to a foster home. Mrs. Fred Martini, wife of the Lion House Keeper at the zoo, took them home and turned her kitchen into a model animal nursery, with the latest gadgets for care of the young. The tiger babies got as much loving care as any set of triplets could expect, including bottle feedings every three hours by Mrs. Martini.

Stars in Stripes makes the most of its ten minutes in telling this unusual story. The photography is first rate, not at all amateurish. The tigers are fascinating to watch, and Mrs. Martini is prettier by far than she needed to be in order to hold an audience's attention. The film is well organized, and an adventure that few of us are likely to experience first hand. See it if you can. (C.S.)

SWEENEY STEPS OUT

Produced by Film Associates, Inc. Available from the Museum of Modern Art Film Library. For educational groups only. (Ten minutes.)

Sweeney is a youngster who visits many of the animals at the Bronx Zoo and has quite a time of it. John Kieran narrates the humorous commentary, the photography is excellent, and in every way the film stands out as a model of productions about youngsters and animals. Directed by Joseph Krumgold, edited by Henwar Rodakiewicz. (C.S.)

TOTEMS

Produced and distributed by the National Film Board of Canada. (Eleven minutes, color.)

Something of the history and meaning of the totem poles which were first discovered in British Columbia about a hundred years ago is told in this film, which was produced and directed by Laura Bolton with the technical assistance of Dr. Marius Barbeau. Shown in their natural colorful landscape of snow-capped mountains, majestic fir trees, and clear, still lakes, the animal figures are explained casually and sometimes not too clearly.

An excellent musical background of drums and chants in Indian style adds to the effectiveness of the film, which, compared to *The Loon's Necklace*, for example, is more a travelog than a really creative film.

(C.S.)

2. art, music, and film

art films

ART TREASURES FROM THE VIENNA COLLECTIONS

Produced by Regency Productions, and distributed by National Film Distributors. (Forty minutes, color.)

Like the Berlin art film (p. 145), but twice its length in running time, this one selects highlights from an outstanding collection of European paintings.

Nineteen paintings are shown and discussed in some detail. The timing seems to be just right, for the film neither drags nor is overpaced. Again in color, again with an intelligent commentary by Thomas Craven read by Basil Rathbone, this, too, is a satisfactory production.

The paintings are shown in the following order: Belloto's "Vienna," Teniers's "Archduke Leopold's Gallery of Pictures," Veronese's "Christ Healing a Sick Woman," Del Piombo's "Cardinal Rudolfo Pio of Carpi," Dürer's "Martyrdom of Ten Thousand Christians," Titian's "Pope Paul III Farnese," Caravaggio's "Madonna of the Rosaries," Savery's "Landscape with Birds," Steen's "World Upside Down," Rubens's "Francisco IV Gonzaga," Vermeer's "Artist in His Studio," Velasquez's "Philip IV of Spain" and "Infanta Margareta Teresa," Rembrandt's "His Son Titus," Jordaens's "Feast of the Bean," Correggio's "Jupiter and Io," Titian's "Danae," Tintoretto's "Susanna and

the Elders," and Rubens's "Feast of Venus."   (C.S.)

1848

Produced by La Cooperative Generale du Cinéma Français. Released by A. F. Films. (Twenty minutes.)

This is a little gem of a film. Taking its visual substance from engravings, etchings, and ink drawings of a contemporary Paris, it revives one year out of a past century with a feeling of historical realness and rightness which the camera has probably never before accomplished. Parisian boulevards, cafés, parks, evening parties, the monarchy and its ministers, financiers, the beggars and hawkers and unemployed, the new railroads, factories darkening the skies, women and children working in coal mines. Unexpectedly the Government is overthrown; the right to work and the right to vote become for a brief moment the new political banner of the nation.

1848 is easily one of the most recommendable films of the year. There are sure to be others using a similar style, and there is room for more.

(C.S.)

FIDDLE-DE-DEE

An abstract color film by Norman McLaren, produced and distributed by the National Film Board of Canada. Distrib-

uted by International Film Bureau. (Four minutes.)

This musical cocktail is guaranteed not to leave even the youngest cinemaniac with a hangover. In dazzling movement and color, to the tune of "Listen to the Mocking Bird," hand-painted bands and spots play in miraculous synchronism across the screen, dancing and scattering to every intricate rhythm of the violin. The film is definitely habit-forming, but being delightfully devoid of meaning, it will make everyone from two years upwards happy.   (R.S.)

FRENCH TAPESTRIES VISIT AMERICA

A *Falcon Production, distributed by A. F. Films. (Twenty-seven minutes.)*

This film provides an excellent record and interpretation in color of the great exhibition of French tapestries recently seen at the Metropolitan Museum. Indeed, the camera eye in many ways excels the eye of the average onlooker, for it is able to pick out detail and unravel the story of many of the complex tapestries.

The work of modern artists is not neglected, and the film, very satisfactorily reproduced in Kodachrome, is accompanied by contemporary music from the French *Anthologie Sonore.*   (R.S.)

HENRY MOORE

Produced by Falcon Films. Script and narration by James Johnson Sweeney. Comments by Henry Moore. Photography by Erica Anderson. Music by Ralph Vaughan-Williams. Distributed by A. F. Films. (Fifteen minutes, color.)

This film has several advantages not afforded to the makers of *Van Gogh* (p. 147). The living artist was available to speak for himself, the photography is in color, and the camera can deal with sculpture, because of

its nature as a three-dimensional art, more easily than with a series of canvases. The film seems to have been photographed largely at the time of the Museum of Modern Art's 1946-47 exhibition of the work of Henry Moore, who, although regarded as one of the foremost modern sculptors, was up to that time relatively unknown in this country. When, after a somewhat confusing opening sequence, the camera and commentary get down to business, the film is pleasantly successful in demonstrating what this remarkable British sculptor has tried to do and why it was worth doing.

As the camera pauses to show the way the grain has been followed in a mahogany carving or turns to show the dance of lights in a construction of lead and copper wire, we see how the sculptor's attention to the qualities of his materials helps determine the form a particular piece is to take. The use of color film makes for some charming effects, as for example in the deep purplish tones of the mahogany displayed against a rose-red wall, and, in general, the close-ups of individual pieces are rich in both color and texture, though as much cannot be said of the long shots.

The camera then shifts to the sculptor himself. He tells engagingly of how during the blitz he went into a subway shelter to escape a raid and began the series of sketches that was to take him into the shelters night after night. While he talks we are allowed to examine some of these sketches, whose great dignity and human quality are emphasized by magnification. Finally, we see some of Moore's sculpture since the war and as the camera lingers over the contours of a group of figures in stone, we note a new interest in classical forms and with it a new quality, almost of warmth. That a film about so slippery a subject as modern sculpture should, without departing from its subject, succeed in having the very real human appeal that this one has, seems to me a genuine accomplishment.   (AMY CLAMPITT)

LASCAUX: CRADLE OF MAN'S ART

Produced by William Chapman and completed with a grant from the Viking Fund. Available from Gotham Films, 31 E. 21st St., New York 10, N.Y. (Seventeen minutes, color.)

The finest examples of prehistoric cave painting yet discovered are those which were found in 1940 by two boys near the village of Montignac in Southwest France. At the end of the war William Chapman, then a correspondent for *Life* magazine, heard about the discovery and, although he had never before made a motion picture, he sensed the importance of the occasion and set about the task of hauling the necessary generators, cables and lights up the mountain and into the cave. The result is a breathtaking reproduction of the most fascinating examples of primitive art yet seen on film. Wild horses, deer, bison, cows, birds, and occasionally the figure of a man ornament the sheltered limestone walls, as vivid as though they had been painted twenty years ago instead of twenty thousand.

The film's commentary, spoken by Mr. Chapman himself, is intelligently helpful to an appreciation of the drawings. Fortunately, it is ample rather than excessive—truly a comment on the pictures rather than a lecture about them. The photography suffers somewhat from the difficult circumstances under which it was made, but all things considered, the film is excellent. To be seen, by all means.   (C.S.)

THE LOON'S NECKLACE

Produced by Crawley Films. Distributed by Encyclopaedia Britannica Films. (Eleven minutes, color.)

This film is based on an Indian legend telling how the loon got his white neckband. The story revolves around an old blind medicine man, his magic shell necklace, and his spirit-father, the loon. But more unusual than the story is the extremely effective device by which this legend of British Columbia is presented. Wooden ceremonial face masks are worn by all the characters, and carved animals and painted backdrops provide authenticity and at the same time create the necessary illusion of unreality.

These brightly colored masks and figures might ordinarily appear static and dead to the unaided eye. But under the skill of the film's director and photographer (Radford Crawley and Grant Crabtree) they come to life in their own stylized way. External movements of the camera, as well as the bodily motions of the human beings who wear the masks, allow the inherent expressions and emotional values in these primitive art forms to show with unexpected forcefulness. Incidental personifications of the blustering north wind and the queenly smooth-faced moon are especially charming.

The Loon's Necklace was recently selected as Film of the Year in Canada, and it has won other honors at film festivals in Edinburgh and Cleveland, indicating a deserved popularity with adult audiences and youngsters alike for some time to come.   (C.S.)

MASTERPIECES FROM THE BERLIN MUSEUMS

Produced by Regency Productions, and distributed by National Film Distributors. (Twenty minutes, color.)

Exhibitions of these famous paintings from the Kaiser Frederick collection last year brought record crowds to the museums where they were shown.

The producers of this film, Jo Schaeffer and William P. Riethof, in association with Spencer Samuels, have skilfully filmed some of the highlights of the exhibition, providing a permanent record for those who want to keep the pictures alive in their memories, as well as for those who did not have an opportunity to see the pictures in the first place. The finished production is a satisfactory film in every respect. While the techniques of color reproduction on film cannot expect to rival the color values of the paintings themselves, this film achieves all that could be hoped for, short of a miracle. The camera work itself is unaffected and unobtrusive, as seems fitting in a film of this kind. A truly informative commentary, written by art critic Thomas Craven and narrated by Basil Rathbone, is likewise appropriately pleasant and unpretentious. One would question only the choice of background music—Bach's D minor Toccata and Fugue played on an organ—for more appropriate music is available, if somewhat difficult to find.

The paintings themselves, shown in full and in detail, are fascinating without exception. Those most likely to attract attention are Jan Vermeer's "The Pearl Necklace" and "Lady and Gentleman Drinking Wine"; Botticelli's "Simonetta Vespucci" and "Venus"; Raphael's "Madonna and Child"; Titian's "Venus and the Organ Player"; Patinir's "Rest on the Flight into Egypt"; Correggio's "Leda and the Swan"—in fact none of them should be omitted from mention and praise. The other paintings are by Albrecht Dürer, Rogier Van der Weyden, Joos Van Cleve, Frans Hals, Vittore Carpaccio (his amazingly Dali-esque "Burial of Christ"), and Lucas Cranach.   (c.s.)

THE MAYA THROUGH THE AGES

Photographed by Giles Greville Healey; edited and written by Kenneth Macgowan. Sponsored by the United Fruit Co. Available to adult groups only from the United Fruit Co., 80 Federal St., Boston 10, Mass., and from the Princeton Film Center, Princeton, N. J. Free. (Forty-five minutes, color.)

This film is the natural outgrowth of the exploration and restoration sponsored in the past by the United Fruit Company in the Mayan regions of Central America. Divided into three distinct sections, *The Maya Through the Ages* first shows glimpses of restored Mayan cities throughout Southeastern Mexico, Guatemala, and Honduras. Temples, pyramids, stately buildings show the distinctive architecture of this unique people, now known to have had a Mongol origin. The second section deals with more specific examples of Mayan art work—figurines, the Mayan arch, textile remnants, ceramics, and the like. The dot-and-dash numerical system of the ancient Mayas is explained, as well as other scientific achievements predating those of the Mediterranean world.

The final section of the film, and by far the most fascinating, involves a visit with the last remaining true descendants of the original Mayan race, the nearly extinct Lacandons. Fewer than two hundred of them still remain, living in small family villages of eight or ten members. The primitive cultivation of corn, the religious festivals, the making of family god-pots, and the yearly pilgrimage to lost Mayan temples reflect the ties which this ancient and weary people still hold with their ancestors. After retreating from the invading Spanish during the sixteenth century, the Lacandons successfully evaded all contact with the outside world.

The photographer, having bribed the Lacandons with guns and ammunition, was able to rediscover a "lost" temple at Bonampak, in Chiapas, Mexico, where the first important Mayan paintings were found. Not unlike early Egyptian profile tableaux, these frescoes show static yet lifelike scenes of a highly organized and civilized life. The film ends by showing work being done to restore, preserve, and copy them.

The Maya Through the Ages is an impromptu filming of an archeological adventure. Its defects, such as the uneven quality of the color reproduction, are more than overshadowed by its uniqueness and the importance of its subject. The narration, read in turn by Ralph Bellamy, Irving Pichel, and Vincent Price, gives sufficiently meaningful interpretation to the film.   (c.s.)

PAINTING WITH SAND

Produced and distributed by Encyclopaedia Britannica Films. (Ten minutes, color.)

The Navajo ritual of sand painting is shown here amid the beautiful landscape of Monument Valley, near the Arizona-Utah border. In a story setting, the medicine man performs his "cure" around a child dying of tuberculosis and malnutrition. His skilled, steady fingers pour the colored clay powders into a huge circular design depicting the healing influences of nature—the sun, the earth, the winds, and clouds.

Painting with Sand is distinguished from other similar films by showing primitive art still practiced and in our very midst. Photographed by white men who were not allowed to stand where their shadows would fall upon the magic multicolored circle, it is another valuable record of primitive attempts of man to illustrate his earthly struggles.   (c.s.)

RUBENS

Produced and directed by Henri Storck. Distributed by Brandon Films. (Forty-five minutes.)

Still another outstanding art film is this almost feature-length study of the painting of the Flemish master Rubens. With two strikes against it from the start (color stock is practically unavailable in Europe, where this was photographed, and in places the film is too long and repetitious), *Rubens* is still a triumph of clarity and beauty. The commentary and photography add greatly to an understanding and appreciation of art form and style.   (c.s.)

VAN GOGH

Produced by Gaston Diehl and Robert Hæssens. Narration by Martin Gabel. Music by Jacques Besse. Available from the Museum of Modern Art. (Eighteen minutes.)

Ideally a film about paintings is a supplement to, rather than a substitute for, the paintings themselves, and some such conviction presumably led to the showing of this film at the Metropolitan Museum in New York in connection with its recent Van Gogh exhibition. Made in France and here given an English sound track, the film is composed entirely of images from Van Gogh's work.

Since the paintings and personality of this unique genius are usually thought of as inseparable, the film is also a biography in brushwork. To accomplish such a *tour de force* obviously meant a close acquaintance with the paintings and drawings and also some careful handling of the camera if the total effect was to be more than that of a succession of lantern slides, without, on the other hand, indulging in meaningless acrobatics. The camera does move, but in general it approaches the pictures with a respectful, unhurried, and sometimes studious gaze. As the biography becomes more feverish the pace increases: The images begin to move in and out of focus, to pile upon each other, and to spin around their own centers—all in an effort to dramatize the painter's state of mind.

The fact that we are given an opportunity to look carefully at a good many pictures, among them a number not otherwise to be seen in this country, is sufficient to make the film worth seeing despite certain defects. It is regrettable, first of all, that it is in black and white. The color, whether painful or exuberant, gives Van Gogh's paintings their special quality, and without it the film suggests that a doom-driven, obsessed strain is found equally in all his work. This suggestion is heightened by the quasi-poetic style of the commentary ("the lonely wanderer sets out again, headed toward his own destiny") and by the over-urgent tone in which it is delivered. Having balked at this evidence of romantic distortion, one fresh from the Van Gogh exhibition may well be irritated to notice among the paintings chosen to portray the height of his madness an orchard scene dated several years earlier.

(AMY CLAMPITT)

WHAT IS MODERN ART?

Produced by William Riethof. Distributed by The Princeton Film Center. (Twenty minutes, color.)

"Isn't it beautiful!" . . . "You can have it!" . . . "That's a masterpiece!" . . . "That's a laugh—it's abnormal!" . . . "Crazy, that's what it is, crazy!" All these comments are familiar as more or less average views on modern art. This film, photographed in beautiful color at the Museum of Modern Art in New York City, starts its discussion with this interesting interplay of comments.

In the film a photographer and a painter speak out in words of one syllable and express their own ideas about modern art and its many "isms." The role of the photographer is played by Neva Patterson, an attractive young actress, and the modern painter is Vladimir Sokoloff, veteran stage and screen actor. . . .

The film opens with one of Picasso's most controversial paintings, "Girl with Peacock." Here is a portrait in which the face is seen simultaneously from different viewpoints. The artist points out that the painting is not supposed to be a portrait in the traditional sense, but is a visual image of the spirit of a girl. "Some pictures are not supposed to delight you, but to haunt you," he tells the perplexed photographer.

The film points out that the concept of the artist divorced from reality, isolated in his ivory tower, belongs to a century that is past. Today's painters are of a different type. Such painters as Stuart Davis and Peter Blume are pointed out as leaders among those who have become involved with the images of a more and more complex life, feeling the pulse of the age and reflecting its problems. The photographer says that she can understand this kind of painting. But abstract and other difficult painters like Miró, Klee, Chagall, and Dali bother her. The painter explains that these artists are painters of the subconscious mind, using all the poetic, haunting reminiscences of unearthly fantasy and dreams.

Some people may disagree with the comments on Picasso's famous black-and-white mural "Battle of Guernica," but few will deny his sympathetic expression of the horror of the Spanish War. Some may say that the distortion in the picture borders on caricature. That is a matter of opinion. All that the film attempts to show is that artists are forever inquisitive, and they use their creative powers to investigate, dissect, and analyze the things they feel as well as the things they see. . . .   (BERTHA LANDERS)

music

CARMEN

A condensation of Bizet's opera, produced at the Royal Opera House, Rome, and distributed by Official Films. (Twenty-five minutes.)

One of a long series of potted operas produced in Italy, *Carmen* is a laudable attempt to make the world's most popular opera equally popular on the screen. By using different actors and singers for each part, and combining the voices and lip movements by post-synchronization, the producers planned to make the best of both worlds—the voices of mature singers, the appearance of young and handsome actors. Olin Downes, famous music critic and composer, supplies a brief commentary to explain the plot.

It cannot be said that all these excellent intentions have been realized in *Carmen*. The condensation into twenty-five minutes of film is so excessive that little of the plot remains, and the *verismo* for which the opera became famous disappears under a heap of gorgeous stage trappings. However well the singers may look in repose, their distorted grimaces in close-up make many of the arias look rather ridiculous. And lastly the narrator breaks in most disturbingly on several emotional scenes.

Nonetheless, the opportunities of hearing opera are for most people so slender that any attempt to bring it to the home and school screen is welcome. The voices in *Carmen* are fine and resonant, and are quite faithfully recorded on the 16mm. sound track. Moreover, enough of Bizet's magnificent score remains to give the audience some idea of the enthusiasm which a good performance of *Carmen* always creates.

(R.S.)

HYMN OF THE NATIONS

Produced by the OWI Overseas. Distributed by Castle Films. (Thirty minutes.)

If this film did nothing but present the excellent camera studies of Arturo Toscanini, it would be a remarkable film. The greatest living conductor, together with his NBC Symphony Orchestra, interprets Giuseppe Verdi's *Hymn of the Nations*. The picture was produced in honor of the liberation of Italy; for this worthy cause Toscanini allowed himself to be filmed at work. In addition to one of the best recorded musical sound tracks, the film traces the conductor's life and his part in the anti-Fascist movement.

The film was produced by Irving Lerner, directed by Alexander Hammid, and photographed by Peter Glushanok.   (R.S.)

INSTRUMENTS OF THE ORCHESTRA

Produced and distributed by the British Information Services. (Twenty minutes.)

This is the first film to be directed by a conductor—Muir Mathieson, permanent conductor of the London Symphony Orchestra, whose name is familiar to all who remember credit titles of British feature films. It offers an excellent introduction to orchestra music appreciation; Dr. Malcolm Sargent acts as commentator as he explains each instrument, the sounds it gives, and the family to which it belongs. These groups, that is, strings, woodwinds, etc., are then combined and blended to get the full effect of the score. Dr. Sargent mounts the podium and conducts the London Philharmonic in Benjamin Britten's "Variations and Fugue on a Theme by Purcell," composed especially for this film. (R.S.)

JOSE ITURBI

Distributed by Official Films.

Before Señor Iturbi joined MGM and made the classics interesting to the millions, he made two short films (each about ten minutes) for those who wanted to study his technique. In the first he plays Albeniz's "Sevilla" and Chopin's "Fantaisie Impromptu"; in the second he plays three pieces for the harpsichord by Rameau, and on the piano, Liszt's "Hungarian Rhapsody No. 11."

(R.S.)

LISTEN TO THE PRAIRIES
Produced and distributed by the National Film Board of Canada. (Twenty minutes.)
A CITY SINGS
A short version of Listen to the Prairies. *(Ten minutes.)*

At the opposite end of the musical scale from *Carmen* we find this unassuming narrative of the part which music plays in the life of a typical prairie city, Winnipeg. As the annual Manitoba Musical Festival comes round, we see the city's youngsters busily preparing their parts in choruses and orchestras, solo performances, Gilbert and Sullivan opera. Here and throughout the film, the stress is on music.

The festival begins. The performers are nervous, then gradually relax. The judges go into learned huddles. In a series of brief vignettes, we see a number of well-known choral societies and a group of young performers, several of whom have already made their mark in the musical world since this film was produced.

In the final sequence the audience does indeed "listen to the prairies" as the magnificent music of a chorale from Bach's *St. Matthew Passion* floats out over the vast stretches of the plain and its wheat fields, where another harvest is gathering. (R.S.)

MUSIC IN AMERICA

Produced and distributed by March of Time Forum. (Eighteen minutes.)

Music In America offers a quick panoramic view of the music that appeals to Americans. The film opens with sequences of a symphony audience, of a school orchestra in rehearsal, and of neighborhood music shops with their classical and swing recordings. Most popular and characteristic of the music that appeals to Americans, the film continues, is the product of Tin-pan Alley. What, asks the film, was the origin of this popular or swing music? As the forerunner of swing, the film records the beginnings of jazz with the Dixieland Jazz Band which moved from New Orleans to Chicago and then to New York, where it became a Broadway attraction.

Many thousands of Americans, the film continues, prefer more serious music. We have our community and school orchestras and our great concert halls. Artists like Marian Anderson, it is pointed out, have a large and devoted public. Chamber music is growing in popularity, and through radio and recordings, the music of symphonies like those in

Minneapolis and Boston, and of opera companies like New York's Metropolitan, is shared across the nation.

This story of *Music In America* is told against the background of sequences showing great and famous artists in concert and dance halls: Perry Como as a song plugger; Benny Goodman and Art Tatum giving their own interpretation of jazz; George Gershwin in a memorable sequence playing "I Got Rhythm"; Serge Koussevitsky rehearsing the Boston Symphony Orchestra; Eugene List playing for his fellow members of the Armed Services; and Marian Anderson singing for an enthusiastic audience. . . .   (F.F.R.)

MYRA HESS

Available from British Information Services. (Ten minutes.)

Beethoven's Sonata in F Minor, the *Appassionata*, becomes a personal thing in the hands of Myra Hess. This film presents more than a perfect rendition of a difficult piece —only the camera is capable of capturing the effort which seems wrung from her very soul as her fingers appear to improvise effortlessly. (R.S.)

PADEREWSKI

Distributed by Official Films.

Unlike Shakespeare's somber admonition that the good is oft interred with their bones, here is a specific instance in which the good that a man did lives after him. Paderewski made only one screen appearance, and the selections he played have been edited for 16mm. users. They have been divided into three reels: (1) Chopin's "Polonaise," (2) Beethoven's "Moonlight Sonata" and Paderewski's "Minuet in G,"

and (3) Liszt's "Hungarian Rhapsody." Each about ten minutes. (R.S)

STORY OF A VIOLIN

Produced and distributed by the National Film Board of Canada. (Twenty minutes, color.)

This film is unique in that it shows, stage by stage, how a violin comes to be built, and as such is especially useful in interesting children in the story of the instruments they are learning to play and enjoy. The framework of the film is very simple. Twelve-year-old Bill breaks his violin in a friendly tussle with his playmates —and they, feeling guilty about the accident, club together to buy him a new one. While the weeks pass and Bill and his friends go about their daily lives, the old violin-maker is bringing to the construction of Bill's instrument all the love and skill which he has inherited from the European craftsmen who first perfected the art.

The central part of the film consists of a long animated sequence which shows a violin springing apart into its separate elements, each of which receives a name on a card. The structure of the violin is thus clearly explained.

Story of a Violin was produced by Eugene Kash, concert violinist and head of the Film Board's music section, and it is he who accompanies the animated sequence on his fiddle in Bach's Gavotte in E from the Violin Sonata No. 6. The sound recording is good, but the color is medium to poor.   (R.S.)

TORONTO SYMPHONY NO. 1

Produced by the National Film Board of Canada, and distributed by Sterling Films. (Twelve minutes.)

Sir Ernest MacMillan conducts the Toronto Symphony Orchestra in three modern compositions: Benjamin's "Jamaican Rhumba," MacMillan's "A St. Malo," and Kabalevsky's "Colas Breugnon." Interesting camera studies supplement music.

Film

ANIMATED CARTOONS:
THE TOY THAT GREW UP
(*Eighteen minutes.*)
THE BIOGRAPHY OF THE
MOTION PICTURE CAMERA
(*Twenty minutes.*)

Produced in France by Les Films du Compas. American versions distributed by A. F. Films.

These two films won a Grand Prix at the Brussels Film Festival in 1947, and the second was additionally awarded first prize at the Chicago Film Festival the same year.

The Toy That Grew Up is a fascinating reconstruction of movies before Eastman and Edison—of the elegant toys into which lorgnetted ladies and choke-collared gentlemen peeped and peered throughout the Victorian era. Starting with Greek friezes, the film ranges the centuries down to those strangely named devices, like zootrope and the phenakistoscope, by which ingenious inventors struggled to recreate life and movement mechanically. It ends with a fine sequence on Emile Reynaud, the precursor of Walt Disney.

The Biography of the Motion Picture Camera takes up the tale and reviews the successive instantaneous photography of Marey and Muybridge's famous experiments with Governor Stanford's horses at Palo Alto, California. By means of expert reconstructions and a lively commentary, these earliest of motion pictures vividly come to life, along with the very first true motion picture, *Leaving the Lumières Factory*, made in

TORONTO SYMPHONY NO. 2

Available as above. (Ten minutes.)

In this reel MacMillan directs the third movement of Tchaikovsky's Sixth Symphony in B Minor. (R.S.)

1895, which is included in the film. The work of Edison and Eastman is also well portrayed. (R.S.)

BASIC MOTION PICTURE TECHNIQUES

Produced by Celluloid College. Available from Sterling Films. (Thirty-nine minutes, color or black-and-white, sound or silent.)

This film demonstrates the dos and don'ts of amateur film-making, covering such topics as indoor lighting, panning, screen direction, use of the tripod, and so on. Much of the film is intentional comedy, thus making its limitations less objectionable than they would otherwise be. Home-movie enthusiasts and beginning students of film will find the material interesting and the rules simple enough. (C.S.)

FACTS ABOUT FILM

Produced and distributed by the International Film Bureau. (Ten minutes.)

Everyone who puts on 16mm. shows, or who teaches others to do so, will appreciate this concise and pertinent film on good projection techniques and film care. It begins by explaining the differences between 35mm. and 16mm. film, emphasizing the latter's fragility and non-inflammability. Correct threading of several kinds of 16mm. projectors is demonstrated, as well as some basic rules for preventing film damage and breakdowns in showings. As more than one producer has pointed out, a film is only as good as it looks on the screen. Better see this one!   (c.s.)

FILM AND YOU

Produced and distributed by the National Film Board of Canada. (Twenty minutes.)

Every time an audience gets to look at some good 16mm. films, the unanimous reaction is "Why don't we see films like this more often?" This film shows how a community can get the most that the non-theatrical film offers through an organized film council. (See "Film Councils at Work," by Glen Burch, p. 58).

At the initial meeting of interested community representatives we see the planning and organizing of a film council. Arrangements are made to have a 16mm. projector for the use of all groups in the community, and a small circulating collection of films is started. The film council also trains projectionists, puts on film demonstrations, and sees that information about films is available to interested local groups.

Once a project of this kind is under way, there is a wealth of material on 16mm. film to meet every interest in the community—and we see that film can play an exciting role in helping explain many phases of today's complex living and in providing much needed recreation.

Film and You doesn't tell that story as excitingly as the subject warrants, but it gives the best all-around coverage on the non-theatrical field yet available on film.   (c.s.)

FILM TACTICS

Produced by U. S. Navy. Distributed by Castle Films. (Twenty-two minutes.)

The seemingly dull topic of film utilization is transmuted by this brilliant film into a highly amusing comedy of errors involving every Naval rank from the admiral down. Four instructors are told to use a single film in teaching a simple P.T. boat maneuver to their four classes. In a series of wonderful surrealist sequences, the camera gets inside the head of four members of these classes and displays the bewilderment, boredom, inattention, and exhaustion which can result from the wrong use of film.

The subsequent carrying out of the high-speed P.T. boat maneuver by a set of hopelessly muddled trainees results in a comedy of averted collisions of truly Mack Sennett proportions, resulting in apoplexy on the part of the Naval brass and frantic directives to Washington.

Though the film is thus geared to a specific Navy training problem, its lessons are of much more general application. Its fresh and imaginative approach will impress the fundamentals of film use on all who have to employ film in teaching, sales training, and in industrial demonstration.
(r.s.)

HOW MOTION PICTURES MOVE AND TALK

Produced by the Bell and Howell Corporation, and distributed by Castle Films. (Eleven minutes.)

An easy-to-understand explanation of the fundamentals of 16mm. projector design. Why does film move intermittently? How does the sound track work? What is the function of the different parts of a projector? This film will help all projector users to handle their machines more effectively.   (r.s.)

MARCH OF THE MOVIES

Produced and distributed by the March of Time Forum. (Twenty minutes.)

In its relatively short history, the motion picture industry has accumulated an estimated seventy million patrons each week in this country alone. *March of the Movies* shows some of the many production activities in Hollywood, and also tells of the work of the Museum of Modern Art's Film Library in preserving and circulating a large collection of the world's outstanding films to educational groups in the United States.

Among those outstanding films, we see excerpts from many which are little more than names to the present movie-going generation, and nearly forgotten memories to their elders. Beginning with scenes from *The Great Train Robbery*, the film highlights the great movies and stars of the past several decades—*The New York Hat*, with Mary Pickford and Lionel Barrymore; William S. Hart in *The Fugitive*; Theda Bara in *A Fool There Was*; Charlie Chaplin and Marie Dressler in *Tillie's Punctured Romance*; Rudolph Valentino in *The Four Horsemen*; Douglas Fairbanks in *Robin Hood*; Greta Garbo and John Gilbert in *Flesh and the Devil*. Then excerpts from the "talkies"—Al Jolson in *The Jazz Singer*, the magnificent *All Quiet on the Western Front*, Will Rogers in *David Harum*, Paul Muni as Emile Zola.

Europe's recent challenge to Hollywood is exemplified by scenes from the Italian *Shoe Shine*, the French *Volpone*, and a long black-and-white sequence from the British *Henry V*, starring Laurence Olivier.

March of the Movies doesn't attempt to do an important critical job of reviewing these fifty years of the film, but it provides a good bit of material for anyone who wants to do so. And it gives further impetus to increased revivals of worthwhile films in theatres and film societies.

(c.s.)

four british documentary classics

GRANTON TRAWLER (1934)

A carefully edited, excellently recorded sound-and-picture study of a fishing expedition off Scotland, with no spoken commentary. Produced and photographed for the [British] Empire Marketing Board by John Grierson; directed by Edgar Anstey. Available from the British Information Services for purchase only. (Eleven minutes.)

LEVER-AGE (1942)

A model teaching film, showing the development of the lever of ancient times to the highly complicated gear of today's industrial world. Originally produced in 1939 by Arthur Elton for the British Petroleum Films Bureau under the title *The Transfer of Power*, the American version is available without charge from the Shell Oil Company, 50 West 50th Street, New York. (Twenty minutes.)

NIGHT MAIL (1936)

Produced for the British GPO Film Unit by John Grierson; directed by Basil Wright and Harry Watt; sound direction by Alberto Cavalcanti; music by Benjamin Britten; verse commentary by W. H. Auden. Available from the British Information Services. (Twenty-seven minutes.)

The overnight run of a London-Glasgow mail train is used as the vehicle for some interesting experiments in documentary techniques.

SONG OF CEYLON (1936)

Produced for the Ceylon Tea Propaganda Board by John Grierson; directed by

Basil Wright. Available from the Museum of Modern Art Film Library to
educational organizations only. (Forty
minutes.)

This film contrasts the graceful and

dignified life of the people with
external influences brought by international and Empire commercial
trade, using a film form which can
most readily be described as sym-
phonic.

3. christmas and religious films

(Editor's Note: Although churches are
among the leading users of non-theatrical
films in this country, the so-called religious films have consistently been of
the poorest imaginable quality. Most of
them are crude re-enactments of Bible
stories, or modern-dress stories deriving
from Biblical sayings and teachings.
However sincere they must have been in
the planning stage, the final results can
only be classed as utter fiascoes. The
casual viewer hesitates to condemn them
for fear of implying criticism of their
basic motives. And we cannot say that
the Bible doesn't lend itself to dramatization on film—D. W. Griffith's silent
classic, Intolerance, has some extraordinarily moving episodes from the life
of Jesus. But magnificent film work of
this kind cannot be copied merely by
using the same text.

The occasional amateurishness of
many kinds of films is easily overlooked,
but films which are insensitive and offensive can never be excused. The films
reviewed below are reasonably good exceptions to this sad rule about religious
films and perhaps will serve to indicate
a better direction for future production.)

ANSWER FOR ANNE

Produced by Caravel Films for the National Lutheran Council and released by
the Religious Film Assn. (Forty minutes.)

Answer for Anne was made with
great concern for two kinds of people: those who have been cut off
from creative normal lives as a result
of the past war, the so-called displaced persons, and those who prefer
not to think about them in any
realistic and constructive way, that
is, you and I.

It could hardly be asked that a
more convincing and appealing film
be made. This is a "message" film
with much to say and a slick, professional manner of saying it. There
are only a few scenes which get
bogged down in amateurish acting
and they are certainly forgivable.

The story in brief: Anne, an attractive high-school student, is as-
signed a term paper on "Why Our
Town Should Take in DP's." She
goes out to interview the townspeople and the answers she gets add
up to one thing in her mind—selfishness. Her pastor tells her about
his recent visit to DP camps and
Anne decides that the problems can
be solved. "We can make room, we
can find jobs, we can bear the burden of people—we always could."

(c.s.)

CHRISTMAS CAROLS

Produced and distributed by Castle Films.
(Ten minutes.)

The words of the carols are superimposed over a boys' choir as they sing "The First Noel," "Hark, the Herald Angels Sing," and "Adeste Fideles." Excellent arrangement for group singing; audience may join in. ("Silent Night, Holy Night," prepared in the same format as above, is available from the same source. Three minutes.) (R.S.)

CHRISTMAS RHAPSODY

Produced and distributed by Encyclopaedia Britannica Films. (Ten minutes.)

First in the new Encyclopaedia Britannica Films series of home movies, this black-and-white film tells the story of a little fir tree which thinks itself neglected in the forest until it finds that it has been selected by a forest ranger and his children to be set up in their home and decorated as a Christmas tree.

Though the commentary may be too coy and sugary for some tastes, the film succeeds through its simple and beautiful mountain photography, and the superbly recorded carols which accompany the simple story. Excellent for young children. (R.S.)

CREATION ACCORDING TO GENESIS

Produced by Herman Boxer and released by the Religious Film Assn. (Ten minutes, color.)

Here is a Biblical film which didn't involve building costly sets or re-enacting age-old stories. Its subject matter is as exciting as any—the earth and the heavens, darkness and light, the land and the waters, the cycle of the seasons, the fruits and creatures of the sea and the air and the land, and man created in the image of God.

With deliberate slowness the camera illuminates the spoken words of the text, using the simple details of nature rather than attempting to create an illusion of breathtaking, panoramic, and essentially false splendor.

There is every reason why this film should be shown outside churches at least as much as in them. It stands its ground well as a film, combining sensitive camera techniques and an excellent musical score with one of the most familiar narratives ever told. (C.S.)

HOLIDAY CAROLS

Produced and distributed by Official Films. (Nine minutes.)

Divided into three groups: (1) "Oh Come, All Ye Faithful" and "Noel"; (2) "It Came Upon a Midnight Clear" and "Joy to the World"; (3) "Hark, the Herald Angels Sing" and "Silent Night." No superimposed titles. Boys' choir seen in church and going from house to house singing. (R.S.)

THE LIFE OF CHRIST

Produced by Atlantic Productions. Distributed by Athena Films. (Sixteen minutes.)

Albrecht Dürer's woodcuts are used in this distinctive film to tell the story of the life of Christ. With greatest concern for the material and subject, Robert Hertzberg and Rosemarie Hickson, who wrote and photographed the film, have sought out detail after detail in the intricate Dürer woodcuts, with the rewarding result of new and valuable interworkings of art, religion, and the motion picture. An original musical score by Irving Landau, based on medieval themes, adds much to the over-all tonal beauty of the film. (C.S.)

THE NATIVITY

Produced for The American Bible Society by Anson Bond Productions. Avail-

Robert Flaherty,
documentarian *extraordinaire*

2

3

1. *"Nanook of the North," produced for Revillon Frères, 1922 (p. 173).*
2. *"Louisiana Story," produced for Standard Oil Co. (N.J.), 1948 (p. 32). Photo by Webb.*
3. *Flaherty at work on "Louisiana Story." Photo by Webb, courtesy Standard Oil Co. (N.J.).*

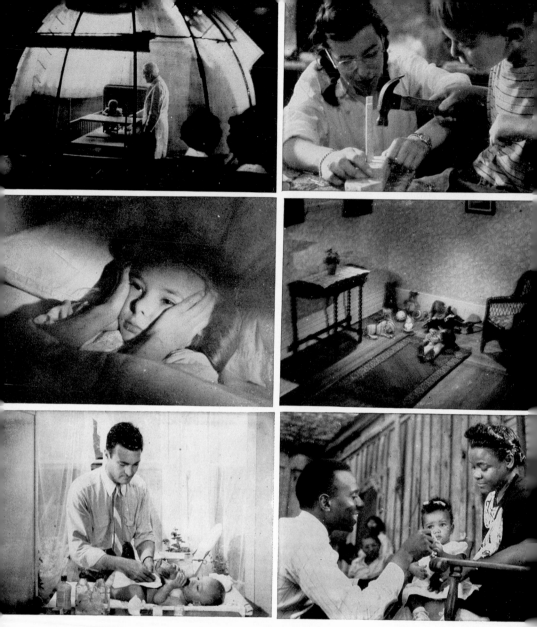

1. *"Sampan Family,"* International Film Foundation, 1949.

2. *"Rhythm of Africa,"* A. F. Films, 1948 (*p. 222*).

3. *"Clearing the Way,"* United Nations Film Board, 1948 (*p. 84*).

4. *"The Bridge,"* produced for the Foreign Policy Association, 1940 (*p. 236*). Photo courtesy New York University Film Library.

5. *"Wind from the West,"* an Arne Sücksdorff production available from Films of the Nations, 1945 (*p. 86*).

6. *"Nomads of the Jungle,"* a Louis de Rochemont production for United World Films, 1949 (*p. 224*).

1

1. *"The Titan: Story of Michelangelo,"* American version produced by Robert Flaherty, 1950 (*p. 176*). *Photo courtesy Michelangelo Company.*
2. *"Rubens,"* a Paul Haesaerts-Henri Storck production, distributed by Brandon Films, 1949 (*p. 147*).
3. *"Hymn of the Nations,"* Toscanini, with director Alexander Hammid in front of the camera, 1945 (*p. 149*). *Photo courtesy Museum of Modern Art Film Library.*

2

3

1. *"The Roosevelt Story,"* released by Brandon Films, 1949 (*p. 209*).
2. *"The Rising Tide,"* National Film Board of Canada, 1950 (*p. 228*).
3. John Ferno shooting *"And So They Live,"* in a rural Kentucky schoolroom, 1940 (*p. 158*). Photo courtesy New York University Film Library.
4. *"Children of the City,"* British Information Services, 1947 (*p. 181*).
5. *"The Quiet One,"* a Film Documents production released by Athena Films, 1949 (*p. 175*).

1. *"Challenge: Science Against Cancer,"* produced by the Medical Film Institute of the Association of American Medical Colleges and the National Film Board of Canada, 1950 (p. 180).
2. *"1848,"* A. F. Films, 1949 (p. 143).
3. *"Brotherhood of Man,"* produced by United Productions of America for the United Automobile Workers CIO, 1947; distributed by Brandon Films (p. 216).
4. *"Boundary Lines,"* a Philip Stapp production for the International Film Foundation, 1947 (p. 215).

1

2

4

3

1. *"The Loon's Necklace," produced by Crawley Films, released by Encyclopaedia Britannica Films, 1948 (p. 145).*
2. *School children in rural Canada watch a National Film Board production.*
3. *Norman McLaren paints directly onto film in some of his unique color abstractions for the National Film Board of Canada.*

1

2

3

1

2

1. *"The Children Must Learn," produced for the New York University Educational Film Institute, 1940 (p. 159). Photo courtesy New York University Film Library.*
2. *"The River," Pare Lorentz' production for the Federal Security Administration, 1937 (p. 208). Photo courtesy the Museum of Modern Art Film Library.*
3. *"The City," produced for the American Institute of City Planners, 1939 (p. 197). Photo courtesy the Museum of Modern Art Film Library.*
4. *"Valley Town," produced for the New York University Education Film Institute, 1940 (p. 212). Photo courtesy New York University Film Library.*
5. *Willard Van Dyke, at work on "The Children Must Learn." Photo by Bob Churchill, courtesy New York University Film Library.*

3

5

4

able from Association Films. *(Nineteen minutes.)*

This simple reconstruction of the events surrounding the birth of Christ, from the Annunciation to the coming of the three kings to Bethlehem, is accompanied by a recitation of the Bible narrative. Faithfulness to the words of the Gospel and the beauty of the unnamed actress who plays the part of Virgin Mary redeem this film from the banality which afflicts so many Bible films. (R.S.)

ONE GOD—
THE WAYS WE WORSHIP HIM

Produced by Farkas Films. Distributed by Association Films. (Thirty-seven minutes.)

Starting out with the important role which freedom of worship has played in the history of this country, the film focuses upon the distinguishing, and often similar, rituals and symbolisms of the Jewish, Catholic, and Protestant faiths, and the minority groups within each of the larger ones. It introduces the audience into churches and temples and meeting rooms, which they probably would never have a chance to know at first hand. The camera serves as an observer rather than an interpreter; spoken comments are simple and explanatory, without emotional overtones. An interesting musical background provides additional significance to the ceremonies pictured.

One justifiable complaint is that the film does not develop its One God theme to anything like the extent to which it explores The Ways We Worship Him. Such a film would certainly be harder to make, probably less acceptable in some situations, but infinitely more interesting and worthwhile.

One God, based on Florence Mary Fitch's book of the same name, was made especially for young people, but it should interest their elders just as much. (C.S.)

THE WAY OF PEACE

Produced by Christian Films, 1947. Distributed by Religious Film Association. (Eighteen minutes, color animation.)

The Way of Peace portrays the Christian concept of the causes of war and appeals to mankind and particularly to Christians to follow the injunction of Christ to love one another. The film first tells the story of creation as related in the Book of Genesis—that in the beginning God created all that was good to live in His light. But man, the film continues, turned away from God and built about himself a wall. In shutting out the light of God man found no peace either within himself or with his neighbors.

The film then tells of the birth of Christ as the Son of God who was to be a new light to the world. His commandment was "Love one another as I have loved you." But mankind, the film points out, has not accepted this commandment. In the past men have continued to fight against men, nation against nation, and race against race. And now in this atomic age, when power has been harnessed for total destruction, time is short to learn to walk the way of peace.

In its portrayal of the Christian concept of the nature of evil and in its appeal to Christians to follow the injunction of Christ to love one another, *The Way of Peace* points out one approach to the problem of war. As an inspirational presentation of its subject the film is excellent and effective. The scenes of creation, of the evil and woes that have come into the world because of man's turning away from God, of the Nativity of Christ, of the failures of Christians to live the way of peace, and finally of the destructiveness of a possible atomic war—all done in color animation—are beautiful and inspiring. . . . (F.F.R.)

4. education

AND SO THEY LIVE

Produced for the Sloan Foundation, 1940. Distributed by the New York University Film Library. (Twenty-two minutes.)

Filmed with a certain poetic realism, this is a story of the harsh and stark world of some mountain peoples in the United States. It is a cold, cheerless life, one of malnutrition and poverty, but not without some music and characterized by warm family ties. Families live in cold, bare wooden shacks. Their diet seldom varies—fat pork, biscuits, corn bread and berries. Seldom are there vegetables, and milk is almost unknown. Pellagra, dysentery, rickets have their way, and the death rate is high.

The land, too, is sick. Burnt stumps and a few saplings show where rich timber has been logged out and burnt over. A few goats are kept, not for milk but to defend the scraggy sheep from vicious dogs. The land is worn out by constant crops of corn. As the farmer in the film says, "A man must raise something."

The one-room school is another bare, cold spot where the teacher tries to help all the children in all the classes struggle with geography and history and poetry, with never a thought for the problems which the children around her face.

But grim as is the prospect, there is a warmth of family life as these people struggle to live on. In the strength and kindliness of the people, aided by a new and vital education, lies hope for their future. This is the burden of *And So They Live,* a film never pretentious, not weighted with wishful thinking or sloppy sentimentality, and powerful in its impact because of this simple dignity and honesty.

Because of the simplicity of its message and the comprehensibility of its images, and because the struggle of man against hunger and want is a universal theme, this is a film which may be used by all types of adult audiences. It is one of those rare films which make their point very clearly and at the same time raise provocative questions for discussion. Commentary, dialog and photography all achieve a high degree of excellence in this film directed by John Ferno and Julian Roffman. . . . (F.F.R.)

A BETTER TOMORROW

Produced by the OWI Overseas. Distributed by Castle Division of United World Films. (Twenty-four minutes.)

Alexander Hammid's film study of three progressive public schools in New York City, although it was made several years ago, has only recently been released in this country. It shows the vast potential educational resources of a large city. *A Better Tomorrow* was made to show people outside the United States the strong points of American education. It presents a challenge to Americans to pursue these goals more conscientiously and effectively. The photography and direction are excellent, as is usual in a Hammid production. (c.s.)

CAMBRIDGE

Produced by Everyman Films, London. Distributed by the British Information Services. (Eighteen minutes.)

This film, like the university it commemorates, bears the scars and erosions of time, for it was made more than ten years ago and the prints have been widely circulated in all parts of the world. Appropriately too, the impressions it leaves are those of ancient buildings overshadowing those who work and live in them. In *Princeton* (p. 162) it is the students and faculty who hold the scene; in *Cambridge* the halls and quadrangles, the great windows and long medieval vistas. This feeling of age permeates everything. No sequence in the film is as compelling as the four episodes in *Princeton.* Yet the spirit of Cambridge, which breathes through the film as a whole, is more compelling. (R.S.)

A CHILD WENT FORTH

Produced by John Ferno and Julian Roffman, 1942. Distributed by Brandon Films. (Twenty minutes.)

This is an intimate study of child life at a progressive summer camp. The two-to-six-year-old boys and girls candidly photographed in the film are allowed a maximum of freedom from supervision by their camp counselors. They are encouraged to express their creative instincts, to solve their problems independently. Each is relatively free to explore where he will within the bounds of the camp. The camera follows them as they splash in a shallow pool and play with their pets. After lunch the children rest. The commentator remarks that the camp emphasizes independence consistent with health and security. The child's natural interest and curiosity are the instruments for his education. Animals on a neighboring farm contend with a tractor in the fields to draw his attention. Camp counselors arrange trips that are both exciting and instructive to the children. In and around the camp, the boys and girls investigate nature for themselves.

Evening brings story-time and then bed; it has been a full day, and, as each day is significant to the child, an important one.

A casually poetic exposition of a child's summer day in the country, *A Child Went Forth* is both artistic and, within its subject-area, provocative. It will probably be most serviceable as an introduction to the general topic of child care. The film's thesis, that children promote their own learning when left to their own devices, provides a fertile field for discussion. . . . (F.F.R.)

THE CHILDREN MUST LEARN

Produced by the Educational Film Institute of New York University for the Alfred P. Sloan Foundation, 1940. Distributed by the New York University Film Library. (Thirteen minutes.)

In isolated rural sections of the United States the economic and social well-being of the community depends in large measure on the productivity of the land. Elementary schooling in these backwoods areas has a real practical significance, for the children are raised to cultivate the land that their fathers farmed before them. Too often, however, community schools, incompetently staffed and equipped with outdated or inappropriate texts, fail to fulfill the need for pertinent, practical education. *Children Must Learn* shows one community handicapped by such failure. . . .

As a serious treatment of its subject the film is a superb production. Photography, sound, and commentary are excellently integrated, yet each carries its own particular share of the burden of exposition. Camera techniques are especially provocative, presenting contrasts effectively and at all times guiding the audience with subtlety and intelligence. The same can be said of the commentary which, quietly and instructively, informs rather than propagandizes.

The treatment as a whole is honest and complete and emphasizes the importance of educational methods designed to meet local as well as general problems. It is suitable material for general adult groups, adult classroom groups, groups on higher levels of educational preparation, and groups interested in the particular subject treated.

Children Must Learn is similar in theme and treatment to *And So They Live*, which was produced under the same auspices. It was produced by Willard Van Dyke and edited by Irving Lerner. . . .

(F.F.R.)

DOES IT MATTER WHAT YOU THINK?

Produced and distributed by the British Information Services. (Fifteen minutes.)

This film demonstrates the various ways in which public opinion is formed in war and peace and stresses the need for the individual's awareness and action in shaping it.

At a Civic War Exhibition in England a guide arrests the attention of several visitors by referring to the power of propaganda. Among his exhibits are a metal "container of propaganda" and a tiny printing press, the latter influential enough to be confiscated by the police. How much more, he adds, can editors of widely circulated papers contribute in molding public opinion!

The wide distribution of print is seen in the shots of news- and magazine-stands and bookstores. Readers in trams, homes, streets, and factories are expressing widely differing individual opinions based on the views of editors and on news stories. The camera halts to witness an orator's speech in the square, and lingers at the statue of Voltaire, with its memorable inscription of the philosopher's tribute to freedom of speech. The media of screen and radio are shown as further examples of opinion-shaping organs.

The spokesman, at the War Exhibition, has by this time won the ready ear of the visitors. He takes them on another imaginary trip to show how reform, resulting from public opinion, has provided organized playgrounds for cruelly treated street waifs.

The narrator reminds John Citizen that, through the ballot, he can do his part in the achievement of the universal four freedoms. "Form into groups," he concludes, "and see that your opinion is felt."

This timely film leaves no doubt in the mind of the audience that it matters a great deal what we think. An appeal is made for transferring the proven effectiveness of wartime propaganda to the winning of the peace. The British commentary is not always clear, but the highly interesting shots of the various media employed in the creation of public opinion reveal imaginative and dramatic production.

Film forums will find little difficulty in discussing the film topic; the discussion leader, however, will need to guide his audience in dealing with several of the more important issues raised on the very general subject of public opinion. . . .

(F.F.R.)

THE FIGHT FOR BETTER SCHOOLS

Produced by the March of Time. Available without charge from the National Citizens Commission for the Public Schools, 2 West 45th Street, New York 17, N. Y. (Twenty minutes.)

The development of our public-school systems on a community basis has resulted in many inequalities of opportunity in education. This film shows how the citizens of Arlington County, Virginia, worked to put through the necessary legislation to insure the kind of schools and educational facilities they wanted for their children. It also explains the program of the National Citizens Commission for the Public Schools in helping communities throughout the country bring their schools to meet present standards and needs. *The Fight for Better Schools* is an important, although necessarily limited, visual introduction to the problems of reorganizing and revitalizing our public-school systems. Follow-up assistance for a real community fight for better schools is also available from the National Citizens Commission.   (c.s.)

LEARNING TO UNDERSTAND CHILDREN

Produced and distributed by McGraw-Hill Text-Films. (In two parts, forty-four minutes.)

How the teacher approaches the problem of understanding the many children she works with in the classroom is told realistically in *Learning to Understand Children*. It is told through the story of Miss Brown, junior high-school teacher, and Ada Adams, a shy, unhappy child in her class. Miss Brown acts as commentator of the film.

Miss Brown is both delighted and anxious as her English class assembles for its first meeting of the term. She muses on the wide variety of personalities and the individual needs of the children. As Ada comes late into the class, fumbling her books and looking as if she didn't have a friend in the world, she catches Miss Brown's attention. Later when the class is asked to tell about their interests and activities, Ada finds it difficult to share her experiences with others. Miss Brown recognizes that here is a lonely, unhappy child for whom she may be able to do something.

Although Miss Brown is aware that there are many personality problems in her class, she feels that Ada's problem is most severe and needs immediate attention. Before she can help her, however, she must find out all she can about Ada. She checks Ada's health records and finds that she is both physically and mentally normal. Finding an excuse to visit Ada's home, Miss Brown discovers that home difficulties are a great source of the child's maladjustment.

Ada's mother is overburdened with housework and the care of a young child. Her father is undependable and disappears for days. Ada's activities are rigidly restricted by the mother. On the visit Miss Brown finds out that Ada has great interest and talent in art. Miss Brown wonders whether this might not be a means of helping Ada find greater adjustment to her school life.

Miss Brown then visits Ada's other teachers. She discovers that her slow school work is due to reading difficulty. By appealing to her interest in art, she is able to help Ada improve her reading. She also asks the help of Ada's other teachers.

To help Ada gain recognition in her class group, Miss Brown suggests that she let her classmates see what she has painted. When the class plans a dramatization of scenes from Shakespeare, Ada is selected as chairman of the costume committee. In the meantime Ada persuades her mother to let her dress differently.

Gradually she becomes more and more accepted by her schoolmates.

The film is an effective dramatization of how the teacher uses all available resources to help "problem" children adjust themselves. It is in two parts, the first called "Diagnostic" and the second "Remedial." The content of the film is correlated with the textbook *Student Teaching* by Schorling.

The continuity of the film is excellent. For reasons of clarity both the problem and the solution are somewhat simplified. Yet the complexity of the problems facing the teacher and an indication of what might be done about them are at least mentioned. Although made specifically for student teachers, the film will be of interest to parents and those interested in child guidance. (F.F.R.)

LESSONS FROM THE AIR

Produced by the British Ministry of Information, 1943. Distributed by the British Information Services. (Fourteen minutes.)

This film deals with the educational program provided for the schools by the British Broadcasting Corporation. Children in cities, children cooped up in hospitals, children set off in isolated rural communities—all may gain valuable experiences suited to their age, interest, and understanding. For the first time mothers are able to know what the children are learning in school and are thus able to follow up and lead on to other activities. A great deal of research goes into each of these broadcasts. The film shows the advisory committee at work deciding on important topics for production; the experts preparing content scripts and checking them with practicing teachers, and the production staff applying their imagination to make these programs *live* in the classroom. . . .

This is a delightful film, produced

with a light hand. It is a well integrated combination of effective visual elements and a sound track that is as imaginative as any good radio program. Its subject matter is somewhat specialized, but most adult groups will at some stage be interested in the education offered in their community. The film does not touch on uses of radio in adult education. It deals with school classes, pointing up the advantages to teachers that are now offered by such organizations as the BBC and the Columbia School of the Air. Nor is any attempt made to give a detailed exposition of the utilization techniques that must accompany such a program if it is to have a place in the school program. An effective point is made concerning the necessity of having teachers and parents decide what shall be the content of such programs, rather than advertisers or government officials. In fact, one of the highlights of the film is the effective way it points up the collaboration in learning which must be achieved by parent, teacher, technical expert, scholar, and the child himself. Teachers and home and school associations will be especially interested. . . . (F.F.R.)

PRINCETON

Sponsored by Princeton University and jointly produced by Affiliated Film Producers, Inc. and International Film Foundation. Available from Princeton University, Princeton, N. J. (Thirty-two minutes.)

This film has been produced by that distinguished documentary team, whose names—Hammid, Jacoby, Van Dyke, Rodakiewicz—are threaded through so much of the film history of the last fifteen years. Associated with them is Julien Bryan, himself a Princeton man, whose travels and lecture tours have made him one of the most warmly respected figures in the world on non-theatrical film.

The problem of the film was difficult enough to tax their best abilities. It was that of compressing into thirty minutes the life and spirit of Princeton, with all its long history, its rich associations, and the gift it makes to those who spend four years within its walls. It must be said at once that they have magnificently succeeded. The opening section evokes the memories of Princeton men who come back for class reunions. The fine camera work by Peter Glushanok lingers on ivied walls, glances up at the stone lions, catches a smile on a young face, or a moment of tense excitement at a ball game.

After reviewing the bicentennial celebrations, the film moves on to inquire what are the characteristics of a great teacher; and in a moving series of close-ups, finds that they lie in wit and wisdom, in the ability to marshal facts and to communicate feelings. Across from the teacher is the student, and the film dwells next on the student side of college life, with its games and examinations (observed by an honor system). So we go back into the past to review some of Princeton's history—a battleground in the Revolutionary War, the home of Jonathan Dickinson, Madison, and Aaron Burr.

All this, however, is but a prelude to the body of the film—a series of four episodes grouped round four members of the senior class. Each has at one time reached a turning point in his life, and it has been Princeton which has made him face the crisis and has helped him to find the solution.

There is Bill Brown, son of a newspaper editor, brash and careless, who is confronted for the first time by a sense of the need to weigh facts, not simply accept them, when he finds that his physics experiments don't square with the theory. Mike Salter, tied to a mother who runs a

bookstore in Dallas, is set on becoming an author, though he has no talents for literature. It is his English teacher who, in a sudden flash of inspiration, is able to discern his real abilities and convince him where they lie. Dick Arkwright, pushing, successful, confident, is maneuvered by a skilful history professor into a series of admissions before a seminar class which are fatal to a pet theory he holds. He learns for the first time that a person can be wrong without losing dignity, and that he doesn't need to push people around to make them believe in him. Finally, George Hammond, brilliant and popular, is inclined to take too lightly the responsibility of writing a senior thesis on labor relations. His professor makes him realize that he cannot write without also knowing life; he spends a summer as a worker in an oil refinery, and his thesis gains a new dimension of reality.

Stated thus briefly and baldly, these episodes may not carry conviction. It is Alexander Hammid's brilliant casting and direction, and Jacoby's sensitive dialog which bring them to life and make them humorous, touching, and persuasive. If the film has a fault, it is an excessive wordiness which results from trying to cram so much into so little space. But it is a fine achievement and deserves the highest praise.   (R.S.)

ROLE PLAYING IN HUMAN RELATIONS TRAINING

Produced and distributed by the Division of Adult Education Services of the National Education Association, 1201 Sixteenth St., N.W., Washington 6, D.C. (Twenty-five minutes.)

This film has most of the defects of an amateur production, but people who are interested in adult group work will probably be willing to overlook them. By presenting enactments of such every-day problems as how parents can keep teen-age daughters at home on week nights and how a foreman stays on good terms with his men, the film shows some of the why's and how's of role-playing. Filmed at one of the informal summer sessions of the National Training Laboratory in Group Development at Bethel, Maine, it is the first to illustrate the values and techniques of this new device for getting at human relations problems in situations where words are not enough.

(c.s.)

THE SAFEST WAY

Sponsored by the American Automobile Association, Pennsylvania Ave. at Seventeenth St., Washington, D.C., and produced by Pennsylvania State College. (Seventeen minutes, color.)

. . . The film shows how school children in elementary grades should plan the safest route between their homes and school, taking advantage of traffic lights, stop signs, and patrolled crossings. Most of this film is carried in dialog between a teacher and her pupils, but a large-scale map she draws helps to make the points unmistakably clear. . . .

(r.s.)

THE SCHOOL

Produced for the U. S. Government by Julien Bryan. Available from Castle Division of United World Films. (Twenty-one minutes.)

A casual and pleasing approach to public education in the United States, as seen in a typical small town. Photographed and directed by Francis Thompson. (c.s.)

SCHOOL IN CENTERVILLE

Produced by the Southern Educational Film Production Service. Distributed by the Department of Rural Education,

National Education Association, 1201 Sixteenth Street, N.W., Washington, D.C. (Twenty minutes, color or black-and-white.)

This is the most recent film on American education and certainly one of the best. Its subject is rural education geared to problems of learning to live in the community. We see classes in action at a model school in rural Virginia, where students are at work on projects which relate both to their need for knowledge and to the future roles they will take in the community they live in. The three R's aren't neglected but are integrated into meaningful work and study and activity. Everything about this film is good—what it shows and the way it shows it—and all parents, teachers, and school administrators should see it. (c.s.)

THE SCHOOL THAT LEARNED TO EAT

Produced by the Southern Educational Film Production Service for General Mills, Inc. Available from General Mills, Minneapolis, Minnesota. (Twenty-two minutes, color.)

While far from ambitious, *The School that Learned to Eat* does a wonderfully good job of exploring its own small piece of territory. The teachers at a school in a country town realize that the children in their charge aren't getting enough to eat. They are listless at work and play, and the attendance records don't measure up to standard.

What the teachers do is reflected in a change of attitude by the whole school. A dietary expert explains to teachers and parents the fundamentals of good feeding, but this is only a small part of her task. She sets out to engage the interest and enthusiasm of the children themselves. She makes them understand that what matters most is not how much they eat, but what they eat. And she starts them off on all sorts of interesting projects.

They compare the growth of guinea pigs which have been given different amounts of proteins and vitamins, they put on puppet plays to show the need of proper diet, and they stage all sorts of exhibits in the classroom. The result is that before long the school is well on its way to becoming one of the healthiest in its locality.

The School that Learned to Eat is technically excellent. It has some of the best color photography ever seen in 16mm. and a warm and understanding (though rather overcrowded) commentary. The handling of the children is exceptionally happy and natural. This film does great credit to the unit which made it and the firm which sponsored it.

(R.S.)

SCHOOLHOUSE IN THE RED

Produced by Agrafilms, Inc., for the W. K. Kellogg Foundation, Battle Creek, Mich. Distributed by Encyclopaedia Britannica Films. (Forty-two minutes, color.)

Schoolhouse in the Red is about rural public-education problems. Specifically, it tells the story of the old-fashioned, one-room Miller School, its twelve pupils, its one teacher, and its ten-minute lesson-hearing periods for each subject and grade. The school is dirty and dilapidated, and the problem is, What to do about it? The parents want to do whatever is best for the children, but what is best? Well, they might raise money to rebuild the school, but they aren't convinced that this is the solution. Or they might join up with the nearby town and send their children to a school where they will have better educational and recreational facilities.

The county superintendent is called into a meeting of the parents, and they decide to pay a visit to the new town school. The improved classrooms, new teaching techniques, library, gym, workshops, and laboratories look mighty fine. But not all the parents are convinced.

The educational advances which the new school offers reflect the change and growth of the modern world and its way of living and working, the film says. If we want to avoid being the victims of change, then we must be its leaders. For indecision will not stop the change. The film leaves the parents voting on what should be done about the school. And however it comes out, the commentary states, it will be what they want.

It is hard to imagine any way in which this film might have taken a more mature approach to its subject. Every scene invites and encourages the best possible thinking on the part of the audiences who see it. Naturally it is intended primarily for groups having a similar problem, but there are many other educational situations in which the film will serve well.

The non-professional cast does a first-rate acting job, and nearly everyone is pleasingly photogenic. But perhaps best of all is the way in which the film demonstrates a basic faith in the democratic way of doing things—all the more convincing because it is unperturbed and consistent. (C.S.)

SCOTTISH UNIVERSITIES

Produced and distributed by the British Information Services. (Twenty-two minutes.)

This is a charming study of Scotland's famous universities—St. Andrew's, Glasgow, Aberdeen, and Edinburgh. The magnificent old buildings tell of an honored academic tradition which ranks with the best. Under new governmental provisions which make higher education available to nearly every young person, the universities have their own problems of too many students and too few teachers—and a great deal of determination to solve them. Like most of the British films this one is a pleasure to see and hear.   (c.s.)

TEACHERS' CRISIS

Produced and distributed by the March of Time. (Seventeen minutes.)

A great deal of money has gone into America's school buildings, the film says, but what happens inside? We see again the overcrowded classrooms and the overburdened and often incompetent teachers. The film also makes an excellent behind-the-scenes excursion into the lives of these teachers. Those with families must supplement their incomes with extra work. Even so, more than 300,000 have left their jobs since 1940 for more lucrative work. In addition to the ignominy of being underpaid, teachers are open to constant scrutiny and criticism for the mildest deviation from the rules about personal conduct which the community imposes upon them.

The film ends with a review of the work of the National Education Association and the United States Office of Education in bringing these facts to the attention of the public. The bill for Federal aid to schools is brought up as one helpful way in which to attack the problems.

The Teachers' Crisis is a good, typical March of Time summary of the educational situation in this country. Unfortunately, only a few 16mm. prints of the film have been distributed; the film has not been publicized by its producer, mainly because they felt that the film is too timely to be of extended use.

Another film, *The American Teacher*, is available from the March of Time and from a wider number of rental libraries—but this one lacks most of the directness of *The Teachers' Crisis*. It ends with the statement of a controversy which at best is mainly old hat—progressive education versus the other kind. This part of the film looks as if it were shot at least two decades ago, and the arguments sound at least that old. So if you are interested in an up-to-date picture of the educational scene, be sure to get *The Teachers' Crisis* instead of *The American Teacher*—if you can.   (c.s.)

WHO WILL TEACH YOUR CHILD?

Produced by the National Film Board of Canada. Distributed by McGraw-Hill Text-Films. (Twenty-four minutes.)

The most pressing educational problems today revolve around the shortage of teachers and the overcrowdedness of schools, with the added disturbing factor that little is being done to attract new qualified and interested people to the teaching profession.

The film tells first about the life of the preschool child. Curious about the world around him, full of a variety of mental and physical energies, he is often a trial to his parents. But he is trying to satisfy his many curiosities. At every moment of his life, even when he is asleep, he is learning about the world and his place in it. When he is old enough, he goes to school, where his normal drive to know the answers to a thousand questions can be channeled into useful learning. There for hundreds of weeks of his life he will be guided by teachers who will influence him in innumerable ways.

We see a variety of means in which teachers meet this challenge. One competent teacher diverts a personal near-tragedy in a boy's life into a lesson-in-living for the entire class, but another teacher, with inadequate training and understanding, finds herself unable to cope with even basic problems of maintaining student interest and discipline. What can be done to see that your children's education is in the hands of competent, well-trained, mature people? Who will satisfy their need to know?

This film is a new version of a Canadian film, revised for American audiences. Parts of the film are excellent, especially in the first half, where the young child's natural expressiveness beautifully shows his impulsive curiosity and his delight with the world and with himself. The commentary throughout is well written and sympathetically spoken. Though the film has some weak moments, it is an effective and important presentation of some important problems in public education today. Teachers and parents everywhere should see it. (c.s.)

5. feature films—american and foreign

available features
Cecile Starr

SINCE feature films on 16mm. are much in demand, this is an opportune time to review the kinds of features that are available and the conditions governing their availability. In general the situation is this: There are many good 16mm. foreign feature films for adult groups and enough Hollywood features for children to see in school during class periods. But there are few of the better Hollywood features for adults, except to show to the invalid and the incarcerated, and practically no full-length films at all for children's non-theatrical recreation programs.

The most widely available feature films are Hollywood productions of the least desirable kind. Local commercial film libraries and camera-supply stores often rent many Westerns, mysteries, comedies of a sort, and miscellaneous Grade C and D productions of independent companies. Most of them were pretty bad in the first place and aren't improved in the reduction to 16mm. gauge. While there are usually no restrictions on the use of these films, their usefulness is certainly limited.

British, French, Italian, German, Spanish, Russian, and Jewish-language features are distributed in 16mm. by libraries specializing in foreign films. A new catalog of its feature—and excellent short documentary—subjects has just been issued by Brandon Films, 200 West 57th Street, New York 19, N. Y. It is one of the most informative and useful catalogs yet published, including descriptions, data, and critic's comments about each film, with a number of illustrations. The last ten pages of this sixty-four-page catalog is a separate "Handbook for Film Societies," written by Thomas J. Brandon.

Among the outstanding foreign films listed in this new Brandon catalog the foremost is the newly released French full-length documentary *Farrebique*, which deserves some comment here. It is a film I fell in love with at first sight, and increasingly each time I saw it. *Farrebique* encompasses one year on a French farm, one round of the seasons, one cycle of working and living. In this film perhaps better than in any other we can see the basic differences between the documentary approach and the non-documentary. The story begins and ends as arbitrarily as the calendar itself, entirely lacking in formulated dénouements and climaxes—approaching the realness, the dull slowness, if you like, or the slow excitement, in my own opinion, of life itself. *Farrebique* was directed by George Rouqier; running time is ninety-one minutes.

Other interesting titles available from Brandon Films include the following: French films—*Crime and Punishment*, starring Pierre Blanchar and Harry Baur; *Grand Illusion*, directed by Jean Renoir, with Jean Gabin and Eric von Stoheim; *Volpone*, starring Harry Baur and Louis Jouvet; the Swedish *Torment*, with Mai Zetterling; the German *Murderers Among Us*; the Italian *Revenge*, starring Anna Magnani; the Russian *Alexander Nevsky*, *Mother*, and *Road to Life* and Alfred Hitchcock's *Thirty-Nine Steps* and *The Lady Vanishes*. All in all, Brandon supplies a large selection of very adult film fare, with no restrictions as to non-theatrical use.

Some other foreign-language features are available from Film Program Services, 1173 Avenue of the Americas, New York—among them, the French *Poil de Carotte* and the British *The Raiders*. Contemporary Films, at 13 East 37th Street, New York, N. Y., has a selection of titles which includes a number of Jewish films; the French *Naïs*, starring Fernandel; the Italian *Rossini*, *A Yank in Rome*, and *Two Anonymous Letters*.

A new Spanish version of *Don Quixote* has been released in 16mm. by the Special Features Division of Azteca Films, 1564 Broadway, New York, N. Y.

The International Films Division of United World Films has a number of interesting, newly released British films for 16mm.

rental. Among them are Noel Coward's *Brief Encounter* and *Blithe Spirit*, Carol Reed's *Odd Man Out*, and *Dead of Night* and *I Know Where I'm Going*. Offices of United World are in New York at 1445 Park Avenue, in Chicago at 542 S. Dearborn Street, and in Hollywood at 7356 Melrose Avenue. The films are usually available except in occasional, if not rare, instances in which theatrical commitments preclude their non-theatrical use.

The magnificent Italian film *Shoe Shine* is available for 16mm. rental through Lopert Films, Inc., 148 West 57th Street, New York 19, N. Y.

The fifteen feature productions of Sir Alexander Korda have recently been released on 16mm. by Ideal Pictures Corporation, 65 E. South Water Street, Chicago. Twenty-three branch offices around the country supply rental prints to nearby film users. These include *The Ghost Goes West*, Charles Laughton's full-blown interpretations of *Henry the Eighth* and *Rembrandt*, Sabu in *Elephant Boy*, and H. G. Wells's *Things to Come*. Ideal Pictures also has a few newly released Hollywood subjects: *Mr. Deeds Goes to Town, Pennies from Heaven, The Howards of Virginia*, and on down. The films are rented with the understanding that they are to be used non-theatrically, with no admission charge and no public advertising. This, it is felt, would constitute intentional competition with local theatres.

The finest library of feature and short motion pictures is that maintained by the Museum of Modern Art, at 11 W. 53rd Street, New York, N. Y. It includes foreign and American films, full-length and short, silent and sound, and all are significant for their contributions to the development of the cinema and their individual merit. Many of these films are available on 16mm., but distribution is strictly limited to organizations showing the films for educational purposes. This means that many borderline groups are deprived of the privilege of renting films from the Museum, and our first reaction is to accuse the Museum of failing to meet the demands we would like to make of it. However, on later thought we can see that it is too much to expect that one educational institution should supply five decades of film productions to the entire nation of 16mm. film users. The fault lies less in the distribution policy of the Museum of Modern Art's film library than in the fact that only a pitifully small number of other film libraries can supply films of so high a quality.

The two major Hollywood companies which permit distribution of their films for non-theatrical showings are RKO and Twentieth

Century-Fox. RKO has its own 16mm. branches in twenty-one "exchange" cities around the country. Its New York office is at 1270 Avenue of the Americas. Films are available to shut-in institutions (jails, hospitals, etc.) and to schools, which must show the films for educational purposes during school hours. Written application must be made and approved before any films can be booked. School people will be interested in knowing that many of the Disney features are distributed by RKO—but since they cannot be shown except for "educational" purposes, there's not much real use to which they can be put.

Films, Inc., which distributes the Twentieth Century-Fox features, has approximately the same distribution policy as RKO and approves each individual account to avoid possible competition with local theatres. New York office is at 330 West 42nd Street.

This, in essence, is what is and is not available in feature films on 16mm. The choice is at least a hundred times greater than the movie theatres of an average town can offer its community at any one time. In planning private or community non-theatrical film programs, this factor of *choice* in selection is the one redeeming compensation for the present discomforts and inadequacies of 16mm. film programs. Forty years ago theatres were as uncomfortable and projection as amateurish as non-theatrical screening rooms and facilities are today. Yet the public put up with the situation because it was getting something it wanted. It is not unreasonable to expect that if public interest in non-theatrical film showings continues to grow, another decade or two will see many communities provided with well-equipped centers for non-theatrical film shows, and film societies on hand to have a say in the selection of programs.

Does this mean competing with the theatres? It doesn't need to. But sooner or later the local managers of theatres and the entire Hollywood film industry will have to concern themselves to a larger extent with community needs, with minority film interests, with a broader concept of the motion picture as a recreational pursuit. Until now motion pictures have been only a business, adhering to a formula of absurdly high production costs, dictated distribution, and advertisement schemes. Hollywood says that it bases its policies upon "mass taste." And here the producers and distributors have made their biggest mistake—they think of mass taste as poor taste. Yet the truth seems more likely that people go to the movies because they like *movies*, not because they like *poor* movies. The result, as Hollywood already has cause to know, is that people go to the movies until they have become saturated with disappointment, and they stop being patrons when they can no longer look forward to an evening of films with fresh anticipation and hope.

While we deplore the ineffectual, sporadic, and unorganized production and distribution of non-theatrical films, let's remember that these adjectives can be applied to any project which it still in the early stages of development. The fact that the non-theatrical film movement is just taking shape means that anyone who is interested can help form it. There is room for participation by interested individuals and organizations in every community. And for each of them there is hope of improving and widening the recreational value of the motion picture, as well as the educational.

Once the community has organized its non-theatrical film activities, perhaps the makers and distributors of theatrical films will have a chance to recognize some specific obligations to their audiences and to the communities which support them. Perhaps then Hollywood will be concerned with producing films to please many tastes, and perhaps then it will want to provide its films to the public on a more meaningful basis—both in and outside the theatres.

THE BANK DICK
(Eighty minutes.)

MY LITTLE CHICKADEE
(One hundred minutes.)

YOU CAN'T CHEAT AN HONEST MAN
(Eighty minutes.)

NEVER GIVE A SUCKER AN EVEN BREAK
(Seventy minutes.)

Produced by Universal-International. Distributed by United World Films.

These W. C. Fields movies didn't make a great pile of money as Hollywood features go, and Fields himself could never understand why they didn't play in first-run prestige theatres. His biographer, Robert Lewis Taylor (*W. C. Fields, His Follies and Fortunes,* Doubleday, 1949), while obviously an ardent admirer of the juggler-comedian, writes that Fields's producers deserve considerable honor "for continuing to turn out products of his that defied every law of the industry." The recent successes of Fields's revivals in small theatres all over New York City may do a little to encourage the big studios to permit more of Fields's kind of free-wheeling. Now it comes as a happy discovery to find that these four films are available for 16mm. showings.

Fields's peculiar ideas about justice and liberty and respectability stand out in every line he rumbles out of the side of his mouth, in every tilt of his cocky head, in every gesture and strut. *You Can't Cheat an Honest Man,* his biographer notes, was one of his own favorite slogans, for he regarded himself in no small way as the victim whose mighty defenses struck down every poor swindler who ever paid fifty cents to see a sword swallower. In the film he appears as Larson E. Whipsnade, just one of the hundreds of criminally ridiculous names he used on the screen and in real life. Around him are dummy Charlie McCarthy, Edgar Bergen, a circus menagerie, and a society family into which his daughter is supposed to marry. In every Fields movie there is at least one scene that can be called "the scene." In this one it is the Bel-Goodie's ball which Whipsnade imperiously crashes, showing mercy to no one. His mission completed, and having rendered his hostess unconscious if not delirious, he makes a dashing getaway in a Roman chariot, cloak and all, across the state line.

Never Give a Sucker an Even Break was, as all of these films, Fields's own creation, title, and plot, written under the pen name of Otis Criblecoblis. Taylor, pointing out that the synopsis of the film was composed on the back of a grocery bill, for which he successfully demanded that the studio pay him $25,000, calls it "as grotesque a travesty of a plot as he could contrive in the brief time allotted to him." The singing child star Gloria Jean appears as Fields's niece and ward, and Fields's real contempt for children (neither children nor dogs ever liked him), as well as his disrespect for Hollywood plots (also mutual), show themselves to Fields's advantage throughout the film. One *non sequitur* follows another in rapid absurdity, and anyone who could successfully summarize the film on the back of a grocery bill deserves $25,000.

My Little Chickadee presents Fields with the Loyal Opposition, Miss Mae West, co-author and co-star. A mild tale of the Wild West, this film gives Fields (Cuthbert J. Twillie) an excellent chance to relate some favorite stories, take a hand or two of poker, wrestle with the lady's feather boa, and pursue her with indifferent diligence. Miss West does all right for herself, too, especially when shooting down attacking Indians from a moving train and later as substitute teacher in a class of male post-adolescents.

But the all-star Fields film is *The Bank Dick*, which he wrote under the name of Mahatma Kane Jeeves. (There must have been hundreds of Fields names. Taylor writes that at one time Fields had more than three hundred different bank accounts in cities and towns all over the world, entered under whatever odd-sounding name happened to strike him at the time.) *The Bank Dick* gives Fields a memorable role—loafer, movie director, unwitting thief-catcher, barfly, embezzler, bank cop, despised and despising husband, father, and son-in-law, Egbert Sousé by name. At the end of the film he has become beloved by his family, respected by the community, high in his own self-esteem—in short, a millionaire.

While Fields's comedy is only rarely in a class with Chaplin's, he had no challenger in the nonchalant art of putting heel to crumpled paper napkin, nor high silk hat to upturned cane, nor alcoholic "depth bomb" to loving lips. Movie-goers who still prize comedy will find many rewards in these films. In even the weakest we find riches, carefully stashed away in hundreds of places. Only Fields's own expletives are sufficiently expressive—"Godfrey Daniel! . . . Mother of Pearl!" (c.s.)

GREAT EXPECTATIONS

Produced by J. Arthur Rank. Distributed by United World Films. (One hundred and eighteen minutes.)

The recent British production of Dickens's famous novel, featuring John Mills, Valerie Hobson, Jean Simmons, and Martita Hunt. The first part of the film, showing Pip's

extraordinary childhood, is definitely best; but this is a good example, as a whole, of a more than adequate film version of a famous literary work.
(C.S.)

THE LONG VOYAGE HOME

A Walter Wanger production directed by John Ford, starring John Wayne, Thomas Mitchell, and Ian Hunter. Camera: Gregg Toland. Available from Film Program Services. (Ninety-two minutes.)

This famous film of the sea, adapted from Eugene O'Neill's plays about the S.S. *Glencairn*, is too well-remembered to need detailed recapitulation. It is presented in a complete 16mm. version, with superb photographic quality and a brilliant sound track. Everyone will remember the death of Yank, the heroic efforts of Ole Olssen to get back home from the sea, and the drunken Englishman, Smitty, whose tragic secret is wrested from him by his crewmates after they have worked themselves into a state of spy-mania in the strained atmosphere of the fo'castle. Indeed, it is a film of atmosphere rather than plot, but it well deserves re-seeing. (R.S.)

MARCH OF THE WOODEN SOLDIERS

May be rented from Films, Inc. (Ninety minutes.)

Originally titled *Babes in Toyland*, this fantasy features Laurel and Hardy as two workmen in Santa Claus's factory. In this fairyland adventure not only does Mother Goose come to life, but she is joined by Little Bo Peep, Red Riding Hood, and Jack and Jill. Victor Herbert's music includes "Toyland," "Castle in Spain," "Little Bo Peep," and, of course, the lilting "March of the Toys." (R.S.)

THE MIKADO

Produced by J. Arthur Rank. Distributed by United World Films. (Ninety-five minutes.)

Kenny Baker stars in this Technicolor Gilbert and Sullivan operetta. The music, settings, and performances are just about all that D'Oyly Carte himself could have wanted.
(C.S.)

MIRACLE ON 34th STREET

Produced by Twentieth Century-Fox. May be rented from Films, Inc. (Ninety minutes.)

To those skeptics who no longer believe in Santa Claus this film is dedicated in perpetuity. When one Kris Kringle upsets the normal business procedure of Macy's toy department, he sets into motion a series of events which are brought to a climax with his trial; in the courts at New York City, he is officially declared to be the bewhiskered old gentleman known and beloved by all. Jurisprudence in such a great metropolis is a complicated and impersonal study; and if they say Edmund Gwenn is St. Nick, who are we to disagree? A delightful comedy which should be seen many times, and if by chance you have not seen it, by all means do so. Several lines to which there had been some objection by the Legion of Decency in the original theatrical version have been deleted; it now has an A-1 rating. (R.S.)

NANOOK OF THE NORTH

Produced by Robert Flaherty for Revillon Frères. Directed and photographed by Robert Flaherty. New sound version produced by Herbert Edwards, with commentary by Ralph Schoolman, and music by Rudolph Schramm. Distributed by Athena Films. (Fifty-five minutes.)

There couldn't be a nicer present to 16mm. film users than the news that

Robert Flaherty's *Nanook of the North* is now available for non-theatrical screenings. However you look at the film—as one of the all-time classics in motion picture history, as one of the great grandparents of the present-day documentary film, as a striking photographic achievement, as an exciting romance of life in the Arctic, or as an epic tale of man against the elements—one thing is certain: *Nanook of the North* is a wonderful film, and Robert Flaherty is a greater man for having made it.

The history of this film is only one small chapter in the remarkable history of Flaherty himself. It has been told and written a number of times, and I shall do my best to summarize it here. Flaherty, according to all accounts, was and still is a man of remarkable wit and warmth, unconventionality, and stoutheartedness. He began working as a mining engineer and explorer, and on one of his early ventures into the Arctic took a camera to record what he saw. The film he brought back from this trip was subsequently destroyed by fire from his own cigarette. The loss was not mourned, however, for Flaherty found that he had taken a series of unrelated shots—"a scene of this and a scene of that." But it was enough to make him decide to go back and make a really good film about Eskimo life.

Flaherty's first concern was for financial aid, and after having been turned down by a number of potential backers, he finally succeeded in interesting a Paris fur company, Revillon Frères, in financing his trip and his film. The Eastman Kodak Company showed him how to develop and print his film as he shot it so he could see the "rushes" as he worked.

Once having reached the Arctic, Flaherty, with his heavy and cumbersome equipment which often had to be carried over long portages, found the hardships formidable, and on several occasions he almost froze to death. He spent another year with the Eskimos, and in spite of the bitter cold and the primitiveness of the life, there is reason to believe that he loved every minute of it.

When he returned to New York, he had a film the likes of which had never before been seen. And within the next few years it was seen and loved by people all over the world. It has been said of *Nanook*, as of the old British Empire, that the sun never sets on it. Perhaps this is an overstatement. But now that 16mm. distribution of *Nanook* has been announced—twenty-eight years after the first release of the film—it seems unlikely that its popularity will ever diminish. And the addition of a sound track enhances the beauty of the film with a remarkably fine commentary and musical score.

Good humor is the keynote of the film, despite the grimness of the setting. Everyone seems to be playing jokes on everyone else. There are so many little jokes, in fact, that sometimes it is hard to tell where they begin and end. In the introductory scene, for example, who can help laughing when about a dozen happy men, women, and children crawl out of the top of what seems to be a bottomless kayak? And who is kidding who when later at the trading post Nanook bites into a phonograph record which he grinningly has mistaken for a new kind of canned food? After trading his furs for civilized products he presumably has no interest in (practically no equipment or clothes or food from the outside world appear in the rest of the film), Nanook sets off in the same jovial manner for a new year of catching fish through ice holes, hunting fur-bearing animals, building magnificent one-night homes, outwitting and outpulling walrus, and in general providing for his family and his dogs as well as a man can be expected to, circumstances being what they are.

There is beauty in *Nanook of the North*—real beauty seldom equaled on the screen: the faces and postures of the people and animals; the skilled hand at work on an igloo; the peaceful dogs rolled up into snowy roundnesses on a stormy night; expanses of snow, hills and valleys, light and shadow. And there is drama such as only a skilled artist can convey: hunting, eating, and sleeping; the training of the child to take the place of the father; the fierceness of starving huskies; the limp, dead seal; the code of the walrus; the menacing sky; the magnitude of the place and the occasion.

As long as films can be preserved, and longer, this film will live as a masterpiece unique in motion-picture history. But my word is not enough; here are the words of other reviewers: "It contains more beauty, drama, suspense and excitement than a dozen average films." "Every shot is composed with the eye of an artist." "*Nanook* is film-making as we had almost forgotten it—a sequence of moving pictures telling their own story through the eye." "What gives *Nanook* its astonishing vitality?—the secret is something in Flaherty himself . . ."   (c.s.)

THE OVERLANDERS

Produced by Ealing Studios, London. Starring Chips Rafferty. Written and directed by Harry Watt. Camera: Osmond Borradaile. Music: John Ireland. Available from United World Films. (Eighty-seven minutes.)

16mm. film users can now rent a picture which, though highly praised by the critics, was so slighted by exhibitors that few have ever had a chance to see it in the theatres. Yet in the history of the movies it will surely stand with *Grass* and *The Covered Wagon* as an epic of human achievement on the world's frontiers.

The Overlanders tells the story of the great trek across Australia when a thousand head of cattle were driven two thousand miles down from the Northern Territories, threatened by Japanese invasion early in 1942. The story is a simple one, and the acting too is simple—naive, in the opinion of many brought up in the lilac-scented atmosphere of Hollywood pictures. But *The Overlanders* is essentially tough, tough in a kind of elemental way which makes the average Western look like a Noel Coward dressing-room comedy. It is dominated by the figure of Chips Rafferty, a tall and muscular figure of immense strength who, as leader of the drive, lashes his little team of helpers along with loud-mouthed oaths and with the force of his own relentless example.

The real heroes of the film, however, are the cattle themselves. Month after month they plod onwards, driven along a few miles each day, dying of disease, climbing mountains and falling headlong from the crest, creeping across a pitiless desert where water-holes are often several days apart. In recording all this, and in painting a picture of the great Australian interior, the camera of Osmond Borradaile has succeeded marvelously. Many sequences are breathtaking in their excitement, and are reinforced by a powerful orchestral score from the pen of John Ireland. This film puts Harry Watt in the front rank of film directors of the outdoors.   (r.s.)

THE QUIET ONE

Produced by Film Documents. Distributed by Athena Films. (Sixty-seven minutes.)

. . . *The Quiet One* is about a ten-year-old Negro boy. On the face of it, he is worthless, stupid, vicious, and a menace to society. He plays hookey from school. He steals. He smashes a store window with a rock. And he is sent away.

He is sent to the Wiltwyck School for Boys, which cooperated in the making of this film. Here under the care of competent psychiatrists and social service workers he is allowed to find himself, and perhaps one day become a useful member of society; we say perhaps rather advisedly, because the school only cares for boys until they are twelve. What is to become of them when they are so eager and willing to be accepted as decent human beings and they are thrown back into a hostile and selfish world? The film cannot pretend to answer this question; it deals with a different subject.

The Quiet One takes its place among the outstanding American documentary films; it ranks with the work of Flaherty and Lorentz. It delves into the heart and feelings of an inarticulate youngster who cannot even fit into a circle made up of other juvenile delinquents; he is the quiet one.

Produced by Janice Loeb, directed by Sidney Meyers, commentary written by James Agee, and music by Ulysses Kay, this film is part of a campaign to raise $1,000,000 for the Wiltwyck School for Boys. In the years since 1942, Wiltwyck has achieved national recognition of its program for sound and intelligent treatment of children with serious behavior problems. Primitive punitive custodial methods are left behind. Affection, understanding, and cooperation are offered instead to the child who has known only rejection and abuse.

This is the first feature production of Film Documents, a group of craftsmen and artists from whom we may expect a steady flow of important Ideas on Film. (R.S.)

THE TITAN—STORY OF MICHELANGELO

An adaptation of the Curt Oertel film. Produced by Robert Snyder. Directed and edited by Richard Lyford. Written by Norman Borisoff. Art interpretation by Michael Sonnabend. Music by Alois Melichar. Narration spoken by Fredric March. Presented by Robert J. Flaherty, Robert Snyder, and Ralph Alswang. Distributed by Classic Pictures, 1560 Broadway, New York, N. Y. (Seventy minutes.)

This extraordinary film, the first of its kind ever to be shown in this country, has opened my eyes to a world of the camera hitherto unexplored and superb in its resources. *The Titan* is an old picture, as pictures go. Yet it is newer in its technique than the latest picture to be produced. It was made between 1938 and 1940, chiefly in Florence and Rome, by the Swiss producer Curt Oertel. In its original form it lasted ninety-five minutes, whereas in the reassembled and re-edited American version, equipped as it is with a new script, an excellent score, and a fine running narrative finely spoken by Fredric March, it runs for only seventy minutes. During the war it is said to have been seized by the Germans, distributed proudly as a proof of Nazi culture, and was afterwards discovered in France by the American Army.

When seen by Robert J. Flaherty, one of the screen's true artists, it won his immediate interest. As a director responsible for welcome innovations in such sensitive and unhackneyed films as *Nanook of the North, Moana, Man of Aran,* and *Louisiana Story,* Mr. Flaherty was quick to appreciate the innovational virtues of *The Titan.* It was he who acquired its American rights. And it is he who, with Robert Snyder and Ralph Alswang, has brought together such a talented group of craftsmen as Richard Lyford, Norman Borisoff, and Alois Melichar to direct and edit and supply the script and music for the picture as it is now shown in the United States.

The novelties, the fascinations, and the excitements of *The Titan* are many and irresistible. Although in procedure no less than in purpose it is a documentary in a stricter sense than those pictures usually so described, it is like none of the documentaries to which we are accustomed. We have had documentaries which have dramatized geography and elevated the travelog into the realm of art. We have had documentaries which, because of the eloquent use to which they have put newsreel clips, have presented us with history in the making. We have had documentaries which in their animated maps and diagrams have demonstrated the unrivaled role they can play as swift elucidators of complicated problems. We have seen them do their stirring part as propagandists, watched them breathlessly as they have recorded battle exploits or true sagas of adventure. We have grown increasingly grateful for the sense of truth their methods have created in fictional scenarios. Until *The Titan*, however, we had never sat before a documentary in which the chief concern was beauty and an artist's biography was told in terms of his art.

The screen, of course, has offered us biographies galore—some good, some bad, some tasteful, some tasteless. But all these previous re-creations of the past have depended upon living actors; actors dressed up and bewigged; actors pretending to be Pasteur, Queen Christina, Henry VIII, Madame Curie, Woodrow Wilson, Thomas A. Edison, Zola, or George M. Cohan. *The Titan* is different; wonderfully, stirringly different. It dispenses with flesh-and-blood players as completely as if it had taken to heart Duse's famous hyperbole: "To save the Theatre, the Theatre must be destroyed, the actors and actresses must all die of the plague. They poison the air, they make art impossible."

In *The Titan*, although no one impersonates Michelangelo, Lorenzo, Savonarola, or Pope Julius II, each

of these great Renaissance figures seems to be present. Their struggles, their hopes, their plots, their cruelties, and, above all, the works of art which they either created or commissioned are present, too. Florence, Bologna, and Rome in all their glory supply the settings. Portraits, prints, paintings, architectural details, and statues emerge as players. The dialog is written not with a scenarist's pen but by Michelangelo's chisel and brush.

The tragic tenderness of his first "Pietà," the vigor of his "David," the pagan abandon of his "Bacchus," the power of his "Moses," the agony of his "Slave," the richness of the Sistine ceiling, the brooding profundity of his "Dawn" and "Night," the soaring greatness of the dome of St. Peter's, the fury of his "Last Judgment," and the final sorrow of his "Deposition"—all these speak both for themselves and for Michelangelo. Without seeing him we see what he was. With the aid of the narrative and especially due to the camera's chaperonage, we follow his life and sense the grandeur of his genius. The result is a masterpiece composed of masterpieces. In it a period writes its own history even as the art of an artist writes his biography.

All of us who have made our pilgrimages to admire Michelangelo's works may have felt that we were well acquainted with their marvels. But most of us would, I suspect, now have to confess we had never really *seen* them until we saw *The Titan*. As highlighted by Klieg lights, as surveyed through the camera's eye, as approached from unexpected angles or viewed in dramatic close-ups, they leap and lunge into a life even more amazing than that which we had prized as theirs.

One can only hope that what *The Titan* does so magnificently for the work of one magnificent artist will be done again and again with the same brilliance and integrity for other artists and their works.

(JOHN MASON BROWN)

John Mason Brown is the drama editor of the Saturday Review of Literature. *His weekly column, "Seeing Things," has dealt with a number of the arts, including film.*

THE TRUE GLORY

Produced by the combined film units of the Allied High Command. Distributed by Castle Division of United World Films. (Eighty-four minutes.)

This massive and powerfully wrought film tells the story of the Allied campaign in Europe from the preparations for invasion to the capitulation of Germany. When there is so much talk of another war, it is wholesome to remind ourselves sometimes of what the last one was really like.

Consciously constructed in the style of Hardy's *The Dynasts,* the film puts its explanatory passages into blank verse, spoken over finely conceived picture maps which show the grand strategy of attack. The body of the film tells of the soldier's war. It is a tapestry of voices: every variety of American accent and British dialect, Polish, Czech, Canadian, Australian, French—each recounting his own episode in the advance. And through them all weaves the kindly, reassuring voice of Ike Eisenhower.

"Now the time has come," says the narrator near the end, "to put our victory to the test of peace." Six years have passed since those words were written. What have we to show for them? (R.S.)

ZERO DE CONDUITE
(ZERO FOR BEHAVIOR)

A film written and produced by Jean Vigo. Available from Brandon Films. (Fifty-one minutes.)

Jean Vigo produced only two films that were at all widely seen before he died in poverty at the age of twenty-eight. His life was a continual struggle to get financial support for his own uncompromising view of what film should say, which fell into none of the popular art styles of his time.

Zero de Conduite, which has had a profound effect on other film makers, cannot perhaps be recommended for general screening any more than Auden's poems for general reading, and for the same reasons. It will be enjoyed by all who have felt that the film still has vast unrealized powers of expression, and are interested in seeing them put to use to penetrate the strange thoughts and behavior of children. Vigo here follows the arrival of a new teacher at a boys' school, and involves himself in the turmoil and rioting which surround the school's principal, a dwarf-like creature much smaller than the boys themselves.

The film has no continuity in the ordinary sense. It moves from scene to scene with a logic of its own, viewing the antics of the elders through the eyes of a child. There is the master who creeps around corners peering into the children's lockers looking for candies to steal; the walk through the town which goes faster and faster until the kids can scarcely keep pace with the teacher; and the famous pillow-fighting sequence in which the slow-motion camera is used with marvelous imagination.

Many will be bored and even repelled by Vigo's film; but there will always be a discerning few on whom it will cast a haunting spell akin to that of Alain Fournier's *The Wanderer.* (R.S.)

6. health—physical and emotional

(Including Child Care and Psychology, Sex Education, the Physically Handicapped, and Psychiatry)

ALCOHOL AND THE HUMAN BODY

Produced and distributed by Encyclopaedia Britannica Films. (Fifteen minutes.)

A film of this kind will probably do more to take the false glamour and excitement away from the cocktail lounge and bar, in the minds of the high-school students for whom it is primarily intended, than any amount of lecturing or forbidding could possibly do. The technique is simple and the information factual. Animated drawings show how various amounts of ethyl alcohol affect the body and brain, and live photography shows how these in turn affect the behavior of the drinker. We see why and how moderate or "social" drinking results in a mild relaxing of inhibitions. Excessive drinking, far from easing social tensions, involves loss of muscular control and memory and, as more and more of the brain becomes affected, ends in unconsciousness. A brief sequence on the problem drinker explains that his dependency upon alcohol constitutes a disease. However, the film deals with only the most superficial aspects of the causes of alcoholism and its proper treatment.

All in all this is a successful film, cleverly interweaving straight scientific information with dramatic re-enactments which translate the information into terms of commonplace reality. Adult groups will find the film every bit as useful for their own information as teachers will for classroom use.   (c.s.)

ATTITUDES AND HEALTH

Produced and distributed by Coronet Films. (Ten minutes.)

This is a simplified, non-technical explanation of some of the ways in which emotional problems affect physical health, with some practical advice on the subject. Marvin Baker, a young high-school student, overhears the family doctor outlining the causes of his sister's psychosomatic illnesses to their mother. Marvin thinks of his own ill health, his disappointment at not making the first-string basketball team at school, and his subsequent failure to do well in other activities. After discussing this with the doctor, Marvin learns that his attitudes do affect his health. And he understands that he can avoid disappointment by not expecting to do well in everything, and by working hard to succeed in things for which he has special aptitude and interest.

Because the film directly relates its subject matter to its intended audience, and particularly because it offers intelligent, easy-to-understand answers to the questions it raises, this film is sure to be a valuable addition to youth health programs— and to many adult programs as well.
                    (c.s.)

CAREERS AND CRADLES

Produced and distributed by the National Film Board of Canada. (Ten minutes.)

Personal problems often are the direct result of social changes to which the individual must adapt himself. The role of women in society is an outstanding recent example of change to which we have not quite become adjusted. The film shows the characteristically interested glances which an ordinarily attractive woman gets from men as she walks down the street, in contrast with the uncomfortable stares she gets from seated males in the trolley or subway while she stands or hangs as best she can.

The problem goes more deeply than merely whether a man should offer his seat to a woman, who may earn more money at her job than he does. It goes even more deeply than a mere matter of reconciling society to woman's new dual role as a responsible citizen and as a wife and mother. For not only are men confused about the new status of women, but women themselves have to face problems which formerly were relegated to men—and more and more of them are finding themselves successful. The film shows a number of famous Canadian women at their work as scientists, musicians, even deep-sea divers.

Some interesting questions are posed in this film, humorously as well as seriously. But *Careers and Cradles* is only a brief introduction to a subject which certainly deserves fuller film treatment.   (c.s.)

CHALLENGE: SCIENCE AGAINST CANCER

Produced by the National Film Board of Canada and the Medical Film Institute of the Association of American Medical Colleges. Distributed by the International Film Bureau. (Thirty minutes.)

The struggle to conquer cancer has been dramatized on film many times, but never with the depth and sensitivity of this film. *Challenge: Science Against Cancer* does more than warn against the dangers of ignoring recognizable symptoms and shows what can be done to cure some cancers. It goes far beneath the surface to present cancer as a special medical problem. Striking new techniques in animation show how the growth of the cell by mitosis in a predetermined pattern makes us grow in the ordinary way. What causes one set of cells to grow and multiply into malignant cancers, the film explains, is still a mystery as great as life itself. But patiently and perseveringly men all over the world are tracking down the answers to thousands of questions.

By allaying fears rather than aggravating them, by being specific rather than vague, and by relating the problem of cancer to many other problems, the film achieves an overall excellence which earns for it the highest praise. Excellent as it is, however, the film is not organized and edited as precisely as it might be. A less obtrusive musical score would also have improved it, since the film without the music would be about as dramatic as an audience could take.

More than any other film yet produced, this one is an inspiring account of science at work for the good of all. High-school and college students should all be given a chance to see it. A shortened version has been prepared for theatrical use. Credit for this outstanding production, which recently won an award at the Venice film festival, goes to Guy Glover, producer; Morton Parker, director; Maurice Constant, script writer; and medical consultants Bernard Dryer, Dr. David Ruhe, and Dr. V. F. Bazilauskas. Music was composed by Louis Applebaum, and the commentary is read effectively by Raymond Massey.   (c.s.)

CHILDREN GROWING UP WITH OTHERS

Produced by British Ministry of Information, and distributed by United World Films. (Twenty-five minutes.)

As matured adults we are self-reliant members of our family and community. We have learned to live cooperatively with others. Happiness has come through confidence and security. But for children, learning to live cooperatively and happily is a long story. *Children Growing Up With Others* tells this story simply and pointedly. Its purpose is to help adults recognize the problems children face in learning to forego privileges and in adjusting to people and things. The commentary suggests ways in which we can be of help through advice and guidance.

From the moment the child is born, the film shows, it has an individual life of its own. This life has an all-or-nothing quality. The child is self-centered, absorbed in its own feelings and desires. As he grows older he learns what is approved and not approved. He finds out that the world is full of things that won't go right. He finds himself thwarted and flies into a rage. At these times, the commentary points out, the child needs wise and patient handling and guidance.

At four or five, the film continues, the child enjoys being with other children. His world begins to widen beyond the immediate family. At the same time he becomes less dependent on others. He learns basic skills of ordinary living. He grows in self reliance and can satisfy his own needs. Yet he is still baffled when he finds that there are things adults do that he cannot or is not allowed to do. At these times, we are reminded, the

child turns to grown-ups for understanding. . . .

The film clearly and poignantly develops its theme of growing children and their problems. At each step, from the complete introspection of infancy to the social consciousness of young adulthood, the film is full of insights, managing to capture the mood of each age it talks about. Sequences of children at play, of a child being caught smoking, of adolescents day-dreaming, and of young men and women discussing the problems of adulthood that face them are warm, human, and real. Parents and teachers—in fact, those in *any* way responsible for children will find the film a rich storehouse of material.

Because of the large area covered, some aspects of the film's presentation are necessarily incomplete, and the continuity is at times difficult to follow. Nevertheless, with proper supplementation, the film will serve as an excellent introduction to the area. . . .   (f.f.r.)

CHILDREN OF THE CITY

Produced by Crown Film. Distributed by the British Information Services. (Thirty minutes.)

Children of the City is a thorough and intelligent investigation into problems of juvenile delinquency, based on conditions in a large industrial city in Scotland. The story told is that of three young boys who have broken into a shop. What started out as a mischievous prank becomes a crime in the eyes of the law. But how responsible are these children? the film asks. We are shown the houses in which they live, the pitiful struggling existence of their parents, the lack of guidance and recreation provided for the boys —and then we are shown the measures that the community has taken to help prepare them for healthy and profitable lives.

The youngest boy, who suffers from an eye ailment, is put under the care of a child guidance clinic. Duncan, who is twelve, is placed in the hands of a probation officer, who must win the confidence and respect that the boy would normally have for his own father. But Alec, who has been brought before the juvenile court for previous misdemeanors and whose home life is intolerable, must be placed in an "approved" school. By giving him the discipline which his home is not able to provide, it will perhaps be possible to restore his self-confidence through training and the development of skills which will enable him to earn a respectable living for himself.

But, the film asks, what about the many other children who are being brought up in these same conditions? What can be done to prevent their normal lapse into anti-social behavior? The school can do part of the job, but play centers, clubs, and workshops are needed in every neighborhood of every community. For in that way, the film tells us, these energetic children of the city can be guided into discovering for themselves the excitement of building their own world, rather than destroying the world of adults which has always been cruel and forbidding to them.

The film is highly recommended as an aid to adult discussion. It states its vital problem clearly and shows one way in which attempts have been made to solve it. Its presentation is stirring, informational and provocative. Sensitiveness on the part of the camera and the script prevent the film from resolving itself into a pat and final solution of the problems of juvenile delinquency. Responsibility, problem, solution—terms which are often used unquestioningly in films of this type —are employed here with caution and discretion.

Technically the film is excellent.

Some audiences may have preliminary difficulty in understanding the Scottish voice used in the spoken commentary, but the film is so intelligently planned and so warmly presented it can hardly fail to hold the interest and stimulate the minds of the most isolated audience.

(F.F.R.)

CLEAN WATERS

Produced by General Electric in cooperation with the United States Bureau of Health. Distributed by General Electric, Nela Park, Cleveland 12, Ohio. Raphael G. Wolff, producer. (Twenty-three minutes, color.)

Here are flowing rivers, rippling brooks, torrential waterfalls, glistening lakes—beautiful, clean waters. And here too are aquatic sports and abundant wild life. The picture changes: Now we see muddied streams, scum-covered brooks, and stagnant lakes. There is no sign of life, for without clean waters nothing survives. This, says the film, is the price of neglect—a price which we have paid not once, but over and over again, by failing to maintain pure water supplies. . . .

Pictures, sketches, and diagrams are then used to explain the process of decontamination. Emerging from the processing plant, polluted waters are clean and beautiful again.

Although it contains useful information. *Clean Waters* suffers from uneven, often distracting production techniques. The pace is too deliberate, the development continually lags. The commentary tends to rely on lyrical verse of dubious quality to emphasize the attractiveness of clean water—a point, incidentally, which several excellent photographic sequences make much more effectively. Also, it should be noted that the equipment recommended by the film is both elaborate and expensive. The average community will scarcely be able to afford decontamination plants as large or as complex as the one shown. Nevertheless, the film does make a strong indictment of careless use of water resources, and, in this sense, is appropriate for any community audience. The diagrammatic explanation of the decontamination process is a model of clarity. . . . (F.F.R.)

THE ETERNAL FIGHT

Produced by Carroll Productions for the United Nations. Distributed by the U. N. Film Distribution Unit. (Eighteen minutes.)

An epidemic in Egypt or Malaya or India can mean danger to anyone anywhere in the world now that, for better or worse, international trade and travel bring all countries so much closer together. This film shows how the World Health Organization roots out communicable disease wherever it may exist before it reaches epidemic stage. As thrilling as a detective story, this is one of the more important of the United Nations films, which as a whole have, unfortunately, been disappointing. (C.S.)

FEELING ALL RIGHT

Sponsored by the Mississippi State Board of Health and produced by the Southern Educational Film Production Service. Distributed by the Columbia University Press, 411 West 117th Street, New York 27. (Twenty-two minutes.)

Not many of our readers are likely to see this film. Its subject, venereal disease, is highly specialized; its intended audience, the Negro population of the Mississippi delta country. Yet, despite the forbidding subject, this is one of the most delightful Negro films ever made. Done by the director and cameraman who made *The School that Learned to Eat*, it is cast entirely with colored people.

Apart from a slight stiffness in the dialog, the acting is wonderful, and the warmly told story carries the audience right along with it. Its frank and simple appeal is a welcome relief from the histrionics with which producers usually overburden the subject of syphilis. (R.S.)

THE FEELING OF HOSTILITY

Produced and distributed by the National Film Board of Canada. Directed by Robert Anderson. (Thirty-two minutes.)

The protagonist of this film is a successful businesswoman who is incredibly lonely and sees no way out of her loneliness. We see typical incidents in Claire's early life which helped cause her emotional insecurity. They revolve around her father's sudden death, her mother's remarriage, the birth of a baby brother, and Claire's increasing inability to express her need for love and attention. In sharp contrast to this area of emotional neglect we watch Claire come to rely more and more upon her mental and critical powers to earn for her the attention she so desperately wants and so obviously needs.

A trailer at the end of the film recapitulates the factors in Claire's life which contributed most to her emotional immaturity. Like *Over-Dependency* this film raises more than enough problems to make it worth everyone's while to have a mental-health specialist on hand at the showing. (C.S.)

THE FEELING OF REJECTION

Produced and distributed by the National Film Board of Canada. Directed by Robert Anderson. (Twenty-three minutes.)

Produced for the Canadian Department of National Health and Welfare, *The Feeling of Rejection* illustrates the function of psychiatry and guidance programs in helping overcome many of the normal problems of adjustment to responsible adult life.

Margaret, twenty-three, seeks relief from the headaches which symptomize her maladjustments. With the aid of a psychiatrist, she is able to trace their origins back to her early childhood. "Be a good child," her parents constantly admonished. It was a lesson she learned too well. For Margaret at the age of twenty-three was still a good child. She had not learned to face difficulties, to make her own decisions, to stand up for her opinions, or to enjoy her life.

In school Margaret grew more and more incompetent at the task of securing her position with her contemporaries and with the rest of the world. She did not dare assert herself for fear of losing friends. At home she grew to resent her younger sister, who was not as bound as she by habits of blind obedience and submission. At the office her relationship with her fellow-workers was restrained and immature.

With the aid of psychiatric and group guidance therapy, she became aware of these stunted developments in her personality. Once aware of them, she could analyze and eventually conquer them. Her headaches became less frequent, for fewer conflicts bring fewer symptoms.

The Feeling of Rejection, first of a series of films on mental health, is an excellent presentation of the normal kinds of adjustment problems faced by many adults today. It serves as a much-needed introduction to discussion of the function of the psychiatrist and the guidance clinic in the community.

The film is particularly excellent in its skilful commentary, its direction, and its dramatization. A magnificently quiet and unstrained quality is found in the performances of the non-professional actors in the film.

Timely and important, it should be of enormous interest to parent-teacher groups, to social and medical organizations, as well as to general adult audiences. (F.F.R.)

FIRST AS A CHILD

Sponsored by the State of Virginia Health Department, in cooperation with the United States Children's Bureau. Produced by The World Today, Inc. Available from Film Program Services. (Twenty-two minutes.)

This sensitive study of crippled children shows how orthopedic cases are treated with proper regard to the child's psychology and his home life. All too often the crippled child has been regarded by his playmates as an object of derision, and by his parents and teachers as a hopeless case who can never lead a full life.

Singling out a twelve-year-old boy, Alexander, who has been lamed as a result of an injury, the film shows how the public health nurse and social welfare worker cooperate to overcome the parents' natural reluctance to try further medical treatment, and explain how the community will bear most of its cost since they cannot afford to pay it. Alexander, too, benefits from this humane and understanding approach. In the hospital his mind is taken off the unpleasant prospect of another operation, and the foster home to which he goes for convalescence keeps him in touch with his own family.

The film broadens out at the end to show how much remains to be done if all our crippled children are to receive the capable and kindly treatment Alexander did. (R.S.)

FIRST STEPS

Produced by Frederic House for the United Nations. Directed by Leo Seltzer; script by Al Wasserman. Distrib-

uted by the U.N. Film Distribution Unit. *(Ten minutes.)*

Crippled children need not remain helpless; through treatment they can learn how to take care of themselves and gain the happiness which independence brings. This is the message of *First Steps*. The learning process is shown to be slow and painful, calling for a high partnership of endeavor—courage and an adventurous spirit in the child, sympathy and faith in the therapist and social worker.

This film shows us an American therapeutic center at work. We see first a shady, grassy playground, swings moving against a summer sky. Children are heard at play and soon we find them sporting in a shallow pool. Normal children they appear, until they are lifted out and we see in their limbs the pitiful evidence of infantile paralysis and cerebral palsy. That is the problem. We watch next how it is attacked. At first sight the treatment seems delightful—massage and group games accompanied by music. But a glance at the children's faces shows that these exercises are accompanied also by strain and courageous effort. A little girl with paralyzed arms learns how to lift a block of wood as part of a game. Presently a slice of bread is substituted—and she is feeding herself, torturously but also triumphantly.

The film moves into the epic of one little boy's struggle to walk. When he walks alone for the first time, leaving behind him the support of his familiar apparatus, we are reminded of the tenseness of a Lindbergh take-off. At last he leaves the Center, walking with clumsy dignity along the sidewalks of his town, a proud little citizen, smiling at the freedom he himself has achieved.

It is not surprising that *First Steps* won the Academy Award for 1947. It does a magnificent job. It is dif-ficult to realize that its running time is only ten minutes, so penetrating a journey into experience does it offer. Its emotional impact is unforgettable; its message, one of universal inspiration. The agonizing effort of a handicapped child to regain normality serves as a symbol of human striving against great odds. This film, in addition to enlarging sympathy for crippled children and their helpers, will give vision and encouragement to any group engaged in social action. It was made by the United Nations at the request of the Government of India. This origin, springing as it does from international cooperation, adds to the inspirational appeal. . . .   (F.F.R.)

FITNESS IS A FAMILY AFFAIR

Produced and distributed by the National Film Board of Canada. (Nineteen minutes.)

Most people who do not know how to enjoy their home and community life lack opportunities for help provided by organizations such as the Peckham Centre. Without help these people are apt to remain unaware of the causes of their restlessness, loneliness, and fatigue.

In this film, for example, Ed Logan and his family spend most of their time and energy making life unpleasant for each other. Left to themselves the Logans probably would never change. But fortunately for them, the Joneses next door are a happy family, and the spirit of cooperation which characterizes work and leisure hours in their household gradually infects the neighbors.

From the rumpus room in Sam Jones's basement we see evolve the idea for a community workshop and recreation center. Naturally enough, grumpy Ed Logan gets interested despite himself, and his transition to a more active and pleasant person is easily credible in view of the hum of interesting activity which has surrounded him. Family life at the Logans becomes more enjoyable too, as a result of this cooperative community undertaking.

A lot of food for thought and activity is packed into this nineteen-minute film, and many audiences should be inspired to get started on their own projects of this kind. Some situations in the film, particularly in the Jones's happy, happy home, are overdone, but the dreary Logans are just about perfect. (c.s.)

HIGHLAND DOCTOR

Produced and distributed by the British Information Services. (Twenty-two minutes.)

Highland Doctor tells the story of how the "Highlands and Islands Medical Service" was brought to the rural and seafaring inhabitants of the isolated sections of the Scottish mainland and the Hebrides. The evident needs of the scattered population, the financial problems in the way of meeting those needs, the study and planning done to get around the difficulties are all described as the film recounts the bringing of specialist aid and modern advantages to a stricken woman of one of the islands. . . .

This frank exposition of the good results which followed a socially-minded attack upon medical problems in scattered parts of Scotland exhibits much technical competence. A limitation for many American users might be the strongly marked Scottish accent of the principal characters. This factor should not prove too great a deterrent for groups with a special interest in widening opportunities for medical services, but for people less familiar or concerned with the matter in hand it would be a serious hindrance. Certainly the topic is of more than passing interest and the film should provoke lively discussion for some time to come. . . . (F.F.R.)

HUMAN BEGINNINGS

Produced by Eddie Albert Productions. Distributed by Association Films. (Twenty-two minutes, color.)

The men who were responsible for the production of *Human Growth* have come up with something that is certainly an eye-opener. It is *Human Beginnings*, a film designed to help six-year-olds express and clarify their ideas and feelings about how a baby grows. Based upon research among young children in the public schools of Eugene, Oregon, and filmed with pupils at the Walt Whitman School in New York City, the film first shows a class of boys and girls working out, through drawings and clay models, their ideas of how a baby grows inside its mother. Each child holds up his drawing and tells the others what it means to him.

The film indicates that all the children have a fairly sound basic idea about human growth, but each idea has been distorted according to how much the child feels he must hide and by how many disturbing emotions hinder his expressing what he knows. The difference, for example, ranges from a gentle and naive drawing which shows three lumps in a mother's "pocket" (when the owner of the drawing is challenged by another child that there are too many babies he lisps, "But they're twiplets!") to the very complex drawing of a decapitated mother who obviously never could and never did love her own child.

After all the drawings have been displayed and talked over, the teacher in the film calls on one of the boys to tell about his own new baby sister. As he talks the film shows his mother and father helping prepare him to understand about the new personality that is on its way to share their home and their lives. After the baby is born, he even has a chance to help select her name and he chooses "Marilyn." As in *Human Growth*, the film ends with children asking questions.

The drawings and the children's comments about them are the real meat of the film, something quite new for the public to see and hear. And undoubtedly they will help other six-year-olds get started on a similar project. Yet, before the film is shown to youngsters, or even to parents and teachers, it should be remembered that the film is an experimental one, based upon experimental research findings. It points to ways in which what we are learning about six-year-olds can help us in helping them grow up, but much more preparation than just the film alone is needed before this can be achieved.   (c.s.)

HUMAN GROWTH

Produced by Eddie Albert Productions for the E. C. Brown Trust, 220 West Alder Street, Portland 4, Oregon. (Twenty-one minutes, color.)

Human Growth is a film intended for the seventh to ninth grades, and may be shown as early as the fifth to sixth grades. It starts with the easily observable facts of human growth from childhood onwards, and then points out that growth does not begin at birth, but that in fact the first nine months of life are among the most important. So the film traces in simple and graphic animation the process of human reproduction and the development of the embryo.

The chief importance of this film, however, lies in the effort it makes to rid its audience of the embarrassment and restraint which often overtake talks on sex education. The prolog and epilog of the film show an early teen-age mixed audience before and after they have seen the film. Their reactions, and the behavior of their teacher, are so natural and likeable that the real audience of

the film is bound to go along with them and warm up to the business of asking questions.

An analysis of a large group of parents and teachers in Oregon showed the group as a whole to be 97.2 percent in favor of a child seeing the film during his school career. Men teachers voted 100 percent. Ninety-one percent thought the film should be shown at the beginning of adolescence.

Almost 98 percent of the group thought that the success of the film depended in large measure on the competence of the person using it, 54 percent favored separate screenings for boys and girls. (Rather surprisingly, fathers voted 65 percent on this issue, women teachers 45 percent.)

As an introductory film, *Human Growth* deserves the widest possible controlled use, and should continue in circulation for many years. (R.S.)

HUMAN REPRODUCTION

Produced by Audio Productions for Mc-Graw-Hill Text-Films. (Twenty-one minutes.)

Human Reproduction is intended for use in the freshman year in college, but it is also suitable for the final year in high school, as well as for adult instruction. Like *Human Growth*, it starts with a sequence designed to put the audience in a relaxed and receptive frame of mind —this time a very poorly directed and awkwardly acted scene in which a young couple (intended to represent the college-student audience a few years on) find themselves under the fire of questions from their seven-year-old son. . . .

However, the gist of the picture is in its long animated sequences, which are excellent. After a description of the sex organs in both men and women, the film deals rather fully with the menstrual cycle and the mechanism of fertilization. It then shows (much more briefly) the growth of the embryo, and ends with a perfunctory sequence on the process of birth.

The animation throughout is exceedingly clear and well paced. (Many animated films are far too rapid.) The commentary avoids the pitfalls of being coyly reticent or medically abstruse. This film must be given very high marks for making so much basic information so lucid and simple. (R.S.)

INVISIBLE ARMOUR

Produced and distributed by the National Film Board of Canada. (Twenty minutes.)

This is the story of how one woman managed to inaugurate an effective campaign against diphtheria among preschool children in her small home town. Pleasantly, and step by step, the film shows how everyone, doctors and citizens, worked together to put over a community-sponsored health service. (C.S.)

JOURNEY INTO MEDICINE

Produced by the Affiliated Film Producers for the State Department. Distributed by Castle. (Thirty-nine minutes.)

This is an extraordinarily moving account of one man's journey into medicine as a life's work, from struggling student to full-fledged doctor with a career in public health. Produced for overseas use, the film is now available here and should be of particular value in introducing medicine to those who may be considering it as a career for themselves. Exciting and often brilliant, *Journey Into Medicine* was directed by Willard Van Dyke, with script by Irving Jacoby, and photography by Boris Kaufman. (C.S.)

KNOW YOUR BABY

Produced by Crawley Films and distributed by the National Film Board of Canada. (Ten minutes, color or black-and-white.)

This film touches upon some of the important factors in the care of the new infant. Feeding, bathing, clothing, and loving all help determine the child's future physical and emotional well-being, and the film gives some practical examples to bear in mind. In addition, it dramatizes the relationship of the new baby to other members of the family, particularly to older siblings who are likely to become jealous and demanding. The film packs a great deal of information and experience into its single reel. (C.S.)

LIFE WITH BABY

Produced and distributed by the March of Time Forum. (Eighteen minutes.)

The content of the film is provided by the work of Yale University's Clinic of Child Development, founded and headed by Dr. Arnold Gesell. Here specialists have worked for over twenty years, charting the behavior patterns of children from every kind of environment.

Through a special one-way vision dome, photographic records have been made which have enabled Dr. Gesell and his associates to determine a pattern of growth common to most normal children. *Life with Baby* shows some of these tests being given, and briefly records some of the stages which produce the changes from infancy to childhood.

Similar studies of children's minds and social behavior help to guide parents in their relationships with their children, and help reduce risks of maladjustment in cases of adoption. . . .

There can be little doubt as to the importance and timeliness of this film for adult discussion purposes. It should be extremely useful with parent groups and teacher groups, as well as general audiences.

Although the film deals with material obtained through scientific research, it is non-technical in its presentation. Humorous and appealing, *Life with Baby* is interesting from start to finish.

Technically the film is out of the ordinary. Because of the particular film mechanism which has been installed in the Clinic, much valuable uninhibited reaction material is presented which could not otherwise be obtained. (Other films, more detailed in nature and more useful for actual research and study of child development, have been produced in the Clinic, but this March of Time Forum film is more appealing for non-professional audiences.) . . .
(F.F.R.)

LIFE WITH JUNIOR

Produced and distributed by the March of Time Forum. (Eighteen minutes.)

Produced in cooperation with the Child Study Association, this film shows a busy day in the life of a ten-year-old. Junior hates to get up just as much as he hates to go to bed. His addiction to the comics and the radio seems as much a part of his development as his love of candy. He finds new responsibilities in his work at school, as a cub member of the Boy Scouts. No one thinks of him as adorable any more. If he is lucky, his family and teachers are genuinely interested in him as a person and he feels the effects of their interest and guidance. But his need for a feeling of freedom is manifested in a variety of ways during his strenuous day, and it looks as if Junior is more or less on his own. *Life with Junior* is typically an American movie, for Junior himself is truly an American concept. The film is amusing but hasn't a great deal of warmth. (C.S.)

THIS CHARMING COUPLE
(nineteen minutes)

MARRIAGE TODAY
(twenty-two minutes)

CHOOSING FOR HAPPINESS
(fourteen minutes)

IT TAKES ALL KINDS
(twenty minutes)

WHO'S BOSS?
(sixteen minutes)

Produced by Affiliated Film Producers for McGraw-Hill Text Films. For rental, consult nearby educational or commercial film libraries.

This series of films was made for discussion use in college and upper high-school classes in connection with Henry Bowman's textbook *Marriage for Moderns.* Typical American homes and situations were chosen to help de-glamorize the typical youngster's notions about love and marriage in offering material for a positive approach to solving marriage problems *before* they happen. So important is the subject and so novel its treatment in these films that they have been widely screened by groups other than the colleges and schools for which they were primarily intended. In comparing them with other films by Producer Irving Jacoby, Directors Willard Van Dyke and Alexander Hammid, and Photographer Peter Glushanok, we are apt to lose sight of the fact that these are educational films. Although they do not achieve the excellence of such films as *Valley Town, Valley of the Tennessee, The Pale Horseman,* and other landmark documentaries made by these men, as teaching aids they set a new high.

This Charming Couple reviews our alarming divorce rate, which increases sharply with every new set of statistics. The film singles out one unhappy couple, Winnie and Ken, now face to face with the failure of their marriage. But the film reminds us that before they were bride and groom they were "in love," and it flashes back to scenes of their courtship. There were misunderstandings based on greatly differing interests and backgrounds, quarrels based on selfishness and lack of understanding. There were also the lovely days when it was easier to forget problems than face them.

This Charming Couple is a most provocative introduction to marriage problems. Expertly directed, well acted (especially by Winnie), and sensitively photographed, it is this reviewer's choice as the best in the series. An appealing touch is added by the effective use of a folk ballad with a truly haunting refrain—"For I was nothing to him, and he was the world to me."

Marriage Today is not so successful a film. In an effort to present a three-way contrast of the economic and social realities of the present day, one young couple's dream of living in a love-nest, and two successful marriages, the film has bitten off a good deal more than most audiences can chew. The Burns and the Hartfords, however, do come over as two credible couples who realized that marriage is, first of all, an adult undertaking in a real world.

Choosing for Happiness is of major interest to high-school and college girls. Eve has a lot of boy friends at school, but none of them seems to last for very long. Her cousin Mary listens sympathetically as Eve describes them and their shortcomings. Only when Eve begins to understand her own selfish and demanding behavior does she see that she has been expecting too much from other people.

A humorous touch is introduced in *It Takes All Kinds*, elaborating upon differences in behavior and personality by showing how a number of young people react to the frustration of running out of gas on a lonely road (in broad daylight, by the way). Mac, the inevitable boss; Irene, the peevish girl who must have her own way; Lily, who makes the best of everything; Gerald, the strong silent type—they and the others are all distinct personalities, and each has his own values. The world is full of people, and everyone has the right to choose among them. But, the film reminds us, the important thing is to know what you are getting when you ask for that one "special" person.

Who's Boss? ends the series with the problem of two successful careers in one family, and solves it on the basis of partnership instead of competition. Ginny and Mike Jackson go through the kind of quarrels and reconciliations that are familiar to us all. Both of them are able to make concessions down the line, and manage to win the struggle to preserve their marriage.

The acting, by non-professionals, is uneven—often exceptionally good and sometimes falling flat. The real importance of these films lies in the fact that they are among the first to deal honestly with some of the human-relations problems which this younger generation must attempt to solve. One tendency throughout the films which bothered this reviewer was that the leading women in the films seemed excessively dominant. Winnie is the girl who always gets what she wants, including Ken; Phyllis Burns helps her husband with his work and acts as his conscience in the final scene; Kathy Hartford is more intellectual and sensitive than Frank; Eve quite obviously dominates men, and even her good cousin Mary seems to get along well because she knows how to dominate in the right way; and in the last film it is Ginny who has the more successful career. Undoubtedly there is room for many more marriage films.   (c.s.)

MEETING EMOTIONAL NEEDS IN CHILDHOOD

Produced by the Department of Child Study, Vassar College. Distributed by the New York University Film Library. (Thirty-three minutes.)

This film is one of the Vassar College Studies of Normal Personality Development Series. Our citizens are products of their childhood, the film states. If they are not interested in the welfare of others, if they are wasteful and have no sense of responsibility, it may be due in part to their early lack of security. The film points in turn to the typical kinds of behavior in an elementary-grade class— the clown, the sassy kid, the daydreamer. It investigates situations in the home which intensify "problem" behavior and shows how teachers and parents can help remedy them.

The child must feel free to come and safe to go, the film says, for confident people make competent people. *Meeting Emotional Needs in Childhood* leaves much to be desired in the organization and filmic presentation of its material, but it is an important film not yet equaled in the significance of its message. (c.s.)

A MESSAGE TO WOMEN

Produced and distributed by the U. S. Public Health Service, Washington, D.C. 1944. (Eighteen minutes, color.)

The "iron curtain" that shrouds venereal diseases has for years effectively silenced open discussion of their prevention and cure. Only recently have films been produced that do not play peek-a-boo with this important subject. *A Message to Women* is one of these films, frank and factual.

A young girl is examined by her doctor and learns from him that she is infected with gonorrhea. Shocked and frightened, she at first refuses to admit that she has exposed herself to the disease. The doctor, however, wins her confidence and assures her that it is not too late for complete cure. The girl confesses that her family has always avoided mention of

venereal disease, that she knows very little about it. The doctor speaks to the girl's mother and convinces her that the parent's duty is to inform her children. The public must know the facts, he declares. The mother joins a group of women in her community who resolve to find out about venereal disease. The group goes to the local hospital. There a doctor shows them (and the film audiences) how infection occurs. With diagram and photograph he traces the progress of chankroid, gonorrhea, and syphilis. The ladies are told that infected expectant mothers can often bear normal children if treatment is administered before the fifth month of pregnancy. They learn that prophylaxis is not a foolproof prevention. Continence outside of marriage, the doctor states, is the only completely safe course. What if medical care is too great an expense? asks one of the group. Free clinics are maintained by the Public Health Service for those who are unable to afford private care, she is told. The ladies are further instructed in the importance of blood tests, and when infection is uncovered, of remaining under a doctor's care until complete cure is effected.

A Message to Women deserves the widest possible circulation. It is intelligently narrated with good color photography and sound. But, more important, its approach is refreshingly candid without being offensive. The presentation is factual, and, in consequence, extremely interesting. Although the film is angled to female audiences, there is no reason why fairly sophisticated mixed groups cannot use it. The clarity and honesty of the film's treatment does full justice to the importance of its subject. . . . (f.f.r.)

A MODERN GUIDE TO HEALTH

Produced by Halas & Batchelor for the British Ministry of Health. Distributed by the British Information Services. (Ten minutes.)

This delightful cartoon manages to give some good health rules and make them seem worth following, even to the laziest person. In episodic form it considers the need for outdoor exercise and activity away from city smoke and dirt; it urges clothing properly geared to weather and comfort; and gives some tips for safeguarding against insomnia.

The animation has a pleasant and glowing style of its own, and the film is cleverly persuasive. Highly recommended for working adults.

(C.S.)

NOBODY'S CHILDREN

Produced and distributed by the March of Time Forum. (Seventeen minutes.)

High in every society's casualty lists are its unwanted, unclaimed children. Every year illegitimacy, orphanage, and divorce victimize many children in the United States, putting them into the hands of state or private agencies for support and perhaps eventual adoption. It is to these conditions and to the work of the social agencies designed to improve them that the March of Time directs its attention in *Nobody's Children*.

At their best, child care institutions have done an excellent job, the film indicates. The procedure of adoption is administered cautiously, with every regard shown for the happiness of the child and his future parents. Many childless couples want to adopt children, the commentator declares, but are morally or temperamentally unsuited for parenthood. It is the duty of the agency to investigate every couple that makes application to it. In a typical case, staff workers are shown visiting the applicants in their own home, talking with their friends, and questioning business associates. . . .

Adults who criticize agencies for taking too much time do not realize the often tragic consequences of a hasty or unprincipled adoption procedure, the film points out. Diseased or mentally retarded infants may be adopted by couples who make application to unlicensed, fly-by-night agencies.

In conclusion, the film scans some of the activities of the United States Children's Bureau, and briefly notes the need for adoption of older children as well as infants, who are usually preferred by couples anxious to adopt a child.

Considering its brevity, this is an extremely comprehensive, well-organized film. It presents a considerable body of pertinent information from which issues are drawn with clarity. Production techniques are generally effective, although one may regret the rather heavy tone of the commentary. Altogether, the film should have real value for groups interested in its subject-matter.

(F.F.R.)

OVER-DEPENDENCY

Produced and distributed by the National Film Board of Canada. (Thirty-two minutes.)

Following the very popular *Feeling of Rejection* and the less well-received *Feeling of Hostility*, *Over-Dependency* gives another informal case history of a "normal" neurotic person. We see Jimmy first as he reaches out of bed to turn off the alarm. He doesn't want to get up and go to work; he doesn't feel well. He can't face calling his boss to say he is sick, and he is forced to lie his way out of the situation. His wife comes to the rescue by arranging a visit to a doctor, to whom Jimmy confides his secret feeling that he has some dread physical ailment. But the doctor finds out that there is nothing physically wrong with Jimmy.

Fortunately for Jimmy the doctor doesn't tell him to go home and stop worrying. Instead he arranges a series of meetings with his patient, in which Jimmy talks informally about the things that are on his mind. From these discussions Jimmy is able to recognize a pattern of over-dependent behavior based upon his relationship with his mother, his sisters, and later his wife. A dream gives him some insight into his early jealousy of his father. Then Jimmy learns to regard these over-dependent tendencies as danger signals in his daily adult behavior, and at the end of the film we see him on the way to becoming a more independent and mature person.

As can easily be seen from this very brief outline, *Over-Dependency* is filled almost to overflowing with highly complex ideas. And it should be pointed out that the film raises far more questions than it answers and implies much more than it states.

Like the others in this series, *Over-Dependency* is not an instructional film; it does not define or explain, except incidentally. It is not an entertainment film; technically it is undistinguished, and cinematically it is only adequate. The film reconstructs, in story form, a certain type of neurotic behavior and shows one way in which it can be properly treated. It is certain to evoke some sort of emotional reaction from everyone who sees it. For that reason it seems almost imperative that every group planning to show the film arrange to have a competent specialist on hand to bring out and answer questions arising in the minds of the individuals in the audience. Otherwise, through haphazard showings to casual audiences, the film may do more harm than good in terms of mental health.   (c.s.)

PAY ATTENTION

Produced by Vassar College. Distributed by the New York University Film Library. (Thirty minutes.)

Sixth in the Vassar College Normal Personality Development Series, *Pay Attention* deals with the education of deafened children. It shows a variety of remedial techniques associated with preschool, elementary, and high-school children, taking into account special personality and emotional difficulties connected with deafness among children. Suitable for general audiences, as well as teachers, psychologists, and other specialists, the film is interesting throughout and pleasingly presented.   (c.s.)

PROBLEM CHILDREN

Produced and distributed by the Ohio Department of Public Welfare, available outside Ohio from Pennsylvania State College Film Library, State College, Pennsylvania. (Twenty minutes.)

There are no problem children, argues this film, only problem schools, homes, and communities. These social groups are charged with the responsibility of noting individual differences among children and working together to keep the child well adjusted.

To show the differences in needs that must be studied and met, Jimmy and Roy, two problem children, are described in detail. We see Roy, active and aggressive, as a calculating show-off in the classroom, playing tricks on the weaker children. His above-average brightness allows him to finish his work before the others, leaving him time for mischief. Jimmy is shy, pushed around by others, and lives in a confusion of self-doubt and fears, the kind of boy that the teacher might ignore because he gives no trouble.

Some of the home conditions that, we are told, helped create each boy's problem are dramatized. Roy's father is a successful business man, who feels that his responsibility to his child is discharged by granting him a generous allowance; his mother treats him as she would a six-year-old. Roy's desire to be regarded as a grown-up emerges in a pattern of petty delinquency, in his smoking, his aggression toward other boys. Jimmy, on the other hand, whose parents were separated when he was five, lives with an aunt who cannot adequately substitute for real parental attention. Because Jimmy feels unwanted and lonely, he slips into a dream world to find compensation, and seems to accept his condition of defeat and inferiority.

Situations such as these can be resolved only by closing the gap between school and the home, the film warns us. Not only can the school find work that will challenge Roy's ability and energies, and give him a feeling of recognition, but the teacher can help both parents to understand his needs. Jimmy can be brought back to the real world by drawing him into group activity, and by letting him do his work at his own pace to give him a sense of achievement.

The responsibility of the home and the school to help the child adjust is wider than the boundaries of the community, the film tells us, because the future of our world depends upon how emotionally mature our children will be. . . .

The commentary is sober, and the photography is adequate, if unexciting. . . . (F.F.R.)

PROBLEM DRINKERS

Produced and distributed by the March of Time Forum. (Eighteen minutes.)

Problem Drinkers is a series of dramatized episodes, at times overacted, in the life of a confirmed drinker. In this case there are no apparent reasons for his drinking; like many others, his problem is that no matter what he starts out to do he finds himself having a drink first, and he doesn't know he has had enough until he has had too many. The film

traces some of the efforts that have been made to solve the problem of alcoholism—from temperance unions to Alcoholics Anonymous, emphasizing the work of this latter group and its remarkable number of successful cures. While this is not the whole solution to the problem of alcoholism, psychologically speaking, it has one of the most impressive records of any self-help movement (that is, helping oneself by helping others). (C.S.)

SMALL FRY

Produced and distributed by the National Film Board of Canada. (Ten minutes.)

When parents are not able to look after the needs of their own children, whose responsibility is it? *Small Fry* points out the great inequalities of opportunity among children all over the world and shows the Canadian Government's provisions for family allowances, improved schools, medical care, and facilities for sports and recreation for children who otherwise would be deprived. In addition to well-organized information on the subject of the ever-present need for child-welfare programs of all kinds, the film includes some really delightful shots of young children, one of the most memorable of which shows a youngster on her way to her first day at school. (C.S.)

STARTING LINE

Sponsored by the State of Virginia Health Department in cooperation with the U. S. Children's Bureau. Produced by the Southern Educational Film Production Service. Available from Film Program Services. (Eighteen minutes.)

. . . The problem in *Starting Line* is the treatment of premature birth. Forty-six percent of the babies who die during the first month of life die as a result of pre-maturity. Seven percent of all babies are born prematurely.

These figures throw into sharp relief the importance of the treatment to be obtained at such centers as that of St. Francis Hospital, Peoria, Illinois, where most of this film was shot.

The layman will watch with interest the elaborate methods of maintaining the premature infant under even and sterilized atmospheric conditions, and of feeding it when it is incapable of feeding itself. When the infant reaches the weight of five and a half pounds, it is considered to have been brought up to normal, irrespective of how long this has taken. The child can then safely be returned to its parents.

Starting Line is recommended to all social groups interested in learning how the large loss of life due to premature birth can be checked.

(R.S.)

UNCONSCIOUS MOTIVATION

Prepared by Dr. Lester F. Beck. Distributed by Association Films. (Thirty-eight minutes.)

This film is a miniature experiment, indicating the ways in which inner conflicts affect adult behavior and physical health. Planned and prepared by Lester F. Beck, professor of psychology at the University of Oregon, the film further illustrates how problems of human behavior can be explored on film. Dr. Beck previously prepared the film *Human Growth* and two new productions, *Hypnotic Behavior* and *Human Beginnings*, have just been released.

The experiment shown in the film involves two subjects, Claire and Don, selected for their favorable responses to hypnosis. While in a trance, they are told a simple behavior problem, which is left unresolved. It involves an early childhood episode in which they found a coin purse, spent the money in it, and subsequently lied to their mother. This, Dr. Beck tells them, has bothered them ever since.

After they are awakened the changes in their personalities are shocking. Don, who before the hypnosis had been a carefree and cheerful young man, complains that he feels terrible. His hands are sweaty, he says, and he notices that he is nervously rubbing them together. He feels that he has done something wrong, and he doesn't know what it is. Claire is so upset that she doesn't want to talk about it. She doesn't even want to think about it, and she turns her face from sight.

At a prearranged signal, Claire and Don tell each other about the dreams they had while still under the hypnosis. More readily than Claire, Don begins to piece together bits of the mystery that is bothering them. In an ink-blot test he identifies himself with a grotesque black figure in the center. With other psychological testing aids they are able to work their way through the distressing artificial neurosis which Dr. Beck had implanted. From time to time he asks them how they are feeling. Even without their own comments, it is evident that as they are able to get at the unknown misdemeanors their spirits and appearance improve.

Experiments of this sort are not new, but this is the first one recorded on film. *Unconscious Motivation* is presented exactly as it happened, unrehearsed and unedited. Because of these unique circumstances it cannot be criticized in film terms. Neither Don nor Claire had more than a general idea of what would take place, nor had they ever submitted to similar tests. The film was shot with two cameras working simultaneously, one showing Don and Claire from a side angle, another allowing for close-ups. Although Dr. Beck's voice was recorded as he spoke to them, he does not appear in the film.

What are the implications of *Unconscious Motivation*? To the non-professional it shows beyond reason-

196

able doubt that unconscious fears manifest themselves in any of a great number of ways. Having two subjects in the experiment, the film clearly indicates that people react very differently when confronted with identical problems.

But it remains for a psychologist or psychiatrist to explain the film fully. It is rented only with the understanding that such a qualified person will be on hand to introduce the film, answer questions, and lead discussion. We can only hope that many specialists will be happy to participate in a showing of the film to parents, social workers, physicians, teachers, religious leaders, and other interested adults.   (c.s.)

THE WALKING MACHINE

Produced and directed by Paul Falkenberg for the American Foot Care Institute, 1775 Broadway, New York 19, N. Y. (Fourteen minutes.)

The greatest transportation system of all—our feet—is the subject of this amusing and informative film. Nearly everyone is born with healthy feet, yet one out of three adults— and they are mostly women—complain that their feet hurt. The film gives some pointers on foot care, exercise, medical treatment, and the selection and fitting of shoes. Except for a few shots of highly diseased feet (half a minute at most), I can think of no reason why everyone shouldn't enjoy it.   (c.s.)

YOUR CHILDREN AND YOU
(thirty-one minutes)
YOUR CHILDREN'S EYES
(twenty minutes)
YOUR CHILDREN'S SLEEP
(twenty-three minutes)
YOUR CHILDREN'S TEETH
(fourteen minutes)
YOUR CHILDREN'S MEALS
(fourteen minutes)
YOUR CHILDREN'S EARS
(fifteen minutes)

Produced and distributed by the British Information Services.

This series stands out among studies of children for its simple and human approach. Its theme is Children Are People—people with their own valid ways of thinking and looking at things. The smart young mother wheels out her infant son in the baby carriage, but all *he* sees is an uninteresting expanse of stomach bobbing up and down and blocking his view. No wonder he cries, and she gets miffed. This is only one of the many imaginative touches in *Your Children and You,* which alternately adopts the child's and the parent's camera viewpoint. Very informally, and with a welcome absence of technical jargon, this film takes up many of the preadolescent problems which worry the family: play, discipline, clean habits, meals, sleep, and childhood fears.

The rest of the series fills out these subjects. *Eyes* explains the mechanism of seeing by a series of amusing blackboard diagrams easily understood by children. It especially stresses the problem of squinting, and the serious consequences which may follow neglect of this condition. *Sleep,* a really remarkable film, is pure poetry as well as sound common sense. Explaining the psychological background of anxiety and fear, it uses imagery which is valid for the psychoanalyst and intelligible to the ordinary person. *Ears* explains the mechanism of hearing with admirable clearness, and shows how diseases of the respiratory tract may lead to deafness if treatment is neglected. *Teeth,* the least interestingly presented of the series, shows in a very graphic sequence just how children should and shouldn't brush their teeth. *Meals* stresses the need for color and variety in feeding, and explains some of the conflicts which may grow up between mother and child. The importance of regular hours for mealtime is pointed up by a very charming clock sequence.

Throughout these films, every parent will find himself saying, "If only I had really stuck to that . . . ," or, "Now I know why he seemed so unhappy then. . . ." They all should be widely seen.   (R.S.)

7. life in the u. s.

(Including Minority Problems, Housing, Labor & Management, Natural Resources, etc.)

THE CITY

Produced by American Documentary Films, Inc., 1939. Directed by Willard Van Dyke and Ralph Steiner, from a scenario by Pare Lorentz; music by Aaron Copland. Distributed by the Museum of Modern Art Film Library. (Thirty minutes.)

Our cities, the jumbled helter-skelter of skyscrapers and tenements, are obsolete. They have grown too big. There is a pressing need for new patterns of urban life, for planned cities without slums, without air poisoned by factory smoke and narrow streets jammed with traffic. This is the theme of *The City*, which contrasts the average metropolis with a model community designed and constructed by the Federal government.

Before the noisy advent of the machine age most communities were compact centers of local industry and private life. "We used our hands," says the commentator. "We found a balance." Here is the water wheel. Up the lane is the smithy's barn. Beyond it, cultivated fields. Down by the river some kids are taking a swim. These are quiet scenes, perhaps a little sad, for much of this life is gone, and the new centers are urban.

Across time to the city. These are homes in the factory district of an industrial community: topheavy, ramshackle houses with narrow porches. There's smoke in the air. "Smoke makes prosperity," says the commentator. "No matter if you choke on it." Down in the railroad basin some kids are playing. The shortest route is over the tracks. And around them are dusty acres of the ugly, wood-frame houses in which they live.

Now, down into the heart of the city. Crowds are going home from work. A jay-walker starts across the street, stops, jumps back, tries again. A short man, chewing a cigar, dodges into the stream of traffic to the island of people who stand on the white line. He saved a minute. "Faster and faster," says the commentator. In the office buildings thousands of private secretaries are taking dictation. Under the streets thousands of commuters are taking the subway. Faster and faster. Noon-time. A half-hour to eat. Bologna sandwich on rye, side of cole slaw. Machines turn out the businessman's-special, machines that vend everything from papaya juice to chewing gum. A half-hour to eat. Then back to work. Take a cab. Traffic jam. Heads are popping out of the open tops. What's wrong? What's holding things up? . . .

But all communities are not like this, says the commentator. "We are in an age of rebuilding." Elsewhere we are designing "green belt cities," cities that don't grow too big. This community for example. It was built by the Federal government. There's plenty of *room* here. There are broad streets with overpasses and quiet neighborhoods with clean air. The housewife does her washing with her neighbors in cooperatively owned machines. There are bicycle paths for boys and girls, and playgrounds. And grass. The homes are small but attractive, each with its own yard and lawn. There's a pond for swimming too. This city was "brought into the country." It is for living. The factories are near enough to reach in the morning, far enough to forget at night. This is a new city. It has grown away from the old. "Take your choice," says the commentator.

Few documentary films have been as effectively produced as *The City*. From a purely technical standpoint it could hardly be better. Expressive photography and a fine musical score complement each other perfectly, and the commentary, written by Lewis Mumford, is both intelligent and unobtrusive. As an aid to adult discussion *The City* is a *must* for almost any group. . . .   (F.F.R.)

THE COLOR OF A MAN

Produced for the American Missionary Association by the International Film Foundation. Distributed by the Congregational Christian Churches, 287 Fourth Avenue, New York 10, N. Y. (Twenty minutes, color.)

For a hundred years, the American Missionary Association has helped combat the social and economic degradation of minority groups. This film shows the plight of the American Negro and his struggles to better himself and his race.

The shadows that men cast show only that they are human beings, but as they walk upon the earth they make color distinctions between themselves. Is one man less a human being because his skin is black? The film answers that if the Negro finds himself in a less advantageous position today than the white man, it is because of the lack of education he has received in the past, the poverty in which he has been raised and in which he is still forced to raise his children. It is true in the North as well as in the South. Even in our nation's capital the Negro has to endure insults, discrimination, and poverty, because of his color.

The film shows in detail some of the conditions in which the southern Negroes live today—dilapidated shacks set up on land which is not theirs, insanitary cooking and living quarters, poor educational facilities, and the like.

But where Negroes are allowed to grow up in good health and free from fear and oppression, they have proved that they are capable of learning trades and professions as well as other men. Church-sponsored schools, for the fortunate Negroes who live close enough to attend them, are virtual oases of learning, sheltering children from hate and fear.

But where in books or schools are the answers to the Negro's problems? The film reminds us that it is the duty of Christians throughout the land to remember that God created all men free and equal.

The Color of a Man is an extremely forceful presentation of one of our major problems. It does not, however, present any clear-cut idea of what can be done in order to fight this kind of discrimination. It shows conditions as they exist, and it asks the white man to "ponder his heart." Successful discussion of the problem, after a screening of this film, would have to involve more than that.

The film is handsomely put together, and the color photography is both beautiful and emotionally powerful. . . .   (F.F.R.)

CROSSROADS FOR AMERICA

Produced by Academy Films for The Research Institute of America, Inc., 292 Madison Avenue, New York 17, N. Y. (Thirty-one minutes.)

Produced as a reply to *Deadline for Action*, this film tends to cast serious doubt on the veracity of the medium itself. Using the same story as the earlier film, the same basic premises, even many of the same visual images, *Crossroads* arrives at diametrically opposite conclusions. Its hero, Dave Nelson, is aware of the cross-currents in American life. But for him strikes are only incidental to a larger unity, the concentration of wealth is an unimportant obverse to the multiplication of wealth by shareholding, while the figure of Lincoln, invoked by Joe Turner as a threat to the Capitol's reactionary occupants, is to Dave Nelson a symbol of the united force of the American Government.

Indeed, the only black spot that Dave Nelson can find is the Communist agitator (not mentioned, of course, in *Deadline*), whose stratagems are effectively exposed. Much of the film, however, is devoted to a defense of the economic status quo, and it has therefore not got the vigor of protest which makes *Deadline* so effective. These are two films which should be shown together, but there is a world of relevant material which both of them ignore.   (R.S.)

THE CUMMINGTON STORY

Produced by OWI Overseas, and distributed by Castle Films. (Twenty-one minutes.)

The European refugees who settled in the United States during the war had many adjustment problems of their own. This film tells the story of a community—Cummington, Massachusetts—which learned to adjust to these strangers in its midst. The handful of men, women, and children who arrived in Cummington had only one friend to greet them, the minister who was sponsoring their stay in the town. The townspeople were not used to strangers. Strangers were not accepted. But in the course of living closely together, the people of the town self-consciously and slowly open their hearts to the strangers. The directors of the film, Helen Grayson and Larry Madison, are to be congratulated on the skilful way in which difficult emotional attitudes are presented in the film.   (C.S.)

DEADLINE FOR ACTION

Produced by Union Films for the United Electrical Workers of America. Distributed by Union Films, 11 West 88th Street, New York, N. Y. (Thirty-two minutes.)

This trenchant and hard-hitting film tells the story of a worker, Joe Turner, who tries to learn the secret of postwar high prices and lay-offs in the history of the depression and the trustification of big business. While the film effectively dramatizes the present concentration of wealth in America, it also exaggerates its political power—as witness the 1948 presidential election. Because it is designed for union audiences, *Deadline* takes for granted a legislative program of reform, and therefore confines itself to destructive criticism.

Nevertheless, the film is packed with action and argument, much of it convincing and true. It is not surprising that the bulk of its very large sales went to company executives who felt that they must get out an answer to it—and quick.   (R.S.)

FLORIDA, WEALTH OR WASTE

Produced and distributed by the Southern Educational Film Production Service, University of Georgia, Athens, Ga. (Twenty-two minutes, color.)

From an arid stretch of wasteland supporting only a few people, Florida has become one of the fastest growing states in the union, known the world over as the nation's playground. But behind the luxury and gaiety which the world sees, is the working face of Florida: the citrus groves, cattle lands, cotton and tobacco plantations, cigar factories and phosphate plants. With all these resources, however, Florida's economy is still far below the level which would bring prosperity to all her people.

Some of the reasons for this can be traced to generations of abuse of her abundant natural wealth. One quarter of all the forest fires in the United States each year occur in Florida. Greedy for quick profits, timbermen stripped many forests with no thought of conserving young trees for the future. Large scale farming in the same spirit left the land impoverished. "Centuries of marsh grass would have to grow and rot before this land would be rich again," says the commentator, as the camera surveys the eroded gullies. No beauty spots for tourists here."

With timber gone and little land left for farming, the future looked hopeless to many farm youths. Embittered, in bad health, with few working skills, they left for the cities, only to find more wastelands—of slums, crime, and poverty.

But this waste of human and material resources can be checked and much of Florida's ruined wealth restored, the film points out, by a generation of effort, planned on a statewide basis. The action then switches to brisk scenes of a rehabilitation program that is now under way, though still in its early stages: new water control and irrigation systems; fire towers and reforestation activities; breeding of improved livestock through importation of heat-resisting Brahma bulls from India, and full use of products formerly wasted, such as the processing of citrus skins for use as cattle feed and fertilizers.

In all our dealings with nature, concludes the film, we must take thought for tomorrow. It is for us to decide whether we shall have wealth or waste.

For a program concerned with conservation there are better films than this which develop the same theme in a more unified way; this film is mainly a potpourri of Floridana which brings in conservation almost incidentally. Its usefulness is probably limited to rural groups in Florida and other southern states with similar economies. As an informational film about the agricultural and industrial problems of Florida, it should help to correct the old stereotype of that state as the land of sunshine, hotels, and blossoming orange groves. . . . (F.F.R.)

FOR SOME MUST WATCH

Produced by Julien Bryan International Film Foundation, for the Institute of Life Insurance. Available from the Institute of Life Insurance, 60 E. 42nd Street, New York 17, for free loan. (Twenty-eight minutes.)

For Some Must Watch reenacts incidents in the lives of three families in Oneida, New York, and shows how the sincere interest of Jack Sutton, a local insurance agent, has made him an exceptional leader in his community and a successful businessman. In the course of one ordinary day's work, Jack visits a young doctor, a widow with two children, and a farmer; and the film flashes back to show how insurance of one kind or another has played an important part in the lives of these people.

The film uses the documentary technique of telling its story within the framework and setting of reality. The home and community life depicted are recognizably real, and characters in the film are real citizens of the town. Jack Sutton plays himself with a friendliness and kindness which must be natural to him, and with a general ease before the camera which is usually the sign of expert direction. There are some fine photographic moments in the film, particularly the exterior shots of the town at night and in the morning. And there are some excellent scenes (the railway accident, for example), which make this much more than a run-of-the-mill "free film."

But something is missing in the film. Perhaps it is that we cannot really believe in Jack Sutton. He is too good, or too important, or too busy. As a real-life hero, he carries much less weight than, say, the county agent does in another Julien Bryan film. (*The County Agent*, one of a series of five films on life in an Ohio town, has recently been released by the Castle Division of United World Films, for purchase only.)

Compared with other public-relations films on life insurance, this one undoubtedly sets a new high. Its approach is completely admirable, and if it falls short of being the best kind of documentary we might expect from its producers, we can only hope that this is because of the difficulty of adapting their methods and skills to a kind of sponsorship which always before had been alien and unfriendly to the documentary.   (c.s.)

FUNNY BUSINESS

Produced by RKO and distributed by McGraw-Hill Text-Films. (Nineteen minutes.)

Sunday mornings in the United States have a new ritual, performed to the rustling of newspapers, dedicated to the consumption of the comic strip. In this film we learn about the history and make-up of the comics and are invited to assess their social significance.

The first comic strip was "The Yellow Kid" in 1896, we are told. Today there are four hundred strips organized by large syndicates for the convenience of the newspapers. We watch some of the artists at work and note their different methods. Harold Gray, for example, the creator of Little Orphan Annie, looks at his own face in a microscopic glass and then draws it. When the drawings reach the syndicate, the comics editor, checks them for dialog and continuity, and exercises censorship. Crime, for instance, must never pay. When the drawings have passed the comic editor, they are photo-engraved and the proofs filed.

We next see something of the great influence of the strips, especially on children. From newspapers the strips have spread into movies and the radio. Literary classics, school history books, even the Bible, are being reproduced as comic books. As a result, Robinson Crusoe is once more marooned—on the shelves of public libraries. People are beginning to be disturbed about the educational effect of this new medium.

The film shows us both sides of the comic strip controversy. Marya Mannes complains that the comic "kills the urge to read books" and is stupid, ugly, and educationally dangerous. Al Capp defends the strips, which contain, he affirms, the best illustrating in America and the best humor. To the charge of their harmful influence he replies that the same argument is true of books. There is good and bad in all forms of expression. As we return to a last glimpse of the "folk-reading" in the Sunday living room, we are left to decide its value or its danger for ourselves.

The best part of the film deals with the printing and distribution of the comic strip and the techniques of artist and editor. For this reason it is likely to please groups of adults who uncritically enjoy the strips. Educators, however, and those who view the comics with concern, will find the film's treatment of the social aspect superficial and spoiled by overacting. The merit of the film is that it introduces a discussion on the subject, which should be easy to follow up in any group, provided the leader is well equipped with material on the educational factors to be considered. (F.F.R.)

HIGHWAY MANIA

Produced by R.K.O., and distributed by McGraw-Hill Text-Films. (Eighteen minutes.)

"You've got to have a car" is a phrase often on American lips. Is "You'll probably have an automobile accident" the necessary corollary? This film is a study of the causes of the high accident rate in the United States and makes suggestions for the greater safety of both driver and pedestrian.

As we watch sequences of traffic jams and accidents, the commentator gives us these facts: More than thirty million automobiles are operated annually in this country, and although the automobile is a comparatively new vehicle, it is responsible for almost as many deaths as all the wars combined. "Who," asks the commentator, "is the villain?" The answer is—everybody. Sometimes the fault is exclusively the driver's. We watch the dangerous antics of a series of people—the driver trying to make up time, the driver weaving his way between saloons, the driver who wants to be the speediest on the road, the driver who cannot read. Many people are unfit to drive, states the commentator, but some states do not even require driving licenses. On the other hand, the fault may be the pedestrian's. We watch a crowd of impetuous, careless people risking their lives at a street crossing. Yet again the fault may be one of road conditions, discrepancies between state regulations, or neglected automobiles unfit for the road.

Having stated the problem and its cause, the film proceeds to outline solutions, reminding us that the whole subject has been discussed at a conference called by President Truman. The cure, the film suggests, is as multiple as the cause. Among needed reforms are: uniformity of state laws, extension of driving tests, traffic lessons for school children, safer roads, inspection of wheel alignment, fines for careless pedestrians, and the appointment of traffic commissioners. All this would of course cost money—but is not that more easily spared than human lives?

Considering its brevity, this film gives a comprehensive view of the modern traffic problem. It is full of drama, humor and realism, and its suggested reforms are practical and clearly expressed. (F.F.R.)

THE HOUSE I LIVE IN

Produced by RKO Radio Pictures. Distributed by Young America Films. (Ten minutes.)

This film, starring Frank Sinatra, presents a short but eloquent appeal for religious tolerance.

Opening on a scene in a recording studio, the film presents Frank Sinatra crooning a currently popular love song. During the intermission which follows, he wanders out the stage door into an alley where a gang of young boys are shown excitedly bullying a Jewish boy who, trembling, is standing backed up against a wall. Sinatra rushes to his aid, asking the boys the reason for this "Nazi-like" behavior. He tells them religion makes no difference between people and cites as one example the work of the blood bank agencies, and points out that it may have been the blood of a Jewish donor which saved the life of the gang leader's father who was wounded in the war.

To illustrate further the basic sameness of all Americans and the cooperation between those in the service regardless of race or creed, he then tells the boys the story of a Jap battleship which was sunk by a bomb released by a Jewish bombardier in an American plane piloted by an Irishman.

As he leaves the gang to return to his recording studio, Sinatra sings for them "The House I Live In," a sentimental ballad which presents a strong plea for tolerance and democracy.

The gang then leave, but in going, the leader picks up and returns to the Jewish boy his books which had been thrown on the ground.

Although not primarily a discussion film or one especially suited for adult groups, *The House I Live In* carries a strong appeal for religious tolerance, and might be used as an introduction to a discussion of techniques to promote this amity or to a film showing how tolerance has been achieved. It has a strong emotional appeal, and by starring Frank Sinatra, would be most effective among younger groups and adolescents, who would be able to grasp and understand its message better than they would a more sophisticated film on the same subject. The treatment of the subject is fair, and it is both clearly and interestingly presented. Sinatra gives a good performance and avoids the subtle pitfalls of over-sentimentality. The production maintains an even level throughout, geared to the comprehension of the less mature. . . .   (F.F.R.)

IN BALANCE

Produced by Wilding Pictures for Burroughs Adding Machine Co. Available from the sponsor, 219 Fourth Ave., New York, N. Y. (Thirty-four minutes.)

In Balance argues the case for high business profits and tries to justify the payment to shareholders of comparatively low dividends during a prosperous period like the present [1948-49], at the same time warning employees that profit-sharing schemes are not in their own ultimate interest.

This rather sour-tasting pill is wrapped up in the tale of two Gloucester fishermen, Captain Tad Simpson, who wants to share the profits of a good year with his crew, spending only the minimum on refitting his ship, and his brother Ben, who would spend most of his profits on the ship and let his men be content with the good wages they draw. A writer who has access to the Burroughs Company impresses on the brothers the need for adequate reserves, and the film thereupon nosedives into a narration of company activities. It is rather abruptly wound up to the story's dénouement: The hard-headed Ben goes on from success to success, while the warm-hearted Tad, when his ship's engines break down and his crew deserts, is finally forced to sell out and, too proud to stay in Gloucester, disappears and is never seen again.

The churches may discover with some embarrassment that this unprogressive argument, this false balance between "the head and the heart," is put into the mouth of a minister. But in more ways than this the film is tendentious and unrepresentative of enlightened management. The technique of presentation is uniformly mediocre, but the technical quality is high.   (R.S.)

LIBRARY OF CONGRESS

Produced by OWI Overseas. Distributed by Castle Films. (Twenty-one minutes.)

To foreigners the United States has always been a country without a tradition or a culture of its own. In an attempt to correct that idea, this film focuses upon our Library of Congress and presents it as a symbol of our regard for the non-commercial things in life. Science, painting, music, literature, and history are shown as part of this great institution, which has become a kind of national library to which millions of visitors and scholars come each year. The film does a skilful job of compressing the many activities of the Library of Congress into one short film, without getting bogged down in details. Credit for the production belongs to Irving Jacoby, Alexander Hammid, and Irving Lerner, writer, director, and producer, respectively. American audiences, by the way, are likely to be even more impressed with the film and with our cultural potentialities than foreign audiences.

(c.s.)

MAKE MINE FREEDOM

Presented by Harding College, and produced by John Sutherland Productions. Available from Harding College, Searcy, Arkansas. (Ten minutes, color.)

This animated film presents an idyllic portrait of America with its four perfectly observed freedoms, plus the "freedom to work" and the "freedom to own property." The characters of the film—a Senator, a farmer, a factory worker, and others—are perfectly happy until the appearance of Dr. Utopia, a quack salesman of markedly Latin appearance. . . . Armed with a magic bottle of snake oil labeled Ism, this spellbinder goes to work on his audience and soon persuades the Senator that Ism will win him votes, the farmer that Ism will raise his crop prices, the factory worker that Ism will lower his cost of living. However, just when they are about to sign away their liberties in favor of Utopia, up comes Mr. John Q. Public, who has been slumbering on a park bench.

"What's wrong with the America we've got?" he asks. Didn't Joe Doakes, that proverbial putterer, invent the automobile? Dr. Utopia would take away the freedom to putter. Didn't Joe Doakes build a great city out of the family's savings? Why, even in the Depression, things were really all right; Joe Doakes was still better off than anyone else in the world. His audience, however, is still under Dr. Utopia's spell. "All right," he says, "Go ahead. Drink your Ism!"

And forthwith large and horrible green hands shoot out to bar the worker from his union, prevent the industrialist from expanding his plant, and clap the Senator into a concentration camp. Awaking from their nightmare, the characters hasten to railroad Dr. Utopia out of town.

The propaganda pattern is familiar. It is basically a fallacious "either—or." Either the free-enterprise system is retained in exactly its present form . . . or we must live under the extremist tyranny of the totalitarian state. Mixed in with this is a hatred of foreigners, a contempt for their way of life, and an appeal to bigotry and intolerance at home. The whole unpleasant dish is served up with a crude but appealing humor, calculated to lull an audience into a receptive frame of mind.

(R.S.)

MAKE WAY FOR YOUTH

Sponsored by the National Social Welfare Assembly and produced by Transfilm, Inc. Available from Association Films. (Nineteen minutes.)

Narrated by Melvyn Douglas, this film sets out to tell the story of the formation of a youth council at Madison, Wisconsin. It all starts with a battle between two rival gangs "from the north and south sides of town," in which the local newspaper editor's son gets killed. Suddenly aroused by this dramatic incident, he writes a wrathful editorial, telling the townspeople that they had better get wise to what is happening right in their midst. The kids themselves begin to organize to fight racial intolerance. They organize a youth council, get hold of a recreation director, raise funds, prepare reports, and finally talk the mayor and the city council into letting them have a big warehouse where they can hold their meetings. The film ends with a tree-planting project, which symbolizes the new spirit of friendship between kids of different races and religions.

Unfortunately, the story carries little conviction. The fact of racial intolerance never comes to life in the two brief and unconvincing episodes which are supposed to portray it. The atmosphere of the film is one of simple jollity. Moreover, though the poorer districts of the town are casually referred to, all the children in the film seem to come from the well-to-do levels of society, which are more apt to create intolerance than to suffer from it. However, as a means of showing some of the difficulties of forming a local youth council, and suggesting how energy and enthusiasm can overcome them, this film may do some good.
(R.S.)

MEN OF GLOUCESTER
PUEBLO BOY
SOUTHERN HIGHLANDERS

Three color films in the Americans at Home Series, sponsored by the Ford Motor Co., and produced by Transfilm, Inc., New York. (Twenty-two minutes, twenty-two minutes, nineteen minutes.) Available from Ford Motor Co., Film Library, 3600 Schaefer Rd., Dearborn, Michigan.

This continuing series of Ford-sponsored films seems to have sprung from the laudable desire to make Americans in all their rich variety of background better known to one an-

other. Yet what these films reveal is not so much America as the mind of Henry Ford, Sr. This is not, of course, the Ford of the Dearborn *Independent* and the bitter labor struggles described by Upton Sinclair in *The Flivver King*. Rather, these films reflect the old gentleman of Greenfield Village, meandering along the folkways of America, trying to convince himself that "There's a Ford in Your Past."

Men of Gloucester, for instance, the first and the best film of the three, gives no hint that more than one kind of storm can strike a community dependent on a single source of income—the sea. There is no feeling of a hard and risky economic life for the fisherman, to be countered perhaps by cooperative marketing designed so that he can hold and share what he has won. . . .

In *Pueblo Boy* it is a misty vision of the Spirit of his Ancestors which reconciles the Indian to the denial of his rights by the white man, and the inconsiderable *Southern Highlanders* demonstrates how psalm-singing and the amiable platitudes of the village teacher will make up for a world of poverty and backwardness. . . .

It remains to say that the camera work in color is always beautiful, often magnificent, and that Ford advertising is confined to a title, save that a Ford sedan, no longer of current design, may be seen gliding past the camera now and then.   (R.S.)

A PLACE TO LIVE

Produced by Documentary Film Productions, Inc., 1941. Script by Muriel Ruykeyser; music by David Diamond; directed by Irving Lerner. Distributed by Brandon Films. (Eighteen minutes.)

Based on a survey by the Philadelphia Housing Association, A *Place to Live* demonstrates in human terms the community obligation to provide adequate and sanitary housing for all its people.

Philadelphia, with its magnificent office buildings and its huge industrial enterprises, is truly a city with a future. But it is also a city with a past. That past shows itself in two ways: One is by the monuments and buildings erected to preserve in stone the glory of the city's history, and the other is by the decaying remnants of the old, out-worn city—the slums, the dumps, the unclean and unsightly neighborhoods in which many of Philadelphia's people are forced to live, for want of anything better.

Touring down one of the streets of one such neighborhood, the camera picks up the homeward trail of a young boy out of school, and follows him into his home. There is neither sufficient heat nor sanitation nor space for his family to live comfortably—but it is where he lives. His mother's voice asks what can be done about it. Concrete, electricity, and machinery have changed the city into a center of fabulous wealth, but what about the slums?

The law is on the people's side, the film reminds us, for the housing and sanitary codes of the city make slums a crime. And here and there new homes are going up where the old unusable ones stood. As the boy pauses on his way gathering firewood for the kitchen stove, he sees a new housing project under way, and he imagines his own family living in it.

But, the commentator interrupts, such homes aren't for you—you are worthless and poor.

"We live in a place that is half dead," the boy's mother explains. The boy replies, "Well, it's time to put things in shape, isn't it?"

A Place to Live reminds us that slums are not an inevitable part of our heritage, but are man-made, through careless and selfish living. The guilt for them rests with all of us. The possibility of doing away with slums and of preventing them

in future also rests with all of us. On this basis, the problems of adequate shelter for all its citizens become the problems of every city and of every individual in the city.

Although the film was made before the wartime and postwar housing shortage made people acutely aware of their housing needs, the ideas it presents are still the fundamental issues of our current housing situation. The film is both timely and permanent in its appeal, and will continue so until conditions shown in the film no longer exist.

Music, script and camera-work of *A Place to Live* are excellent, as are the performances of the film's two characters. The film's message is simple and appealing. Although it points out no single set of answers to housing responsibilities, it should be a distinct aid to discussion groups on nearly all educational levels. . . .

(F.F.R.)

POWER AND THE LAND

Produced by the U. S. Department of Agriculture. Directed by Joris Ivens; photographed by Floyd Crosby and Arthur Ornitz; commentary by Stephen Benét. Distributed by Castle Films. (Thirty-nine minutes.)

Until the passage by Congress in 1935 of a bill establishing the Rural Electrification Agency, the vast majority of American farmers were unable to afford the benefits of electrical power. *Power and the Land* shows how this agency has served the farmer.

Scenes of rolling hills unfold on the screen as dawn breaks on the Parkinson dairy farm. Mr. Parkinson goes out to do his early-morning chores by kerosene lamp while his wife begins the tedious work of the day. She is shown doing the laundry, a task which involves the transportation of water from the well, and which will not end until the last iron has been heated on the old wood stove. Meanwhile, Mr. Parkinson has been putting milk in cans which will be picked up by a dairy truck. Due to lack of refrigeration, some of the previous night's milk has soured and will have to be given to the pigs. The film shows other jobs which must be performed—the cutting of the corn, the gathering in of the alfalfa, and finally, after dark, the whetting of knives on a foot-operated grindstone. Work never seems to end.

When electricity first came, the film reports, it cost the power companies too much to bring it to the farm, so that although the vast majority of urban areas received its benefits, seventy-five percent of the farms in America, on whose produce cities depended, were still without its conveniences. With the inception of the REA in 1935, cooperatives were established, and each farmer-member was able to have electricity brought to his farm. Now the farmer could have electric milking machines, an electric grindstone, a brooder for his chicks, refrigeration for his milk, and electric light in the barn to work by. His wife, too, would benefit, with an electric stove, iron, washing-machine and many other appliances that serve to lighten household chores.

Under the cooperative membership system, and with the aid of the REA, "electricity belongs to all the farmers—together."

In addition to presenting a strong argument for the establishment of rural electrification cooperatives, *Power and the Land* gives a clear picture of American farm life. The photography, sound, and music are all superb, and Stephen Vincent Benét has written a fine commentary to go with them. Although this film might be criticized because it fails to mention any electrification programs undertaken by private companies, a wealth of absorbing material conducive to discussion on co-

operative planning is dramatically and interestingly presented. . . .

(F.F.R.)

RADIO BROADCASTING TODAY

Produced and distributed by the March of Time Forum. (Nineteen minutes.)

In this frothy and funny survey of American radio broadcasting, the March of Time has turned up some of the most embarrassing of the industry's faults, and pointed out some of the good things about it, too.

Americans can stand anything but silence, the commentator remarks, as the camera satirically shows us a vastly irate, dripping citizen, dragged from his bath to answer the telephone inquiry of the Hooper audience measurement poll. The Hooper ratings show, we are told, that Americans stick pretty much to the same entertainers. The camera flits from Jack Benny to Fibber McGee, from Bob Hope to Walter Winchell and Fred Allen, all among the top fifteen in popularity year after year.

The most often criticized feature of American radio is the advertising without which these top programs would not exist. The necessity which the radio writer and artist face of satisfying both sponsors and censors creates problems which are graphically portrayed as we see two writers struggling with the ending of a skit. The kind of power the sponsor exerts over radio material is shown in a scene in which a dreadful girl trio jingles the praises of canned sardines to a beaming sponsor, whose only suggestion is that the brand name might be mentioned just a few more times.

While radio critic John Crosby tells us from the screen that "bad programs outnumber good ones twenty-to-one . . . broadcasters don't own their own souls," the commentator nevertheless points out that many noteworthy programs *are* broadcast. Shots of news programs, sports coverage, town meetings of the air, documentaries, and symphonies are shown in proof of the fact that radio is not wholly bad. We are left with the impression that perhaps these valuable public services make up for the poor taste of even the audience participation shows in which, as the camera reveals, people are encouraged to make monstrous fools of themselves.   (F.F.R.)

THE RIVER

Produced by the U. S. Department of Agriculture, 1937. Distributed by Castle. (Thirty-three minutes.)

The River is a motion picture about the Mississippi and the inhabitants of her basin, and it shows how the United States Department of Agriculture has, through the Tennessee Valley Authority, begun to govern one branch of the river. From St. Paul to Vicksburg, the lumbering, slow-to-anger Mississippi has for almost two centuries carried produce to the port of New Orleans. A million farmers along her banks are at the mercy of the old river's whims, dependent on her good nature, in constant threat of her disturbance. The story of the river has been the story of these people.

The film etches some of the epochs in the Mississippi's long history: her early transports of tobacco, whiskey, pork, flour, hemp and potatoes, and the rise to majesty of King Cotton. The river stimulated industry in the days before the Civil War. She served to route raw materials directly to southern markets and to distribution centers in New Orleans. But while the Mississippi carried the farmer's produce to market she also carried his topsoil into the Gulf of Mexico. Her receding flood waters washed away rich, cultivated soil and left only wasteland. By 1870 much of the South was barren and its settlers were pushing west, out of the river's terrain. The Reconstruction and the Mississippi had impoverished the South. But in the North, in Ohio and Minnesota, a new industry was growing—lumber. The trees that were felled in Wisconsin floated down the Mississippi to southern mills. More industries arose—iron and coal for steel mills and railroads. And these industries began to replace lumber, for northern forests of Douglas fir and Norway pine were depleted and their ugly stumps looked down to the Mississippi, now feeding the industrial revolution with other fuel.

Through these changes the river herself was a constant. Her many tributaries continued to swell her waters to flood level, and the farmers who still clung to her southern banks saw their homes and fields washed away to the Gulf. The need for control persisted. At last, under the New Deal, this need was faced. TVA built dams along the Tennessee River which for years had poured its waters unrestrainedly into the Mississippi. CCC workers replanted the ruined forests, planted new roots to hold back rain water. And, through the Farm Security Administration, farmers were granted long-term loans to fight their way back to self-sufficiency.

The big river was being bridled. Now land was growing new crops. The farmers of the Mississippi Valley were, for the first time, receiving electrical power. It was only the beginning, but the Mississippi *was* working again.

This famous documentary film seems to ripen with age. It has suffered little in effectiveness in the years since its production in 1937. The musical score of Virgil Thomson and the commentary and direction of Pare Lorentz blend with superb photography by Willard Van Dyke, Floyd Crosby, and Stacey Woodard to produce a film which is not likely to be forgotten by audiences. This is a superb documentary, structurally sound, artistically exciting, and highly provocative. . . .   (F.F.R.)

(Editor's Note: These two films, one of feature length and one a short subject, are noteworthy attempts to edit and re-use ordinary newsreel camera material to interpret recent history and the outstanding political leader and international figure of the times.)

THE ROOSEVELT STORY

Produced by Tola Productions. Distributed by Brandon Films. (Eighty minutes.)

For many reasons this film is extraordinary and unique. First, it is made up of scenes from the life of an extraordinary public man who in an almost magic way evoked immediate and deep emotional responses from millions of contemporaries. In addition, the film outlines the recent political and social history of this nation and of the world in larger-than-life dimensions. And perhaps most impressive of all, although without the sensitivity it might have shown, the film charts the development of a man, one man, from his youth to his death. In all respects this is an important film.

To abbreviate Franklin Delano Roosevelt's dynamic and overwhelmingly full life into eighty minutes is like reducing a banquet meal to merely the seasonings. We see only the highlights, and in this man's life it means every moment is an occasion, every utterance a byword. But even so, Roosevelt emerges as less of a myth in this film than he did during his lifetime.

As the somber funeral procession goes down Pennsylvania Avenue on April 14, 1945, an unseen cabdriver speaks out: "This is a day to remember, . . ." But there were other days. And the film goes back to Roosevelt's early life: Hyde Park, Groton, Harvard, marriage, and a family. It

shows him as Assistant Secretary of the Navy during Wilson's Presidency; campaigning for Al Smith; a smiling candidate in 1920 for the Vice Presidency; and in August, 1921, at the age of thirty-nine, stricken with infantile paralysis.

The Roosevelt we all knew makes his first appearance in the film at the Democratic National Convention in Chicago in 1932. Will Rogers gives him a faltering impromptu introduction, apologizes for his own lack of eloquence, and reminds Roosevelt that he really doesn't deserve any better. "Remember you're only a candidate." Franklin Roosevelt throws back his head and laughs. The tenseness is over; the personal crisis is dispelled; a new dramatic figure appears on the political scene—a great leader, a voice heard by millions, a name known and respected and loved around the world.

The film continues: Unemployment is at an all-time critical point. The opposition declares that prosperity is just around the corner. In Florida a deranged man's bullet misses the President-elect — and Mayor Cermak loses his life. The bank holiday, beer, NRA, WPA, and the rest of the alphabet. And in Germany another powerful man makes his mark on history's pages. Roosevelt tells the story of a gardener who thumbed his nose at the President. The fireside chats. War brews in Europe. The people elect. And Hitler begins his march; too soon he is dancing at the downfall of France. Pearl Harbor. Roosevelt and Churchill. Casablanca. Cairo. Teheran, then Yalta. The President's last message to Congress. A gaunt, worn face. Unbelievable. The long, slow procession. Streets of the world lined with the friends this man made in his lifetime. They grieve and they weep. He had spoken for millions of inarticulate people. Now they must learn to speak for themselves.

The task of assembling this film

was not a simple one. Roosevelt was a master performer before the camera and the microphone, and he acted out his story every day of his life. What we see in the film are only excerpts from the real Roosevelt story. There is some mush in the film, too, moments of excruciating over-sentimentality — the episode about the draftee and his sweetheart, for example. But the whole film has a terrific impact, and I should think that everyone in the world would want to see it for one reason or another.

The Roosevelt Story was produced by Martin Levine and Oliver A. Unger, with Elliot Roosevelt as editorial consultant. Musical score is by Earl Robinson, and short choral selections were directed by Robert Shaw. Walter Klee compiled and edited the film.   (c.s.)

FDR—THE LIFE OF ROOSEVELT

Produced and distributed by Official Films. (Fifteen minutes.)

This is an interesting super-newsreel, with many of the same shots which were used in the long film, but without the dramatic narration. If *The Roosevelt Story* is merely excerpts, this film is something like a glimpse of a glimpse.   (c.s.)

SEMINOLES OF THE EVERGLADES

Produced by Alan Shilin Productions. Sponsored by the P. Lorillard Co. 1949. Available from Alan Shilin Productions, 450 W. 56th Street, New York, N. Y. (Twenty-one minutes, color.)

This film tells the story of the Seminole Indians, who sought seclusion and independence in Florida's swampy everglades and who now are being forced into a new world and a new way of life. After retreating into the swampland to escape American armies which sought to remove them to the new Indian Territory in Oklahoma about a hundred years ago, the Seminoles found more than adequate protection against their human enemies. But nature provided other dangers: the coiling coral snake, deadliest creature of North America, the diamond-back rattler, and the ever-present alligator. The Seminoles were able to survive in this almost uninhabitable region, building their villages on the flat island-like hills of dry land. Their homes, ingeniously planned to suit the environment, are the only dwellings which have been able to withstand the seasonal windstorms and hurricanes.

One of the most exotic and colorful in the United States, the everglades region provides beautiful camera material. And we learn that only a few things from the white man's world have been accepted by these Indians: tobacco, first smoked in pipes of tribal ceremony now being replaced by the white man's cigarette; the hand-operated sewing machine, which is used to make intricately colored garments for the tourist market; the air boat, a flat-bottomed boat driven by an airplane propeller, permitting travel through the swamps at the speed of fifty miles an hour, and the headlight, a storage-battery device worn on the Indian's head in coal miner fashion to hunt frogs for Florida's wealthy restaurant patrons. Little else of the white man's world has penetrated into the Seminole world.

But this nearly private world is fast disappearing. Reclamation projects are draining the land to make it habitable and arable, thus drying up the waterways which for years have been the Indian's only roads. The Seminole is losing his seclusion, his home, and his livelihood. In this connection the United States Office of Indian Affairs (which cooperated in the production of this film, as did the Everglades National Park Authority), is attempting to help the Seminole adjust to a new geography and a new world. Indians are being trained in cattle-raising, and reservations may obtain loans with which to start operating their own ranches. Economic problems are not the only ones. There are matters of health and education to be worked out if the Seminole is to become a useful and happy citizen of the white man's world, which he has so long avoided.

The film's introductory title states, "Out of gratitude to the people who gave tobacco to the world, the P. Lorillard Company presents this film as a public service." The film has almost everything to recommend it: excellent color photography, a pleasant and simple continuity, and subject-matter which can hardly fail to interest all audiences. Neither superficially traveloguish nor over-bearingly didactic, the film achieves a successful blending of the surface tourist sights and the sociological implications behind them.

Good as the film is, there are one or two uncomfortable moments of mawkish romanticizing about a bewildered Indian in the big city who finds companionship in a carton of cigarettes he buys at a drug store. Since this is the first of a series of films on the American Indian, we can hope that such episodes will be eliminated in future.

The ideal sponsored film is yet to be made, but *Seminoles of the Everglades* takes several firm steps toward that goal. It should give the sponsors, producers, and the public something to think and talk about.   (c.s.)

SWEDES IN AMERICA

Produced by OWI Overseas and distributed, for purchase only, by Castle Division of United World Films. (Sixteen minutes.)

Ingrid Bergman lends an informally glamorous touch to this film by narrating it and appearing before the camera much of the time. Telling the story as her own search for information about the Swedish people in this country, Miss Bergman first visits the famous Sweden House in New York's Rockefeller Center, where fine Swedish glassware and other imported items are on display. Then at the American-Swedish Museum in the Midwest the camera singles out evidences of Swedish-American contributions to our culture and industry. And finally with Miss Bergman we visit "little Sweden"—that lovely Minnesota region where Swedish is taught in the schools, where the town's merchants sweep the sidewalks clean, where Swedish ways have become part of the American way. The film is charming throughout.   (c.s.)

THERE WERE THREE MEN

Produced for the Cooperative League by Tomlin Film Productions. Distributed by the Cooperative League. (Ten minutes, color animation.)

Prices and profits are no longer straws in the wind of supply and demand. They are controlled factors, subject to the regulation of a monopoly business. Because this regulation is arbitrary rather than natural, the farmer and the laborer are often discriminated against. To prevent such discrimination they must band together. They must form cooperatives. This is the message of *There Were Three Men*, which illustrates its theme by a simple cartoon story of a farmer, a laborer, and a monopolist. . . .

At its conclusion the film summarizes the principles of the co-op system: Anyone can buy . . . anyone can join . . . everyone has one vote . . . every year savings are divided according to purchases . . . limited interest is paid on shares." And, the film adds emphatically, "we learn to work together."

There Were Three Men presents

a lively argument for the formation of cooperatives. Although the material in the film is much simplified, even oversimplified, the approach is honest and seems to have a sound basis in economic fact. Whatever the individual's attitude on cooperatives, it is certain that he will find ample matter for discussion in this timely, expert little film. . . . (F.F.R.)

UNION AT WORK

Produced and distributed by the Textile Workers Union of America (CIO), 99 University Place, New York 3, N. Y. (Twenty-four minutes.)

This is the official film story of the Textile Workers Union—how it works and why. With more than eight hundred locals, involving 450,-000 members, the TWUA has yet a big job of organizing to do: More than three-quarters of a million workers are still without the benefits of union contract.

Union at Work gives as sincere and convincing an account of a union's activities and aims as has yet been done on film. Issues, such as organizing, strikes, political action, and the rights and obligations of working men everywhere, are calmly and forthrightly presented. More than that, the film is imaginative and pleasing. Produced by Al Hemsing and directed by Rosemarie Hickson, it shows more craftsmanship than is usual in a film of this kind. A background of guitar-accompanied union songs adds to the film's mobility, yet avoids the pitfall of overemotionalizing. The first-person narration by the voice of a union organizer is precise and earnest, with only one objectionable flaw—its repeated use of the phrase "my people," referring to TWUA members.

While lacking the photographic splendor of most industrially sponsored films, *Union at Work* is a first-rate attempt to communicate ideas and influence attitudes, a film the labor movement and the entire nation can look to with satisfaction.

(C.S.)

VALLEY OF THE TENNESSEE

Produced for OWI Overseas. Distributed by Castle Division of United World Films. For purchase only. (Thirty minutes.)

The contrasts of poor land and poorer people with the skilled workers and fabulous machines which built the dams of TVA provided excellent material for both camera and sound track, and director Alexander Hammid has made the most of them. But the film is more concerned with the development of attitudes than with material construction. It concentrates on the farmers' reactions to TVA, to the noise and activity, to the new ideas of contour plowing and crop rotation, to tractors and electricity. Their reluctance to participate in something they could not understand, and could hardly be expected to understand, is clearly and frankly shown in the film. But we see also that there are always a few men who become the pioneers, who dare to try something new because, among other reasons, they have nothing to lose. These men led the way in the valley of the Tennessee. The rest is the history of the rebirth of an entire section of our country in one of the most impressive experiments ever undertaken anywhere.

(C.S.)

VALLEY TOWN

Produced by the Educational Film Institute of New York University and distributed by the New York University Film Library, 1940. (Twenty-seven minutes.)

This serious study documents the situation that arises when labor-saving machinery replaces manpower without regard for the effects upon the lives of the men, women and children directly concerned. To this end the film presents an American steel-mill town and its people before, during, and after a depression, and before and after new techniques and devices have lessened the need for human labor in the mills.

Introductory scenes establish the background: the dulness of a smoke-covered mill town; men and women whose day to day existence is geared inescapably to machines, whose tempo of living is set by machines. These men and women live tolerably well when the mills are running at capacity, but are wholly lost when the plants shut down.

Good times are exemplified by Christmas-shopping sequences. The commentator makes clear that these people who live by machines also buy machine-made goods, and that as local merchants prosper more job opportunities appear in local stores. Rolling lines of loaded freight cars signify the economic interrelations of the community with other parts of the United States, and suggest the expanding prosperity, which in pre-depression days was expected to continue forever.

Then, reflecting the onslaught of economic panic, the film changes to show frieight cars empty and idle on railroad sidings, factories out of production, bewildered workers whose faces reveal the strain of long weeks without employment. Even with the eventual coming of business recovery this bewilderment of the men is not erased, because for them there is no let-up in depression. The industry has adopted new processes of steel-making and the old-type mills remain closed. One man can now do the work that thirty were required to do before.

The film singles out a discouraged, unneeded steel worker and his wife, their morale crumbling as they stand helpless before a misfortune they can neither comprehend nor fight against. Other jobless mill workers,

young as well as old, with hard-earned skills that have now become worthless, are pictured watching an old-style mill being dismantled. As the building comes down the last hopes of the men fall with it. The film asks whether or not it is unavoidable that these capable men be discarded and disregarded. An answer is indicated in the example of a railroad engineer whose job was lost through motorbus competition, but who is now working at turning out parts for diesel engines for the buses that replaced him! . . .

New productive processes, while helping men in general, frequently hurt man in particular by bringing with them the modern problem of technological unemployment. In *Valley Town* the issues which thus arise are dramatized with force, clarity, fairness, and a high degree of photographic simplicity. In the treatment of its theme the entire film is straightforward and unpretentious, with the possible exception of the technique which superimposes a woman's voice in song to express the rebellious thoughts of the steel worker's wife. For the most part, the musical score complements the film with unusual aptness. The film was directed by Willard Van Dyke, photographed by Bob Churchill, and edited by Irving Lerner, with music by Marc Blitzstein. . . .   (F.F.R.)

WHOEVER YOU ARE

Produced by V. F. T. Films. Available from Film Program Services. (Eighteen minutes.)

This is a frank report of how a single New York community got to grips with its race problems. The initial statement is clear: It is the parents who stir up racial intolerance, not the children; still less, mysterious "Nazis." Therefore it is the parents who get together, hesitantly and reluctantly at first, then with a growing sense of confidence. They gain the support of the churches, the schools, the magistrates, the business leaders; and though the district is evidently a very poor one, they manage to raise sufficient funds to pay a full-time recreation director. The film does not claim that these measures solve all the problems. The district is still no paradise for its Negroes, Catholics, and Jews. But a solid beginning has been made.

The film has a warm and persuasive honesty which more than compensates for its amateur camera work and cutting. It convinces the audience that what can be done here can also be done again if the approach is both hard-headed and sincere.   (R.S.)

8. peoples and places

mutual problems

ATOMIC POWER

Produced and distributed by March of Time Forum. (Nineteen minutes.)

This film presents a survey of events and discoveries behind the manufacture of the first atomic bombs.

The film opens with the now familiar sequence of the ruins of Hiroshima. This is followed by a cross-section of press and public opinion in the United States after the announcement of the bombing. A brief explanation of the principle of nuclear fission is given with the aid of animated diagrams, and there is a discussion of the possible use of nuclear energy in industry.

The main body of the film is given to a series of historical reenactments in which Einstein and other prominent scientists and administrators appear in person. These sequences sketch the progress of research in atomic energy in the years before the entrance of the United States into the war, early experiments with the principle of atomic energy and the stages of government support which led finally to the great secret project at Oak Ridge. The first desert test of the bomb provides the dramatic climax.

This film is primarily a story behind the news, that is, a superficial survey of historical events from the journalist's point of view, which finds the explanation of events in the decisions of a few prominent men. The appearance of these men on the screen gives the film some of the timely interest of a newsreel, and real value as an historical document, in spite of clumsy and unconvincing dramatization.

Because of the amount of space given to these reenactments, however, the scientific explanation has been made too hasty and incomplete to be of use to laymen without some previous knowledge of physics, while the political and moral problems which provide issues for discussions are touched on very lightly at the beginning and the end.

In spite of these obvious weaknesses, the importance of the subject and the facts presented raise inescapable issues for discussion by adults on all educational levels. . . . (F.F.R.)

BOUNDARY LINES

Produced and distributed by International Film Foundation. (Eleven minutes, color animation.)

By means of animated cartoons and supporting dramatic musical score, this color film satirizes man's intolerance for man in all its repulsive manifestations. Taking the theme that a line is what we make it—it is only an idea—the film calls attention to the various imaginary lines which divide people from one another, and endeavors to show that the distinctions thus emphasized have no true basis in reality.

Two boys, Jim and Joe, are playing marbles. They get into a dispute. Boy-fashion, a line is drawn on the ground. It is promptly crossed. Fists fly. A background chorus chants in staccato repetition, "Oh well, boys will be boys!" But boys will also be men, and the lines that men draw mark off more than just arguments over marbles.

The film ridicules the senseless tendency of mature people to draw lines setting apart fellow men because of superficialities of, for example, color, origin, wealth or poverty. Fear-lines are stressed as being particularly malicious. Boy gangs form in neighborhoods and the fear motive is clear and sufficiently deplorable in these juvenile associations; but when the pattern is repeated on the adult level, it widens in area and deepens in bitterness. Grown men do not fight with toys.

Not all boundary lines are bad. The friendly, backyard fences of good neighbors are offered as a case in point. We see cheerful little animated figures of men and women engaging in over-the-fence gossip and easy fellowship. In sudden contrast martial music roars and an ominous, black, fortresslike wall shoots up as symbolical of dangerous, impassable barriers between nations. Lines which say, "Keep out!" are bad lines. They breed mistrust and lead to wars; and the progression in deadliness of man's weapons is shown from prehistoric crudity to atomic finesse.

Men, too, the film states, as well as their weapons, have made progress —progress in nobility. It poses the question: Will men be able to overcome their greed, fear and hate? And, the implication is, in time? Boundary lines, the commentator repeats, are what we make them. We can plan dividing lines between us, or we can draw a circle around all our differences. A line is only an idea.

This highly imaginative piece of film work (by Philip Stapp), with its interesting and venturesome animation and music (by Gene Forrell), gives direction to discussion on present intergroup relations. The commentary is crisp and well edited, and no one is likely to find fault with the fairness of the general handling of the picture's theme. The originality and impressionism of the treatment in certain sequences are such, however, as perhaps to cause conservative audiences to lose track of the film's message. Inasmuch as it is a one-reel film it might more readily implement discussion for some groups if shown twice, because in the rapid handling of so many phases of the topic it does fall short of complete clarity. . . .   (F.F.R.)

BROTHERHOOD OF MAN

Produced by United Productions of America for the UAW. Distributed by Brandon Films. (Eleven minutes, color, animation.)

This film, opening with the statement, "The future of civilization depends on brotherhood," depicts in cleverly animated sequences the basic similarities of the races of mankind. Prejudice and racial hatred are personified by small green demons who perpetually attempt to break up friendly relations and distort expressions of good will between the various races.

Beginning with the common parentage of the first man and woman, the film traces the development of various peoples and cultures, indicating that the dissimilarities we note between peoples today are not differences in fundamental human nature, but merely superficial changes resulting from environmental influences. The only essential difference conceded by the film is that of skin pigmentation. Down through the centuries cultures have been developed to a high level, each by a different group of people. Once again asserting that the physical differences between us are of surface importance only, the film offers in support the cases of an American child brought up from infancy in China and of a Chinese boy raised in this country. It is demonstrated that when children such as these

have matured, they behave the same as other members of the culture in which they have developed, regardless of their physical or racial differences.

Therefore, since there are no basic differences, the film recommends that racial injustices be stamped out. Let there be equal opportunity for all from the beginning—let there be good education, equal medical care, and an equal chance for a job, for then, the film says, "We can all go forward together."

Based upon the pamphlet "Races of Mankind," which was prepared by Ruth Benedict and Gene Weltfish, *Brotherhood of Man* attempts to present a solution to the problem of racial antagonisms and to dispel ideas of inherent racial differences. When used primarily as an informational film, it can be shown with equal advantage to audiences composed of either adults or children, and to those both on higher and on lower levels of educational preparation. The subject is fairly treated and is of universal and lasting interest. Technically, this film is well above average, and the animation sequences used are cleverly thought out and carried through. . . .

(F.F.R.)

ONE WORLD OR NONE

Produced by Philip Ragan, 1947. Distributed by Film Publishers. (Nine minutes.)

One World or None is an animated film which employs a few photographic shots for realistic effect. It was produced with the technical assistance of the Federation of American (Atomic) Scientists.

Stressing the international character of atomic research, the film tells us that the atom bomb grew out of the work of scientists of many different nations, including Japan, Germany, Russia, Great Britain and the United States. . . .

Then the film traces the history of warfare from the days of Alexander the Great, when soldiers armed with swords fought singly, one against one, to the present time when it is possible for one single atom bomb to kill nearly 100,000 people. Therefore it is imperative, the film says, that all nations unite to control atomic energy and thus avert catastrophe. The United Nations must control all weapons of mass destruction, must make laws to abolish war. Such control would benefit all mankind and all nations. The choice, according to the film, is clear. It is life or death that we must choose—one world, or none.

There can be no doubt as to the importance and timeliness of the subject of this film. *One World or None* presents to the film audience the urgency of the situation with regard to control of atomic energy, but in its short running time it does not touch upon possible proposals for that control.

By means of animation, diagrams and maps, some important issues are raised relating to control of atomic energy. However, the evaluating committee felt that the film did not do a clear and thorough job. The few photographic shots are impressive and well placed for maximum effectiveness. . . . (F.F.R.)

THE PALE HORSEMAN

Produced by Irving Jacoby for UNRRA. Distributed by Brandon Films. (Twenty minutes.)

In this, one of the many films on the activities of UNRRA, the spread of pestilence in the war-stricken areas of Europe and the Orient is described.

Against the background of the Axis surrender are seen rows of crosses, less fortunate victims buried under heaps of debris, and pathetic scenes of wounded civilians. The camera catches a bird's-eye view of city streets reduced to acres of gaping craters and rubble. The retreating armies have left a trail of destruction and famine. Uprooted millions form the swelling refugee-trains, stretching for miles along the roads of France and China, or drifting on improvised rafts over the flooded fields of Holland.

It is here that the pale horseman starts on his deadly ride. Exposure and hunger breed and hasten the spread of tuberculosis, cholera and malaria. Into their midst come teams of scientists and relief workers to cooperate in checking the rising toll of disease. Water is again made drinkable, immunization is enforced, malaria-infested swamps are cleared, maternity hospitals are reopened, and children's wards are established where food is more important than medicine. The problem of displaced persons is equally challenging. Location files and communication are provided to facilitate their return home.

UNRRA, we are told, is a cooperative effort to fight pestilence with prevention, for "the care of one case today prevents a thousand cases tomorrow." Health, as an international responsibility, is recognized in the establishment of a United Nations Health Organization. It is only through the combined efforts of the more able countries that the death rate from diseases in war-ravaged areas can be effectively checked.

As a starkly realistic presentation of human suffering from the after-effects of war this film has perhaps few equals. This is a reason for recommending it for adult audiences only.

The film rates equally high in its selection of subject material and its photography. . . .

(F.F.R.)

THE PEOPLE'S CHARTER

Produced and distributed by United Nations Film Board. (Eighteen minutes.)

The People's Charter reviews the events that led up to the organization of the United Nations. Country after country refused to submit to the demands of Japan, Germany, and Italy, the film recalls, and found themselves blitzkrieged and conquered. The peoples of the world who were still free banded together to stop the conquerors. The extension of battle fronts brought more misery and devastation until the aggressor nations were stopped and forced to surrender. Out of this common effort and experience came the determination, as expressed in the charter of the United Nations, "the people's charter," to save future generations "from the scourge of war."

The first expression of long term goals in the war, the film points out, was the announcement of the Four Freedoms in the Atlantic Charter. This was followed in January 1942, by the plan adopted at Quebec for a united effort against the enemy. Under this plan, the film continues, men of many nations fought together and the enemy felt the power of an aroused, unified world. The continuation of this united effort for peace and reconstruction, both human and material in the postwar world, was assured in Moscow in October 1943. At Dumbarton Oaks in 1944 planning and organization for the peace were begun with the establishment of the World Bank and the laying of plans for world economic cooperation. Finally, at San Francisco the following year the charter of the United Nations came into being.

This story of the founding of the United Nations is told against the background of scenes of civilians being bombed, the lines of refugees seeking safety, of concentration camps, of devastated areas, and of men on the battle fields, in the factories, and around the conference table. The film shows the first meeting of the General Assembly, where representatives of the nations expressed their hope and determination to make the United Nations "the pathway to a secure future." As the film ends, President Roosevelt is shown declaring that the United Nations is an "association not of governments, but of peoples."

As the first in a series of films on the nature and problems of the United Nations, produced and made available by the United Nations Film Board, *The People's Charter* offers only a general survey and introductory material. Much of this material, both photographic and commentary, has been seen and heard in other films on related issues. The selection and editing of this material, however, is excellent. The commentary is very satisfactory. . . .

(F.F.R.)

PICTURE IN YOUR MIND

Produced and distributed by the International Film Foundation. (Fifteen minutes, color, animation.)

Picture in Your Mind is a complex approach to the complex problem of man's prejudices. It speaks in terms of some of the best knowledge and thought currently available—stemming from Darwin, the Bible, Freud, and current anthropological, sociological, and political roots. Philip Stapp, who planned and executed this film and the earlier *Boundary Lines,* has forcefully blended color and pictorial form, music and spoken commentary, in a distinctive manner, easily described as the Stapp technique. Gene Forrell's music is excellent.

No man is all bad or all good, the film states. And it seeks to find deep reasons for the fears, intolerances, and prejudices which lie behind our immature concepts of other people and of ourselves. And, we can continue, no film is all bad or all good. What strikes us as good about this one? First of all, its courage to have no truck with the comfortable one-point-of-departure routine. If the film does nothing else, it at least acts as an introduction to an interpretation of prejudice as a complex attitude with a complex past.

What's wrong with the film? Despite the fact that almost every scene is artistically and informationally significant, the connectives and transitions are poor—the film does not flow. It leaps backward and forward, it starts and stops, it jumps around. This, I believe, is as much an indication of this generation's shortcomings in dealing with complex ideas as it is an indication of Stapp's shortcomings. He has shown much creative talent in making this film at all, plus a remarkable amount of meaningful sympathy with contemporary problems. The film is at least several steps ahead of most of the rest of us. It is not the answer to all problems involved in our getting along together socially and politically, although occasionally we feel that it attempts to be. It is not a perfect film. And if we come to the film with our own prejudged attitudes about what constitutes prejudice, art, and human nature, we shall almost certainly tend unjustly to underrate it or overrate it.

See *Picture in Your Mind* yourself; see it several times. You'll be able to think of half a dozen ways in which the film might have been improved, clarified, made more meaningful and compact. But bear in mind the fact that this film has made a valuable first attempt to link up many important avenues of thought and knowledge; it has not taken the easy way. And remember to keep an eye out for Phil Stapp's next films. (C.S.)

ROUND TRIP

Produced for The Twentieth Century Fund by The World Today, Inc. Distributed by Film Program Services. (Twenty minutes.)

Complementing the general argument of *Stuff for Stuff* (page 220), this film discusses in human terms the pros and cons of foreign trade. Why should a machinist in Detroit export a lathe with which another fellow in Coventry may make some gadget which, exported to America, will help to put a New Yorker out of business? Isn't a worker in Brazil who gets a tenth the wage of an American worker likely to undersell on the world market and so contribute to American unemployment? The film uses the screen itself as a medium for an international free-for-all, in which the argument may sometimes get a little too involved.

The broad argument, however, is clear enough. Trade is a round trip in which goods must keep coming as well as going. Nations cannot unilaterally change their trade policies. They should work with the United Nations' International Trade Organization to hammer out a joint economic policy. Above all, the fellow behind the lathe, whatever language he speaks, should realize that protection isn't the answer to more general prosperity; rather, it is a means of hogging what we have already, thus risking a general depression. (R.S.)

THE STORY OF MONEY

Produced by Gryphon Films, London. Available from the British Information Services. (Fifteen minutes.)

Tracing the history of money back to primitive man, this film shows how in the earliest times barter became inconvenient, and objects of rarity and small size, like cowrie shells and silver ornaments, came into use as a medium of exchange. At first valued only for the weight of precious metal it contained, money came later on to acquire a token value, and pieces of paper—promissory notes—began to be accepted in lieu of the money and goods which backed them.

In a series of vignettes of early trading practices, the film traces the growth of banks out of goldsmiths' shops, and the gradual establishment of the idea of credit as a means of transferring goods without the passage of any property of real value. Although quite elementary in treatment, *The Story of Money* makes clear and precise a lot of ideas that float rather vaguely in the back of most people's heads. (R.S.)

STUFF FOR STUFF

Produced by Philip Ragan Assoc. Available from Film Program Services. (Sixteen minutes.)

It was Stuart Chase who coined the vivid phrase which titles this film, and it is Chase's philosophy of the very concrete basis of world trade which underlies the film's thinking. In it Ragan has carried further than ever before his lucid use of animated figures to dissect complicated economic ideas. He starts by showing us on a series of friezes the expanding trade of the Egyptians and Phoenicians, who were the first peoples to use river and ocean traffic as a means of adding to their material stock of goods. Then, sweeping across the centuries, he traces how the great explorers and adventurers opened the markets of the world and multiplied a thousandfold our economic choice.

The world is now inextricably tied together by its trade routes. But two great wars, bridged by a boom and a depression, have taught us that this skein can become hopelessly tangled if nations think only of themselves in settling their economic relations. A thousand men laid off in Detroit will mean less purchasing of imported articles, fewer American goods indispensable to the rest of the world. A factory may thus have to close down in Coventry or Turin or Hamburg or Lille. Unemployment can be exported just as easily as automobiles.

The film is notable for its interesting animation and for an excellent score by Louis Applebaum. It demonstrates convincingly that foreign trade is indeed stuff for stuff. (R.S.)

A TALE OF TWO CITIES

Produced by the U.S. War Department. Distributed by Castle Films. (Ten minutes.)

Hiroshima and Nagasaki—a tragic story of two cities! But it started before that—in the laboratory, the pilot plants, the trial explosion in the desert sands of New Mexico. Rushed over Japan in a B-29, a horror was unleashed to put an end to further and greater sorrow. The atom bomb was dropped on Hiroshima. In one flaming second an area from the center of the city to more than a mile in every direction was completely destroyed. The film shows the unbelievable force of the blast, the incredible destruction of the searing heat. An entire barracks was flattened, the twenty thousand men of the garrison obliterated. A priest, one of the eye-witnesses, is interviewed before the camera and describes the experience.

But still the Japanese refused to yield and another bomb was dropped, this time above the industrial buildings of Nagasaki. Overwhelmed by terror, the Japanese sued for peace.

Now, the film asks, what of the future? Will this new discovery bring power and plenty to peaceful lands or will all of mankind be overwhelmed by a fate similar to the one depicted here?

This is a sober, faithful record of a turning point in history. It does not seek to be a shocker and its treatment of its subject is rather dispassionate. Nevertheless, it does not gloss over the horror. It is an attempt to give a brief picture of what happened and ends by asking the question, "What next?" Its simplicity makes it potentially useful for most adult groups and it should hold the interest of any audience. . . . (F.F.R.)

africa

ACHIMOTA

Produced and distributed by the British Information Services. (Eighteen minutes.)

This film shows us the work of a progressive school on the Gold Coast of West Africa. Negro and white students work together learning the vocational skills needed to develop a better life in a society still very primitive and undeveloped.

Students are shown in day-long activities: taking breakfast together, attending classes and working on the farm. Every boy and girl in the secondary school learns a craft such as weaving, pottery, basket-making, carpentry, spinning, weaving, and sewing. In West Africa the inhabitants depend largely on farming. Agricultural methods are still in the primitive stage. The film shows us how the school adopts new implements for plowing and growing crops. Organized groups of students are seen operating these new implements and keeping pigs and poultry. Others are taught better ways of cooking. The commentator remarks, "Educating women teachers means educating many families." Singing, painting, carving, and modeling are some of the activities of the school. Groups of students are shown performing traditional tribal dances and ceremonies.

The film shows how active the students are, and the significant amount of self-direction that has been developed. Even the young students take a hand in the routine work of keeping the grounds clean and ordering meals.

This film illustrates an experiment in the application of progressive methods of education in a primitive, underprivileged, and illiterate community. It could be used valuably for provoking discussion on questions of better school planning and teaching in such areas.

Sound and photography are good. The subject will be of interest to groups concerned with international educational problems. . . . (F.F.R.)

DAYBREAK IN UDI

Produced and distributed by the British Information Services. (Forty-five minutes.)

The British Government has made a number of films about British Colonial Africa, but *Daybreak in Udi*, the 1949 Academy Award winner in the feature-length documentary field, is the best of the lot so far. It has many unusual qualities, not the least of which is the fact that it interests and entertains its audience instead of bombarding them with impressive scenery and statistics.

Daybreak in Udi is an enacted documentary, with a plot, a number of capable actors, and even a villain (perhaps the best actor of the lot). But the village in Nigeria where the action takes place is the real hero of the film. The story concerns the desire of the more progressive villagers for a maternity center, staffed by a trained, native midwife from the city. Sporadic opposition from the leader of the conservatives culminates in an early-dawn attempt to drive away the midwife. However, common sense prevails and after an all-out celebration the villagers pitch in to continue their pursuit of Western progress and begin a road to link them to the next village.

If the plot outline seems less than thrilling it is because an outline of necessity leaves out the people involved, and this is primarily a film of people. Each is clearly drawn and sharply defined—the testy Englishman who is the colonial officer, the intelligent interpreter, the earnest young couple eager to institute reforms, the midwife from the city trying to conceal her terror of the fantastic bush country, the troublemaker who tries to stop the project. The big cast of extras has taken on the job of acting with the same enthusiasm and energy with which they clear the land, build foundations, mix adobe, or stage a celebration.

Seldom has a film about another race or country succeeded so well in imparting a sense of the vitality and humanity of the individuals. The people of Udi, though still in a fairly primitive stage of development, should not be difficult for American audiences to understand, for local pride is the factor which finally swings most of the opposition into line. If they don't build the maternity center the next village will. The song the villagers sing as they work on the road at the close of the film is translated by the interpreter: "We are stronger than the next town. Our road goes far. When we dig, the earth crumbles away. A tree falls and the earth shakes with our strength. . . . We have power and we have spirit. A thousand men dig and the dust from their hoes rises to the sky. Our road goes far. Who knows where it will go? Who knows?"

. . . *Daybreak in Udi* was produced for Crown Film Unit by John Taylor and Max Anderson, directed by Terry Bishop from a scenario by Montague Slater. The musical accompaniment was written by William Alwyn and played by the London Philharmonic.

(EMILY S. JONES)

NEW WAYS FOR OLD MOROCCO

Produced and distributed by A. F. Films. *(Twenty minutes.)*

Another film dealing with new developments in Africa, this French production tells of the joint efforts of two villages, previously enemies, to bring water to their parched valley in North Africa. Working together, under the supervision of government engineers, they clear the land and build the needed canal.

The film conveys vividly the dry and barren quality of the land, and the back-breaking, unending labor necessary to gain the essentials of life. Since it ends with the opening of the canal, there is no opportunity to show the changes brought about by the irrigation. The people are shown always in groups, never as individuals, and as a result the film lacks the warmth and interest of *Daybreak in Udi*. However, it is an interesting picture of the changes coming to the underdeveloped regions of Africa. (EMILY S. JONES)

RHYTHM OF AFRICA

Distributed by A. F. Films. *(Sixteen minutes.)*

A fascinating study of life in French Equatorial Africa, *Rhythm of Africa* was conceived and produced by Jean Cocteau, photographed and edited by Francois Villier, and its English commentary was written by Langston Hughes and narrated by Kenneth Spencer. A French version, entitled *L'Amitié Noire,* is also available. An exceptional film.

asia

FARMERS OF INDIA (MIDDLE GANGES VALLEY)

Produced by Louis de Rochemont Associates. Distributed by United World Films. (Twenty minutes.)

Photographed and directed by Victor Jurgens, a former March of Time cameraman, this film is another in the classroom geography series "The Earth and Its People."

The film focuses on one boy and his family: their work in the rice fields, the mother's preparation of a meal, a trip to market with his father to sell grain, bathing in the sacred Ganges, the boy's glimpse of life in Benares, city of a quarter-million people, a visit at the clothmaker's, the return home, prayers before the shrine, and always the pressing need for enough food to eat. Completely ignoring political affairs, this film gives an impressive account of a way of life.

The photography is commendably sensitive to the inherent beauty and dignity of the people. Digging way below the obvious surface of a day's events, it is the kind of classroom film that makes everyone want to go to school. This film and the March of Time release below should go well together on the same program.

The use of a boyish narration voice with its wisp of a native accent is a matter of personal taste. While it is a good idea in general, at times it seems forced and distracting.

(c.s.)

INDIA, ASIA'S NEW VOICE

Produced and distributed by the March of Time Forum. (Seventeen minutes.)

This new March of Time release on India (not to be confused with the 1944 film entitled *India*) is one of the better examples of pictorial journalism which the editors of *Time, Life,* and *Fortune* have presented to the movie-going public. Beginning where the earlier film left off, it provides an historical summary of events in the Far East. The film starts and ends by indicating that a strong India now means to the Western world the hope of holding back the tide of Communism.

Highlights of these last few years include the departure of the Cripps Mission; Lord Mountbatten's more successful relations; the emergence of an independent India and the rival state of Pakistan; the greatest mass migration in history, involving millions of Hindus, Sikhs, and Moslems; the assassination of the great leader Gandhi, and Prime Minister Nehru's emergence as the new head of a relatively quieted country still, surprisingly enough, a voluntary member of the British Commonwealth. But behind the political headlines are the millions of people, the land, the way of life. The film crowds in as much background information as could be hoped for: natural resources, language, music, communications systems, industry, the ritual of the Brahmin, the life of the untouchable, schooling, need for irrigation and power, luxury among the few, poverty among the millions. Then it returns to the opening theme — India, defense against Communism.

As is often the case, the photography in this March of Time film is excellent — sharp and penetrating. The music used as a background in *India, Asia's New Voice* seems more abrupt and terrifying and banging than necessary, even in a March of Time release. It is an invaluable record of the times, packed with fact and figure and moving so swiftly that there is hardly time to realize that the film is distressingly cold and impersonal. The March of Time voice in itself would surely annoy an oyster.   (c.s.)

MOTHER

Produced in India for the Social Affairs Dept. of the United Nations. Distributed, to social agencies only, by the United Nations Film Division. (Fifteen minutes.)

Photographed in a small village in the Satara District near Bombay, this film shows the training and work of a regional health visitor and her efforts to teach new sanitary methods of midwifery in backward communities. The picture of life in rural India is grim and reminiscent in its honesty and sincerity of Bunuel's *Land Without Bread* and Ferno's *And So They Live*. While its distribution is limited in this country, it is one of the better documentary films of the past year. (c.s.)

NOMADS OF THE JUNGLE (MALAYA)

Produced by Louis de Rochemont Associates. Distributed by United World Films. (Twenty minutes.)

The first, and so far the outstanding film of the "Earth and Its People" series, is this brilliant interpretation by Victor Jurgens of a nomadic family which lives off the produce of the jungle without recourse to agriculture. The family's story is told in the first person by the son of the chief, a boy on the eve of assuming the responsibilities of manhood. Through his eyes we see the simple but effective methods of gathering food, fishing, building bridges, and floating down to the trading post the captured animals and other goods which the nomads exchange for wraps and knives and cigarettes that have come from the remoteness of the outside world.

The film has been magnificently shot with a keen and humorous eye, and the sound track (recorded on location) captures the noises of the jungle and the camp. What emerges from the film is a sense of cooperation and shared responsibility which makes our modern conception of the family look shoddy. The narrative, written with imagination and restraint, is spoken in a dialect which perfectly matches the character of the boy who tells the story. Though aimed at primary-school grades, this film is so well made that any adult group would find it fascinating.

(r.s.)

PEIPING FAMILY

Produced and distributed by the International Film Foundation. (Twenty-one minutes.)

This is one of the more imaginative films about children of other lands, sure to please adults as well as children in this country. Julien Bryan and his staff have shown a middle-class Chinese family since the war with sympathy and sensitivity, capturing the dignity of the Oriental tradition and the new influences of Western culture. The photography and commentary are excellent.

(c.s.)

TROPICAL MOUNTAIN LAND (JAVA)

Produced by Louis de Rochemont Associates. Distributed by United World Films. (Twenty minutes.)

Also the work of Victor Jurgens, this film is by its nature less imaginative than *Nomads of the Jungle*. Strung on the thin thread of the railroad line which connects Java's mountains and lowlands, it describes most of the island's manufactures and exports. Indeed, it is a remarkable accomplishment to have included so much information without giving a feeling of haste or over-compression. Much of the credit is due to the continuously illuminating camerawork, which combines the very best of documentary photography with a refreshing absence of artiness.

The commentary admirably spoken by an Indonesian, reflects the modern idea that the East Indies rightly belong to their own people, while crediting the Dutch for much industrial progress.   (R.S.)

australia and the pacific

HIGHWAY TO HAWAII

Produced by Cate and McGlone for United Airlines. Available from United Airlines, Inc., 80 E. 42nd Street, New York 17, N. Y. (Twenty-seven minutes, color.)

The color in this film is magnificent —some of the best that has been seen in a commercial film. The fruit and the flowers of the Hawaiian Islands, the welcoming crowds of girls, the semi-tropical scenery, appear in a gorgeous resplendence which would warm the cockles of a Hollywood producer's heart.

But when all this has been spelled out, little remains in the film to command any praise. The first five minutes drag by with a wearisome enumeration of the marvels of flight (surely fairly familiar by now), the supreme virtues of United Airlines, the mechanical miracle of the DC-6, and a mouth-watering description of the meals which are served aloft. This is the technique of the radio commercial, excused only because when the eye is blind, the ear must be cajoled into attention. But the camera has an eye; it is, in fact, an eye in itself. If, as an audience, we are convinced by what we see, what need to lay it on so thickly in the sound track with every copy-writer's cliché in the book? But if what we see with our own eyes doesn't convince us, no honeyed narrator is going to do the trick.

So, switching off the sound of *Highway to Hawaii*, and guided by our own good sense and some attractive maps, we may visit Waikiki Beach, go surf-riding out amongst the big waves, make the ninety-mile circuit of Oahu, and tour the less well-known islands, Kauai and Maui. Along the way we shall have visited the pineapple and sugar-cane plantations, watched a spectacular volcanic eruption, seen the giant fern forest, and come away with a sense of the rich backgrounds of native Hawaiian life. But please, no sound track!   (R.S.)

IN THE SOUTH SEAS

Produced and distributed by the Australian News and Information Bureau. (Eleven minutes.)

Australia administers under mandate a number of Pacific Islands, among them Papua and a part of New Guinea. This film takes us with a party of scientists to a small island close to the Trobriands, made famous by the anthropological researches of Malinowski. It seems that the Australian Government has initiated intensive work on the diet of the natives, their state of health, and their economy and methods of trade. No constructive steps to remedy the conditions shown are even indicated in the film, which, however, contains an interesting sequence about native fishermen who place poisoned roots in holes at the bottom of the shallow lagoons where the fish hide.   (R.S.)

MEN AND MOBS

Produced and distributed by the Australian News and Information Bureau. (Fifteen minutes, color.)

This rather ambitious film, in excellent Kodachrome, traces the growth of Australia's wool industry from the twenty-nine sheep which landed with the first settlers in 1788. The early part of the story is told in very pleasantly colored cartoons; but the screen really comes alive when a seemingly large part of Australia's present population of 120 million sheep starts pouring across it. What *The Overlanders* did for cattle, this film does, albeit on a much smaller scale, for sheep. It ends rather pleasantly with a sequence out on the range where 16mm. movies are shown to the ranchers, while the sheep stolidly look on from the back of the crowd. Some of Australia's wild life is shown in color in *Bushland Color Studies*, also obtainable from the Australian Information Bureau.

(R.S.)

NAMATJIRA THE PAINTER

Produced and distributed by the Australian News and Information Bureau. (Fifteen minutes, color.)

Namatjira is an Australian aborigine, a member of one of the most ancient races of men to have survived down to the present day. He is also one of Australia's foremost water-color painters. How he became interested in painting when still a camel-driver in the back country, how he learned to use the tools of a new profession, how he established a great reputation in the cities which he has stoutly refused to visit, is the story of this film.

But it tells also a more interesting story—that of the bushmen themselves and a way of life which has not altered since the Stone Age. The camera seems to transport us back a hundred thousand years to a time when there were no houses, no agriculture, almost no tools, and certainly no international complications! Seldom has the life, art, and feeling for nature of a primitive

people been presented with so much impact on the screen.

It would be pleasant to think that Namatjira, as an accomplished painter, had infused his work with some of this ancient dignity of his aboriginal race. Unhappily, he has followed the sloppy sentimentalism of English water-colorists; his paintings would do credit to Winston Churchill. Of the old life of the wild nothing remains.

Today Namatjira has some money —not much, but enough to buy paint boxes and water-colors and inspire his sons and nephews to take up the brush. Will they carry on the imitative tradition he has started? Or will they turn to their own people and seek inspiration in the strange rituals and passion for the hunt, which have come down to them from ancient times?

Other, more detailed films on Australian aboriginal life are *Tjurunga* and *Walkabout*, obtainable from the same source. (R.S.)

PACIFIC TERMINAL

Produced for the Tourist Bureau of New South Wales. Available from Films of the Nations. (Ten minutes.)

A pleasant, fast-moving picture of Australian life and resources, centering on the southeastern province of New South Wales. We see the capital city of Sydney, where local law limits the height of buildings to provide more sun and air; magnificent mountain scenery; and sports which range within a few miles from skiing to surf-bathing. Hydro-electric projects and shots of Australia's growing iron and steel industry round off the picture. The narrative is refreshingly brisk and blunt. (R.S.)

THE PHILIPPINE REPUBLIC

Produced and distributed by The March of Time Forum. (Sixteen minutes.)

This film is a brief review of the past and current history of the Philippine Islands in terms of its people, resources, and social problems. We see the thriving prewar agricultural economy bringing great wealth to a small group of land-owners and foreign-controlled interests, while the vast majority of natives live in extreme poverty.

Emphasis is placed on the educational and economic advances made in the islands under United States rule, which placed the Filipino living standard high in comparison with other Eastern countries. The film shows how, under the leadership of Manuel Quezon, independent nationhood was attained by peaceful means. War interrupted the United States-Philippine plan for the islands' autonomy, and we see that the new Philippine Republic is now faced with political, economic, social, and industrial problems greater than that land has ever

before known. Coupled with those problems are the enormous tasks of reconstruction after years of war and Japanese domination.

The film presents a wealth of material necessary to an understanding of the Philippine land and peoples. It is primarily informational, but it suggests issues of current importance in international affairs. The film stresses benefits received by the Filipinos under American rule, and the successful pattern for introducing independence to the islands. The film is uncritical, however, in tracing the events surrounding our acquisition of the Philippines. Social inequalities among the Filipinos are commented on, but little attempt is made to relate them to current conflicts among the various active political parties there.

Excellent photography and an exceptionally well-written commentary help assure audience-appeal for *The Philippine Republic. . . .* (F.F.R.)

canada

FAMILY OUTING

Produced by the National Film Board of Canada, and presented by the Canadian Government Travel Bureau in cooperation with The National Parks of Canada. Available free of charge. For a folder listing the names and addresses of libraries from which the films may be obtained, write to the National Film Board of Canada. (Fourteen minutes, color.)

At the Tunnel Mountain Campground in Banff National Park a typical visiting family pays its $1 registration fee, pitches its tent, and sets about the important business of having a good time. The youngsters go off on hikes, bicycle tours, boating expeditions, horseback rides, and swims in an outdoor hot-springs pool. For the parents there are other pastimes—fishing, golf, and scenic trips through woods and along the

river shores. Since all Canada's national parks offer sanctuary to the wildlife, they see many game animals which without the protection of the preservation laws would have been afraid to appear when human beings were in the vicinity. Despite the fault of occasionally stilted commentary the film on the whole is as pleasant and handsome as the people who appear in it and the setting in which it was shot. (c.s.)

INTRODUCTION TO GASPÉ

Produced for Canadian National Railways by the National Film Board of Canada. (Twelve minutes, color.)

The peninsula of Gaspé, Indian for "Land's End," scene of the first French landing in North America, has long been reputed as "quaint," and this film adds its full quota of quaintness. However, there is a pleasant sequence on the famous old fishing village of Percé, with its Roche Percé, and a boat trip to the neighboring Bonaventure Island, a seabird sanctuary, where the birds are so carefully protected from disturbance that even the blowing of boat whistles in the vicinity is forbidden. The film also includes a number of very clear maps. Color: good.   (R.S.)

THE RISING TIDE

Produced and distributed by the National Film Board of Canada. (Thirty minutes.)

Here is a film which successfully combines a significant statement of reality with exceptional photographic beauty. Set in the fishing villages of the maritime provinces of Canada, *The Rising Tide* reenacts the development of the important cooperative movement in that area. In the Twenties, when nearly all the people were close to starvation, a Government commission set about to remedy the situation and recommended the formation of cooperatives, with Government assistance. Father Cody, one of the leading lights in the movement, urged the fishermen and their families to follow this new way of individual and group self-help. "I've come to organize you," he would say. "You're poor enough to want help and smart enough to get it."

The film gives a moving account of what happened afterwards. Unfortunately, it does not develop at an even pace; the first part of the film is definitely superior to the latter. John Foster's seascape photography is breathtakingly beautiful, filtered to a fine point, and there is an excellent musical background based on Nova Scotian folk songs. In short, the film is a fine portrayal of local economic and social problems, celebrating one solution to them.   (C.S.)

ROCKY MOUNTAIN TROUT

Distributed by the National Film Board of Canada. (Fourteen minutes, color.)

Amid the blue-black snow-covered mountains in Jasper National Park, the camera skilfully picks out scenic views which look more like Oriental paintings than the real thing. And in the foreground expert casting and handling of the line are demonstrated.

The film also shows the work of the Canadian Government in restocking streams, rivers, and lakes; other precautionary measures are shown which insure the survival of the fish, at least until they are big enough to be lawfully caught on the hook. There is some interesting and amusing camera work—the graceful motions of the hooked fish, for example; and an original musical score makes this film about twice as good as the usual canned-music travel film.   (C.S.)

SKI HOLIDAY

Distributed by the National Film Board of Canada. (Eleven minutes, color.)

This film will appeal immediately to many tourists. Unfortunately, however, it isn't as believable as a film like *Family Outing*. Although it gives some useful tips on ski techniques, clothing, and equipment, it is little more than a series of calendar-picture settings, complete with two lovely girls in their red and yellow costumes, who take various poses before the camera. The color quality of the photography is excellent, and so are all the other trimmings. There just isn't much to hold them together.   (C.S.)

europe

BREAD AND WINE

Produced and distributed by International Film Foundation. (Fifteen minutes.)

The life of the Italian farmer, as portrayed in *Bread and Wine*, is one of toil, yet it is not without its compensations and hope for tomorrow. The film opens with a farmer rising with the sun to till the soil and prune the grape vines his forefathers have tilled and pruned for generations. Yet the land on which he lives and works, as pointed out by the commentary, does not belong to him, just as it didn't belong to his father and grandfather before him. He shares half of the produce of the land and its profits with the landowner, in whose family the land has likewise been for generations. The landowner, the film shows, supervises the farm, markets the produce, and keeps the accounts. . . .

In contrast with the bare, strenuous life of the farmer and his family the film shows the pleasant surroundings and leisurely living of the landowner's family. On Sundays, however, and on the Feast of the Grapes, both farmers and landowner and their families gather for religious services or to celebrate the successful harvest. Although the relationship between farmers and landowner is for the most part cordial, the film indicates that the Italian farmers are seeking a greater share of the profits of the soil and look for the dawn of a brighter tomorrow.

Bread and Wine underscores one of the social needs of Europe—a wider distribution of land ownership. In terms of one Italian farming estate the film quietly and objectively states the problem. . . .

Made by Julien Bryan, the film is excellently photographed. Sound effects and commentary are very satisfactory. . . .   (F.F.R.)

FARMER-FISHERMAN (NORWAY)

Produced by Louis de Rochemont Associates. Distributed by United World Films. (Twenty minutes.)

The harsh and rugged climate of northern Norway and its phlegmatic people do not altogether come to life in this film, despite the excellence of its photography. Breaking the pattern of the series, the narrative is put into the mouth of an ordinary adult American, though the story is seen through the eyes of Lars, a fisherman's son in his teens, who with his father works the sea half the year and the land the other half.

The film opens in Bergen, with its reminders of Norway's history and traditions, and moves north to a little village scattered round the shores of a fjord close to the Arctic Circle. There Lars and his family plow their harsh acres, live their unexpressive lives, worship in a strict Calvinist tradition, and go about their business in peace and sanctity.   (R.S.)

MAJESTIC NORWAY

Produced for the Norwegian Information Bureau, New York. Availability: Films of the Nations. (Twenty minutes, color.)

Starting high up in the mountains, this film leads us down by tortuous mountain highways toward the sea. On the way we pass the big hydroelectric stations which have made Norway one of the most intensely electrified countries in the world.

Almost everything makes use of water power—grinding mills, sawmills, flour mills, small and large, are operated by the free power of the almost universal waterfall. We see next the little farms where every corner of useful land is tilled, and the farmers take fullest advantage of the short growing season and the twenty hours of summer sunlight. So we reach the fjords, the only highway between many thriving communities and an outlet to Norway's great source of wealth—the sea.

Here the film loses direction and wanders off on a tour of Norwegian cities: Bergen, Trondheim, Oslo. An air trip takes us on a rather breathless visit to Lapland, and the film closes with a picture of Oslo and its fine modern architecture and magnificent schemes of social welfare. Color: mediocre.   (R.S.)

NEW EARTH

Produced by Joris Ivens. 1944. Distributed by Films of the Nations. (Twenty minutes.)

There are two sides to Holland. One belongs to the tourists—the Holland of tulip festivals, Dutch caps, and immaculately clean kitchens. The other belongs to the Dutch people, and it is the Holland that was reclaimed, acre by acre, from the sea. It is this side of Holland that is reflected by *New Earth* as it tells the story of the construction of dikes across the throat of the Zuider Zee.

The key to the story is on the map, the commentator remarks. It shows that most of the Netherlands lies below sea level; that its only defense against the sea is the dikes holding it back. "We Dutch have made our own country," the commentator continues. "We disciplined the elements."

At the beginning it was an almost impossible job. Materials were carried by hand. Brushwood rafts were built to divert the water currents from the infant dikes. Ten yards would be dammed only to have fifty recaptured by the sea. Ten thousand men and women worked to bottle up the Zuider Zee: clay for the base of the sea-wall; then sand; then giant boulders piled on top. The first great dike was ten years in construction.

Nor was one dike sufficient. Many more were built. Water was isolated and pumped from the land, drained off to create new land. In time, crops grew and homes appeared. A nation was built, the commentator concludes, "on what once had been the bottom of the sea."

New Earth is an extremely satisfying information film. The camera has an exciting story to tell, and tells it magnificently. This is, after all, a subject of epic proportions: The history of a nation struggling to survive the elements that threaten to destroy it. In this sense it is considerably more than a film about the Netherlands. *New Earth* attempts—with a great measure of success—to show men rising above their environment, *pulling* themselves above it by their own boot-straps. Today, perhaps more than ever before, it is eminently valuable that we be reminded that this is possible.

(F.F.R.)

PICTURESQUE DENMARK

Produced for the Danish Information Bureau, New York. Distributed by Films of the Nations. (Twenty minutes, color.)

This sight-seeing tour of Denmark starts in Copenhagen, wanders through the islands, and eventually returns to the capital city. Obviously, Denmark is a country with a delicate flavor, like a rare blend of tea, and does not yield itself to the heavy and awkward approach of this kind of film. A few engaging oddities stand out, like the stork nesting on the top of a telephone pole, and the chimney sweep who rides to his work in a top hat on a bicycle. Everyone rides bicycles, as the most practical transportation in a small and flat country; and the bicycle becomes a mark of the absence of class distinctions.

Superficial as this film is, it cannot altogether ignore Denmark's great housing program and cooperative farms, and it pays an uncomprehending tribute to Copenhagen's clean and modern architectural forms. At least two shots are devoted to the famous Grundtvig Memorial Church.

The intending visitor will also find in this film a barrelful of "traditional" and "picturesque" sights, but they cannot altogether hide the simplicity and good sense of a country which has managed to survive the German invasion without ruin or recrimination. Color: good.   (R.S.)

PICTURESQUE SWEDEN

Produced for the Swedish Information Bureau, New York. Distributed by Films of the Nations. (Twenty minutes, color.)

This film follows exactly the same pattern as the other Scandinavian pictures reviewed here. It takes us on a visit to Sweden's great castles and chateaux, pays passing tribute to housing programs and cooperatives, and carries us on a canal trip through the green and pleasant countryside. We briefly see Gripsholm and Uppsala and take a boat trip to Gottland, where more time is spent on a very ordinary looking beach than on the world-famous fortified city of Visby. This film also includes a brief journey northward to Lapland. Color: excellent.   (R.S.)

WINGS TO IRELAND

Produced by Hartley Productions for Pan-American World Airways. Available from Association Films. (Thirty minutes, color.)

Among travelogs that astonish the eye with their brilliance of color, this simple, unpretentious film comes as a very pleasant relief. Even the bold palette of Kodachrome is subdued by the soft green of Irish grassland, and the purple of the moors and hills.

But what chiefly distinguishes this film (and seemingly others by the same producers) is the apt use of natural sound and speech recorded on location. Padraic Colum's name on the credit titles is an assurance of authenticity; and if the educated tongue of some of the would-be country characters marks them as pure Abbey Theatre, others are genuine enough. The result is a convincing feeling that the audience has been carried to the spot and planted down in Ireland.

Accompanying a visiting couple and their young son, we tour western Ireland, watch the home industries and the local thatchers at work, listen to a woman singing her child to sleep with a Gaelic lullaby, and take a trip on the Lakes of Killarney. Cork and the Blarney Stone, the Rock of Cashel and the abbey which sheltered St. Patrick in 450 A.D., the plains of Tipperary and, finally, Dublin's streets, are all part of the tour, which includes a delightfully photographed fox-hunting episode.

The commentary, both in voice and wording, is refreshingly free from plugs, and an audience is likely to be grateful to the sponsor for its rare and welcome restraint. The film leaves the impression that the sun doesn't shine very often in Ireland, but that the country is soft and beautiful in all weathers, and the people, open-hearted and hospitable to strangers.   (R.S.)

europe's children

THE CHILDREN'S REPUBLIC

Produced by Carroll Productions. Distributed by A. F. Films. (Twenty-four minutes.)

This is by no means a typical story of what happened to French orphans after the war, but it is as pleasant an exception to the rule as we might wish for. It is the story of René and François Desbois and their new home in a model school for young people, where life takes on new meaning and hope. Madeleine Carroll visited this French "republic" and was so interested in it that she produced this film. Narrating it and appearing in the final sequences, Miss Carroll adds her own quiet charm and beauty to an already attractive film on the rehabilitation of under-privileged children. (c.s.)

A PENNY'S WORTH OF HAPPINESS

Produced by Roger Leenhardt. American adaptation by Julian Roffman. Available from A. F. Films. (Thirteen minutes.)

This too is an American remake of a foreign film, and like *Tomorrow's a Wonderful Day* (see below), it is disjointed in spots. But its exceptionally good photography and its sensitively subordinate, spoken commentary more than make up for it.

The films tell of a child-welfare program which provides four-month vacations in Switzerland for thousands of children from war-torn Europe. Some of the children go to hospitals, where we see them receiving medical attention. Some go into Swiss homes, where they can enjoy the tenderness and comfort of happy family life. But their stay is so brief, so needed, and so enjoyed that it seems cruel to have to face the time for leaving.

The vacation is over, the film says, but this is not the end. From their new experiences the children will take home with them the spirit of love and happiness with which to remake their own lives.

As is often the case in films about children, there are many delightful shots of activities and faces. One outstandingly beautiful scene occurs at the end of the film—an aged woman in black waiting at the train depot for her boy to return, the emotional tension in their embrace, and the final shot of the two slowly walking away toward the rubble-piled town which is their home.

(c.s.)

TOMORROW'S A WONDERFUL DAY

Produced by Hadassah, Women's Zionist Organization of America. Available from Hadassah Film Library, 13 E. 37th Street, New York, N. Y., and also from Children to Palestine, 1819 Broadway, New York, N. Y. (Forty-eight minutes.)

This is the story of a fifteen-year-old displaced boy named Benjamin, who last saw his mother when he was seven and who long ago forgot how to read and write. He has arrived at Ben Shemen, a children's village in Palestine, along with dozens of other displaced children. Most of the new arrivals are younger than Benjamin, and they seem to disappear into the community. But not Benjamin, who has spent most of his life in fear, resentfulness, and loneliness. Why should he change now? And why should he work in the fields, which only remind him of freshly dug graves? Why should he play, when the fences prove to him that this is merely another kind of concentration camp?

When Benjamin first sees Miriam he begins to see the way back to life.

Miriam is pretty, a warm and smiling girl of about his own age. The film sensitively shows us his feelings, and the girl's charming response, without straining or belittling an adolescent attraction of this kind. Benjamin does of course learn to work with the others in the fields, to enjoy the present and forget the past. And finally, during a religious ceremony which he has been selected to lead, Benjamin is able to tell himself: "I who have known the dark ways of men am now a bearer of light."

The film is essentially such a fine one that it is unpleasant to have to recall its many shortcomings. It seems that in remaking the film for American audiences some of the episodes have been assembled more with a view to including them all rather than to attaining a smooth flow of ideas. Some of the scenes of Benjamin's inner conflicts and isolation are overly dramatized. But the greatest fault of all, one which is being made much too often these days, is the overloading of the sound track. There are several scenes in this film in which every detail, every thought, and problem are explained, leaving no mental margin with which one can look at the picture and have a thought of one's own.

These are defects, but the film essentially is a good one. It tells of some of the really important work being conducted in Palestine by trained specialists and by the children themselves. Printed material giving the history of this exceptional children's village is also available, from both Hadassah and Children to Palestine. (c.s.)

films in french

The films reviewed below are without explanatory subtitles. Apart from their intrinsic interest, they are likely to be of value in French language and literature classes. Many French teachers are also using French feature films, either with or without subtitles, as an aid to conversation. (R.S.)

AUTOUR D'UN CLOCHER

Produced by La France en Marche. Available from French Films and from International Film Bureau. (Ten minutes.)

The life of a village, grouped round its belfry. The film follows the familiar pattern of a day's work, starting with the baker who gets up when it is almost dark, and following in their turn the blacksmith, the saddlemaker, the mailmen, and the children going their way to school. All very charmingly photographed.

LE MOULIN ENCHANTÉ

Produced by La France en Marche. Available from French Films and from International Film Bureau. (Ten minutes.)

This is a brief biographical sketch of Alphonse Daudet, centered around his famous windmill, but radiating out to include his life in Arles and short summaries of his most famous books. The magnificent landscapes of Provence are finely photographed, and as much information is crowded in as could be expected in a ten-minute film.

The commentary is delivered rather more rapidly than in *Profil de la France*, but the technical quality of sound and picture is better.

PROFIL DE LA FRANCE

Produced by Abel Gance and Jean Tedesco. Available from French Films and from International Film Bureau. (Twenty-three minutes.)

This and the above two films on our list may be obtained with a line-by-line transcript of the narrative in French, keyed to a list of the less commonly used words.

Profil de la France, a film of the old master Abel Gance, who is remembered best for his silent *Napoleon*, is a study in French coastal geography. Opening on the rocky shores of Normandy, the camera moves down to the estuary of the Seine, and thence to St. Malo. After this it takes a leap to the sand dunes of Gascony in the far South, and works its way back northwards into Brittany.

But this is no conventional travel film. Rather it is a mosaic of images of France—the medieval churches, the traveling carnivals, and native costumes—narrated in a style which would seem ornate and precious in English, but which suits the French idiom excellently.

The voice is clearly recorded and the commentary is delivered moderately slowly, so that the film should be of use in intermediate grades for language teaching. While the camera work is excellent, the technical quality of the picture image is not altogether up to modern standards.

LA ROSE ET LE RESEDA

Produced in France by André Michel after a poem by Aragon, spoken by Jean-Louis Barrault. Music by Georges Auric. Available from A. F. Films. An English version is also available. (Twelve minutes.)

The combination of some remarkable talents has produced on the whole a remarkable film. The whole bagful of conventional techniques has been thrown out of the window. This is a film poem set to a spoken poem, and it is chiefly as a visual poem that it must be judged. The film starts with a solemn announcement of its theme. Auric's music, borrowed from a Bach chorale, intones over images of a little French village, its church, its tavern, its farmhouses all seemingly deserted. Then the square, tree-shaded and peaceful. Here the villagers are gathered, sitting mute and motionless on benches, facing their captors. The Nazi soldiers march up and down in their jackboots with a ringing precision. The people stare.

The soldiers become a wooden image of tyranny. The camera rushes up to an eyeless figure, dumbly grasping his rifle. The scene dissolves. The countryside is aflame behind the soldier. Peace descends. Across a rocky landscape rides a solitary figure on horseback. Looking down, he sees two men lying on the olive-clad slopes—two comrades killed in action. As he watches, they come to life and rise from the ground. Silently he rides away.

Here Aragon's poem begins. Its theme is the identity of sacrifice between the two men, *celui qui croyait au ciel, celui qui n'y croyait pas*. Believer and unbeliever share the same devotion to France, run the same risk of death, stand shoulder to shoulder. Barrault's nervous high-pitched voice carries the poem headlong forward to its climax, an evocation of pigeons wheeling out together into space, and of *la rose et le reseda*, the rose and the mignonette.

The visual imagery is on the whole spontaneous and effective, carrying the eye and the mind along with a real poetic impulse. The political imagery is less fortunate. It is not very pleasant to see Aragon, who may be supposed to hold God and the Republic in no very high esteem, extending his hand to the Church, and drawing in the sand the figure of Marianne. Politics certainly makes strange bedfellows. (R.S.)

latin america

THE AMAZON AWAKENS

Produced by Walt Disney for the Co-ordinator of Inter-American Affairs, 1944. Distributed by the Institute of Inter-American Affairs, 499 Pennsylvania Avenue, Washington 25, D.C., for purchase only. (Thirty-seven minutes, color.)

This is probably the most ambitious non-theatrical film sponsored by the Co-ordinator of Inter-American Affairs during the war years and distributed widely in America. It is one of the last films produced in the series that is now available on the life and customs of the twenty-one other American republics.

The Amazon Awakens begins with a sequence depicting the geographical position of the Amazon river. Next is an historical account of the travels of certain of the early Spanish explorers and missionaries. It is noted that from their accounts, the Amazon region was estimated to contain immense riches in gold and was thus christened El Dorado. The theme of the film is that El Dorado of the Amazon has not been completely revealed, that its vast riches still await discovery and exploitation.

Starting at Iquitos, in Peru, the camera takes us down the river from the Andes mountains. In succession we pass Manaus, in Brazil, Boa Vista, a government settlement in the Amazon jungle, Fordlandia, the rubber preserve of the Ford Company, and finally Belem, ocean port for the river's commerce. . . .

The film is noteworthy for its technique of alternating animation sequences with real life photography. Much skill was used by the Disney film craftsmen to get a pleasing and exact coloring that would blend with the actual real life scenes in the jungle. Disney has demonstrated that the techniques of producing color training films in wartime have a real place in films for adult needs.

(F.F.R.)

AMERICANS ALL

Produced by Julien Bryan for the Office of Inter American Affairs, 1942. Distributed by Castle. (Twenty-five minutes.)

An objective approach to the establishment of better relations between the Americas, this film shows the rise and progress of the fifty million Latin Americans in twenty republics through four centuries of development. The cultural heritage of the Old World and of the Indian's dress, dance, and art is shown as blending into the pattern of rural and urban Latin America today.

The war, and the substantially increased industrial production of our southern neighbors, the film shows, have resulted in closer trade relations in the Americas. Communications and transportation have played their part in shifting Latin American trade routes from the Old World to the United States. The doors are now open for an exchange of their respective cultural contributions. The commentary throughout urges North Americans to seize upon this new opportunity for good neighborliness in economics, culture, and democracy.

Present and possible exchanges of art, music, movies, missions, and athletics are given as examples. A student demonstration for democracy and an impressive international display conclude this fast-moving panorama of Latin America.

The film is a reliable and highly interesting portrayal of cultural Latin America. Although the political and economic conditions will change, the picture's essential appeal will remain. The excellent photography of the film is offset somewhat by the commentary, which is sometimes too rapid for easy understanding. . . .

(F.F.R.)

THE BRIDGE

Sponsored by the Foreign Policy Association and produced by Willard Van Dyke and Ben Maddow for Documentary Film Associates. Available from New York University Film Library. (Twenty-seven minutes.)

A useful corrective to the optimism of the travelog is this appraisal of Latin American industry and life. The first few minutes of the film are dated by wartime references, but the remainder gives a fine sweeping sense of what makes the Latin American economy go round—the great natural riches supplying primary industries insufficiently balanced by consumer manufacturers, and the vast untapped reservoir of demand among peasants and workers who are today too poor to buy. There is a moving sequence of life in a village, with its drudgery and malnutrition, and the film ends with a survey of some of the continent's new industrial developments, the progress on the Pan-American Highway, and the bridge of the air which will one day link even more effectively the North with the South.

Other films of interest are *Belo Horizonte* (sponsored by the Coordinator for Inter-American Affairs and available from Castle Films), which describes Brazil's planned provincial capital city, and the rich mineral area which surrounds it. Also *Bolivia* with its interesting account of life on the Altiplano, the fifteen-thousand-foot plateau where much of the country's silver and tin are mined. (R.S.)

CROSS-SECTION OF CENTRAL AMERICA (GUATEMALA)

Produced by Louis de Rochemont Asso-

ciates. Distributed by United World Films. (Twenty minutes.)

The little-known countries of Central America are here typified by Guatemala, with its contrasting northern plains and southern mountains, its mahogany forests and chicle and coffee plantations. In this, as in the film below, the commentary is carried by a poor peasant, thus obliquely pointing up the contrast between the landed and the landless. Once again the camera throws interesting light on ways of life and ways of making a living in a country which in part has moved with the centuries and in part has stood still since the Conquest.

(R.S.)

HORSEMEN OF THE PAMPAS (ARGENTINA)

Produced by Louis de Rochemont Associates. Distributed by United World Films. (Twenty minutes.)

This film depicts life on an *estancia*, or great landed estate, through the eyes of a boy of twelve, son of one of the *pamperos*, or herdsmen. It follows in adequate detail the business of cattle-raising, and gives a clear and concise impression of an economy based on a rich soil and a flat terrain. Since the emphasis is on processes rather than people, the film is better suited to the higher grades.

Its photography gives a fine sense of the vast horizons of a prairie country, while the narrative implies with adequate clearness the consequences of absentee ownership and a high concentration of wealth in the hands of the landowners. (R.S.)

TOMORROW'S MEXICO

Produced and distributed by March of Time Forum. (Sixteen minutes.)

The Mexican "revolution," not unmarked by strife, but in the main a revolution by education and industrialization, is the subject of this film. Noting the interests of tourists in visiting this neighbor land, but dealing with an aspect of a Mexico which few tourists ever see or are ever concerned about, the film explains a struggle that has been going on for two generations. Exploited alike by foreign financial interests and feudal landlords, the common people lived in ignorance and dire poverty. A succession of military leaders, good and bad alike, strove to free Mexico from the power of these two forces. But it was not till the presidency of Cardenas that much real progress was made.

Much of the progress of the Cardenas regime came through the famed "revolution by education," a progressive educational program that drew attention of educators everywhere. In addition, huge estates were broken into smaller cooperative farms. Irrigation projects and the leadership of agricultural extension workers began to bring changes in methods of tillage. Foreign oil holdings were expropriated, bringing censure from the British and American owners, but placing important resources under Mexican control.

At this juncture, Mexico entered World War II as an ally of the United States. The years of war brought swift new changes and a rapid growth in industrialization. Mexico gained new status as a nation in the world community and an important place in the Western Hemisphere. But many difficult problems remain, and the film honestly points out that even today vast numbers of Mexicans have failed to profit by any of the changes noted. The education of children and an attempt to make every adult literate are being pushed forward vigorously. The revolution, aimed at achieving "democracy, self-respect, and well-being for all," still goes on.

An honest attempt has been made in this film to present a rapid survey of recent Mexican history and to interpret the meaning of what has happened there. Technically the film is very superior. Its photography has caught something of the beauty of the country, it is cut with pace and attention-holding style, while its commentary is reasoned and factual. Certain American interests may feel it unfair, but the film seems to have been made with scrupulous regard for fact. As an information film it should interest all adult audiences, and as a discussion tool it should also have wide usefulness because of the importance of Mexico in our plans for the future. . . .   (F.F.R.)

WINGS OVER LATIN AMERICA

Sponsored and produced by Pan-American Airways. Available from Association Films. (Forty minutes, color.)

This bird's-eye view of Central and South American travel takes us to almost all the twenty-one republics and the islands of the Caribbean. We see the temples of Yucatan, the native dances of Guatemala, and the ancient Spanish cities of Panama. We ride with the plane southwards to Ecuador, thence to Peru and its famous Inca capital, Cuzco. This fascinating city, set high in the mountains, still shows us the narrow, winding streets the Indians built, and the solid zigzag walls with which they sought to protect themselves against the Spaniards.

Then on to Lake Titicaca, highest stretch of navigable water in the world, to Chile, Argentina, and its capital, Buenos Aires. We pause to watch the carnival season at Rio, then board the plane again for Dutch Guiana, and enter the Caribbean area through the Virgin Islands. In Haiti we climb the hills and stand among the ruins of the French palace built by Henri Christophe, Negro general and king; and we see the clifflike fortress where he shut himself up to escape the revenge of his subjects. And so home by way of Jamaica and Cuba.

It would be pleasant to report that this long tour was filmed in dazzling color and narrated with zest and imagination. Unfortunately, however, the production is exceedingly amateurish, the color is either thin and washed out or harsh and exaggerated, and the commentary limps along, repeating what is already obvious on the screen. Nonetheless, this film is an encyclopedia of visual information about Latin America, and is worth seeing as a guide to out-of-the-way places which might otherwise be missed on a quick trip.

(R.S.)

WINGS TO CUBA AND THE CARIBBEAN

Produced by Hartley Productions, for Pan-American World Airways. Available from Association Films. (Twenty-nine minutes, color.)

This companion film is louder and generally less successful. The traveler this time is a glamour girl, but the continuity is supplied by a rather unpleasant little animated figure, representing the airline, which pops up at unexpected moments and exclaims with dubious rhyme and logic, "It's quicker by Clipper." Even the Calypso singers are roped in to chant the virtues of Pan-American Airways.

However, the rich musical traditions of Latin America furnish some attractive, locally-recorded singing and dancing, and the camera transports us all the way from the Virgin Islands at one end of the Caribbean to Cuba at the other. (R.S.)

WINGS TO MEXICO AND GUATEMALA

Sponsored by Pan-American World Airways and produced by Hartley Films. Available from Association Films.

This film is both more ambitious and more restricted than *Wings Over Latin America.* Confining itself to two countries only, it is able to give much more of the flavor of both of them, and it is produced with a thoroughly professional appreciation of the art of the color camera.

The first section of the film is narrated by a Mexican businessman, whom the heroine encounters aboard her Pan-American plane as she travels southward. There is quite a feeling of reality about it, and we see not only the obvious attractions of Mexico City, the canals, the Spanish dancing, the bullfights, and the modern buildings, but something also of the life of the people as it is lived in the country districts. A refreshing novelty in a travelog is the use of direct sound to capture the voices, songs, and music of the country, as in a sequence where the camera interviews an archeologist supervising the excavation of one of the great ancient temples.

The Guatemalan section of the film is much less satisfactory, for the heroine, a glittering blonde, takes up the narration, which abounds in such remarks as, "I was fascinated by the tremendous loads the women carry on their heads." If there is no appreciation of the harsh economic realities of Guatemalan life, the camera at least manages to capture the life of the marketplace, the mock heroic dances representing the Spanish conquest, and the magnificent mountain landscapes.

The color is remarkably brilliant and satisfying, and the film is in every way technically excellent. (R.S.)

INDEX

index

Film titles appear in italics.